Creation and Evolution

Can religion survive Darwinism? Do scientists entering the lab or heading for the field have to bracket, or reject outright, all religious commitments and convictions? Trenchantly laying out the evidence for natural selection and carefully following and underscoring the themes and theses of Genesis, Lenn E. Goodman traces the historical and conceptual backgrounds of today's evolution controversies, revealing the deep complementarities of religion and the life sciences. Solidly researched and replete with scientific case studies, vignettes from intellectual history, and thoughtful argument, *Creation and Evolution* forthrightly exposes the strengths and weaknesses of today's polarized battle camps. Religious *and scientific* fundamentalisms, Goodman shows, obscure the real biblical message and distort the deepest insights and richest findings of Darwinian science.

Lenn E. Goodman is Professor of Philosophy and Andrew Mellon Professor of Humanities at Vanderbilt University, USA. His previous publications include *Love Thy Neighbor as Thyself* (2008), *Islamic Humanism* (2008) and *In Defense of Truth: A Pluralistic Approach* (2001).

"Many of us feel that the time is long past due for declaring a truce in the war between evolution and theism. But making a cogent and sensible case for this conviction is not as easy as it sounds, so we cannot but welcome the decency and elegance which Goodman's wise and widely informed deliberations come to our aid."

Nicholas Rescher, *University of Pittsburgh, USA*

"Professor Goodman has written an ambitious work that rises far above the current ID/evolution controversy and places (Darwinian) evolution in the general context of the sweep of Western civilization. I would certainly recommend this to many of my colleagues and students; it is a major contribution to the field and is unique in many ways, educating while it entertains and enlightens."

Carl Feit, *Yeshiva University, USA*

"Lenn Goodman is a philosopher in the highest and best sense – a pursuer of wisdom. In *Creation and Evolution* he deftly uses the tools of philosophical analysis to bring much needed illumination to a topic that is as important as it is controversial. The book is a boon not only to his fellow philosophers, but also to scientists, theologians, legal scholars, and general readers who want to think well about creation and evolution."

Robert P. George, *McCormick Professor of Jurisprudence,*
Princeton University, USA

"Drawing deeply on the biblical and rabbinical sources, Goodman beautifully communicates the richness and variety of the idea of creation. At the same time, quoting liberally from Darwin and his followers, he offers a knowledgeable and convincing portrayal of the case for evolution. One walks away from this book with a clearer sense of why evolution and creation are not only compatible but also mutually enhancing. Ranging from genetics to Midrash to birdsong analysis, these pages offer a call to constructive partnership: 'Where evolutionists ask how we came to be, Genesis probes what it is to be human'."

Philip Clayton, author of *The Oxford Handbook of Religion* and
Science and Adventures in the Spirit

Creation and Evolution

Lenn E. Goodman

Routledge
Taylor & Francis Group

LONDON AND NEW YORK

First edition published 2010
by Routledge
2 Park Square, Milton Park, Abingdon, Oxon OX14 4RN

Simultaneously published in the USA and Canada
by Routledge
270 Madison Ave., New York, NY 100016

Routledge is an imprint of the Taylor & Francis Group, an informa business

© 2010 Lenn E. Goodman

Typeset in Times New Roman by Taylor and Francis Books
Printed and bound in Great Britain by TJ International ltd, Padstow, Cornwall

British Library Cataloguing in Publication Data
A catalogue record for this book is available from the British Library

Library of Congress Cataloging-in-Publication Data
Goodman, Lenn Evan, 1944-
Creation and evolution / Lenn E. Goodman.
p. cm.
Includes bibliographical references and index.
1. Evolution (Biology)--Religious aspects.   2. Emergence (Philosophy) I. Title.
BL263.G625 2010
202'.4--dc22
2009032160

ISBN10: 0-415-91380-2 (hbk)
ISBN10: 0-415-91381-0 (pbk)
ISBN10: 0-203-85785-2 (ebk)

ISBN13: 978-0-415-91380-5 (hbk)
ISBN13: 978-0-415-91381-2 (pbk)
ISBN13: 978-0-203-85785-4 (ebk)

Contents

Acknowledgements

Some of the thoughts in this book were presented at a Harvard conference on science and religion chaired by Philip Clayton of Claremont. My thanks to him, and to all the participants in that meeting. Warm gratitude to the three dedicated research assistants who helped me in its production: James Grady, Nicholas Oschman, and D. Gregory Caramenico. Thanks too to Carolyn Cusick, the sensitive and insightful graduate assistant in my Vanderbilt lecture course, Humanity, Evolution, and God. My deep appreciation to the patient editors at Routledge, Lesley Riddle and Siobhan Greaney.

My wife Roberta Goodman continues to inspire all who meet her with her warmth and openness, and her love of truth and truthfulness.

I learned my love of science from my father in early childhood, with his tales of Galileo and Copernicus, Newton and Lavoisier. My deep attachment to philosophy is also part of his heritage. It was my late mother, often through her poetry and song, who linked that love of inquiry, lyrically, to the love of nature's God and the heritage of our people, whose poetry and practice keep that kind of love alive.

This book began its life years ago in conversations with my late first wife, Madeleine Goodman, a geneticist, and later Vice President at the university of Hawali and the first woman dean of Arts and Science at Vanderbilt. Like the great geneticist and evolutionary biologist Theodosius Dobzhansky, who framed today's neodarwinian synthesis, Madeleine believed that "Evolution is God's, or Nature's method of creation." She shared Dobzhansky's belief that "Evolution is God's, or Nature's method of creation." The seeds of Chapter 1 were sowed in an article that she and I wrote for *Zygon*, the Journal of Religion and Science. The book, bringing to fruition one part of the plans that Madeleine and I once made, is dedicated to her memory, in hopes that is proves worthy of her scientific passion. Our daughters, Allegra Goodman and Paula Fraenkel preserve that passion, each in her own way – Allegra in her works of fiction, which have shown how critical religious insights and spiritual values remain in every realm, and Paula who continues with spirit and integrity her mother's scientific battles against disease, as a research and clinical physician.

Introduction

There's a quiet battle going on in toy stores and on bumper stickers. Plush or plastic dinosaurs jostle for shelf space with Noah's Arks, pull toys with colorful carved animals peeking out the windows. Stick-on Christian fish, in silver plastic, decorate car trunk lids, mocked, on other cars, by fish with feet. The evolution fish bear the name DARWIN. They're mocked in turn, by Darwin fish turned upside down, feet in the air, or gobbled by a bigger fish, labeled TRUTH, as they try to waddle off.

Reading the literature on creation and evolution, I find emotions high, patience short, clarity often lacking. Would be literalists cant the biblical text, or the world in defense of human dignity as they see it. Doctrinaire mechanists make a similar travesty of their faith in nature by projecting onto science dogmatic denials of unwelcome spiritual views. My hope is that conceptual candor might help lower the temperature a bit, at least for some who are concerned about the fit of Darwinian discoveries with religious values and beliefs. The wise don't confuse rigor with purism. They use their analytic and synthetic skills to bridge false dichotomies where polemicists see only an abyss.

Powerful motives drive today's controversy. But the extremes feed off one another, even as they darken the hard outlines of rejected views. I can't flatter myself that this book will convert extremists. But for those who seek a middle ground, it may prove helpful. The aim is not to convince readers simply to adopt my own solutions but to encourage others to build alternatives of their own. I think I can show that religion is no threat to evolution and perhaps calm the triumphalism, or defeatism, of those who assume God is dead in Darwin's world. Neither theism nor biology, I believe, is as full and rich as it can be until cognizant of the other. That claim goes beyond a plea for respect and openness. Defenders of science should give up their positivist pretensions and acknowledge that adaptation is a value concept; and biology, inexorably, a teleological science. Defenders of creation need to recognize that randomness has been and remains critical in the emergence of life and the higher life forms that we hold precious.

Like Teilhard de Chardin, Eric Voegelin, Arthur Peacocke, and Mary Douglas, I believe one shouldn't hide one's spiritual candle under a barrel. Religious values can be articulated confidently, in the scientific light. Science doesn't need the invidious tones of scientism to sustain its credibility. Nor will its findings erode the realities religion aims for. Indeed, the conative character of being at large is part of what we learn from the sciences. Nature is always reaching beyond itself, pointing toward transcendence.

Amicable relations between science and religion, and specifically between evolution and creation, demand more than mutual toleration. There needs to be a firmer weld. For both science and religion are core repositories of value, and both are diminished when either is in denial of the other. As Einstein said, "Science without religion is lame, religion without science is blind." I hope this book can help scientists overcome their fear of Godtalk and theists overcome their fear of evolution.

The questions guiding the five chapters of *Creation and Evolution* are also five. Each draws several others in train: 1) What motivates religious opposition to Darwinism? How have evolutionists couched their response? Where have past efforts at reconciliation failed? 2) How should we read the biblical creation narrative? What claims and values are embedded here? What issues are extraneous? 3) What is the evidence for evolution by natural selection? What was Darwin's argument? How did he answer the objections he faced? How do more recent findings bolster the case? 4) What are today's core objections to evolution? Is Darwinism mere speculation, founded on circumstantial evidence? Is it tautologous? unfalsifiable? Does the complexity of organisms pose insurmountable difficulties? Does methodological naturalism warrant metaphysical naturalism? 5) How does evolution complement theism? What can we make of the robust presence of teleology at the heart of biology? Can randomness be a facet of God's work?

The book opens by surveying the backgrounds of today's conflict, tracing the battles back to a time when creation and evolution were allied against eternalism, the view that nature's rhythms have never changed. This view, that the world has always been essentially as we see it, was long presumed a bastion of scientific thinking. But Genesis in ancient times, like Darwin in more recent days, helped us see the world more historically, showing how we can understand things more fully when we know their origins and their histories of development and change.

Does the world have an origin; do species really change? Classically, it seemed natural to answer no to both questions. But our evidence today runs the other way. What we know about the red shift and the expanding universe points back to a beginning. As for living beings, the deeper we dig in the earth's strata, the simpler and fewer are the fossil types. That confirms Darwin's ideas about species change. DNA now joins the older evidences for the kinship of all living beings. What we see is not explained by the ancient notion that all living types have simply cycled on forever, or by the notion often fathered on scripture, of separate creation.

Science likes constancy, especially in basic principles. Scriptural monotheism sees each finite being as contingent. It says, of all things in the world, and of the world itself: This need not have been. So science seems to favor necessity; and religion, possibility. But science also needs contingency: We seek explanations of what need not have been as it is. Religion too looks for causes, but its search is broader and deeper. It pursues an ultimate cause, and values are what it wants to explain: Why is there goodness, or beauty, or that deceptively simple value, being itself, which never seems to stand still but is always moving, pulsating, affirming and expressing itself? Where does all this energy come from? Is there a cause behind the order and liveliness of things? Why is there consciousness, or caring? Theists believe the ultimate cause is divine. In finite value we see signs of an infinite Source. Proximate and ultimate causes need not be rivals. So when we seek the ultimate cause of all that is precious, evolution is no stumbling block. On the contrary it can stand out as a critical modality in God's creative work.

Before the current evidence was available for the world's origination, divine wisdom was regularly sought in constancy. Individual organisms were not eternal, of course. But to Aristotelians it seemed clear that each species, in its own way, reflects some facet of divine wisdom, eternally. The cycle of generations and the interdependence of living beings assured that invariance. Eternalism, long resisted by believers in the world's utter and ultimate dependence on God, was in time absorbed by many a monotheist. Unchanging species were the secularized, biological precipitate of that ancient idea. Fossils of extinct types belie the idea of eternal species. But many a pre-Darwinian naturalist found in the discreteness of species an enduring hallmark of the perfection of each type. The immutability once urged *against* creation was called to testify in its defense. Evolutionists, for their part, often saw in species change clear disproof of creation. Species constancy was called into court on behalf of creation. Evolution was made witness for the prosecution, against a supposed biblical dogma of species fixity – despite scripture's testimony that plants sprang from the earth and that human beings were fashioned from the soil they would one day till.

Special creation was not thematized in Genesis, nor by most traditional exegetes. They pursue interests of their own. Genesis, for example, avoids naming the sun and moon, calling them the greater and lesser light, slighting their pagan worship. The serpent, biblically, was just another of God's creatures. Likewise, the stars, mentioned as if in an afterthought. Scripture has lessons to impart, about the relations of men and women, about fratricide and guilt. It has spiritual teachings, about humanity's affinity to God, and God's love for creation. Speculative biology is not the focus. But some readers, seeing a threat in secular values, seek armor for their moral tenets and spiritual precepts in biblical inerrantism. Salvation, they assume, depends on our isolation from the evolutionary tree.

As science became a shibboleth of secularity, Darwin was made the apologist (and whipping boy) of every sort of abuse, from colonialism to racism, to communism and socialism. The age of reform, the spread of education, emancipation, better hygiene and social services, raised hopes of a coming golden age. Darwinian ideas were often linked with those visions, whether welcomed or feared. But when industry and finance in the West took the bit between their teeth, the golden age became a gilded age. In the wake of World War I, the gilt, for many, turned tinsel. Darwinism was again the herald, and whipping boy of secularity – of eugenics, cutthroat competition, and cruel exploitation. Fascists, communists, and racists coated their violence and rapacity in the patina of science. Darwin became the natural target of those who sought shelter in the gentler persona of Christ.

Today's debates echo the older polemics. The bones of contention have rather little to do with biology. Rival moral and social claims, presumed implications of evolution, strike closer to the bone. America's pragmatist bent exacerbates the problem: We hold ourselves free to believe what we like and often let our preferences drive our judgments. So we're ready prey to rhetoric. Darwin becomes a brand name in debates about abortion, infanticide, euthanasia, the dimensions and meanings of love and language, the sources of aggression, the destiny of individuals and peoples, the relevance of sin and death, the possibility of freedom – and behind all these, the continued relevance of God.

Part of what I want to do, after exploring the stakes in today's controversy, is consider how we ought to read the Genesis creation story. Its distinctive themes are far too readily buried under standard issue brickbats. Darwin's defenders know that evolution needs little help from them within biology. It's the mainstay of every biological inquiry. But in addressing a broader public, some take on a more sweeping agenda. They know that not everyone reads the Bible literally. But they zero in on volunteer strawmen, pilloried to help them make the case that anyone who takes Genesis seriously today must be a hick or a hack, a boob or deceiver.

Anti-Darwinists are often all too cooperative. Many avoid openly citing the texts that inspire them, lest they seem mere Bible thumpers, or jeopardize their chances of injecting presumed biblical teachings into public school classrooms. Those who do reference the Bible tend to quarry it for prooftexts supporting their preconcerted views: Adam fell, the earth is cursed, Eve was formed from Adam's rib; the earth, drowned by Noah's flood; the world, ready in just six days. Strikingly, they ignore many an explicit theme: that God found his creation good, that he sanctified the seventh day, that life is a blessing, that a man's first loyalty belongs not to his parents but to his wife, that nature keeps its course even in the face of human evil. *Soi disant* literalism bypasses such points, hunting for the source of Noah's floodwaters or a way of packing every animal species into the ark.

Traditional exegetes often say that living creatures emerged from the natural potentials God's creation imparted. That thought follows up on the biblical idea that God works through nature. This doesn't mean that scripture somehow anticipates Darwin. But it does mean that today's conflict between naturalism and "supernaturalism" rests on a false dichotomy. What scientists explain by way of natural causes is not what scripture sets out to explain. And Genesis puts much more in play than explanation. The Bible's creation narrative introduces a genealogy and history, as a prelude to its law and way of life. The underlying norms are prefigured here, establishing their context.

Theists need to take evolution seriously. That means reckoning with the scope and power of the evidence. So, after examining the Genesis account and some of the richest readings of that text, I lay out the chief supports of the Darwinian idea: that all living species stem from a handful of simpler types, the main agency of their evolution being natural selection, the differential survival of types that bear some useful heritable trait. Reading Malthus awakened Darwin to the seriousness of the struggle for survival. The work of Lamarck and the reflections of his own grandfather, Erasmus Darwin, had urged the idea of species change. Lyell's geology convinced Darwin that the steady processes of the earth's history allowed time for the transformations that evolution would require. Darwin broke with classical biology when he saw that the natural variations found in every population are not negligible. Heritable variations that afford the slightest advantage in life's struggle prove critical in time. An exception can become the rule. Species are not fixed types but fluid populations whose gradual changes reflect the shifting challenges and opportunities posed by a dynamic environment.

Darwin found his evidence in morphology and taxonomy, embryology and development, vestigial organs, fossils, of course, and the geographical distribution of distinct and kindred forms. The striking structural affinities in the bones of a human hand to those in a bat's wing or dolphin's flipper, the clustering of types in the taxonomic tree, have an explanation if species are related by descent. Alternative accounts offer only feeble, ad hoc rationales. Darwin could explain the resemblance of developmental forms to their presumptive ancestors on the assumption that the conditions faced by larvae or embryos differ critically from those confronted by a mature adult. He could explain vestigial organs as lasting reminders of an earlier organ, now repurposed or disused. He could find among the fossils lost types that pointed to the common ancestry of living species, and evidence of the severity of natural selection and the permanence of its culling of once flourishing populations. In the flora and fauna splayed across continents and archipelagos he could follow the spread of living species and chart their gradual transformation, as if the changes of many generations were frozen in time.

Today's Darwinian synthesis drops the Lamarckian inheritance of acquired traits, an idea discredited even in Darwin's time. He remained too long attached to it, even intensifying his reliance on it in hopes of speeding the pace of evolutionary change, when challenged by claims that there was not world enough and time for natural selection to do its work, unless variation itself was adaptive. Darwin was innocent of the laws of inheritance. But rediscovery of Mendel's work in 1900 led rapidly to the rise of modern genetics; and (after a period of internecine rivalry between Darwinians and Mendelians), to the replacement of Lamarckian assumptions with the findings of population genetics and cellular biology, forging the new synthesis of neoDarwinism. Where anti-Darwinists had challenged evolutionists to produce a missing link, biology found its conceptual missing link, clinching Darwin's argument, in the new understanding of heredity.

Population geneticists calculated the parameters in which a new gene could spread and become fixed in a population if it conferred even the slightest reproductive advantage. Ethologists followed "ring species" about the polar regions, finding reproductive compatibility between adjacent species, but not, in the end, between species meeting at the far ends of the spectrum. Ecologists traced adaptive radiation in island and continental species, and ethologists observed the darkening of pepper moths in England as the landscape was coated in industrial soot – and the return to prominence of the lighter variants when environmental controls returned the blackened woods to their natural colorations. New fossils fulfill the Darwinian promise of tracing the continuity of ancestral kinds, and DNA sequencing now allows geneticists to track natural selection in wild and laboratory populations, confirming Darwin's claim, that classification maps a family tree, a pedigree of living beings, down to and including our own species.

Of course there are objections. Adam Sedgwick, once Darwin's admiring teacher at Cambridge, was among the first objectors, deeply troubled by his former student's seeming erasure of the very idea of purpose – and the immortal soul. The *Origin*, Sedgwick complained, had no inductive foundation. It was one conjecture piled on another: "You cannot," he wrote, "make a good rope out of air bubbles." Natural selection was no more a real cause than the passage of time. Those criticisms persist today, vulgarly when evolution is called a theory, "not a fact"; more subtly, when Alvin Plantinga contrasts evolution with, say, chemistry.

Karl Popper, a versatile twentieth-century philosopher, ran a more distinctive critique – despite the impact of evolution on his own thinking. The theory, he argued (in an analysis often exploited by anti-Darwinists), is ultimately unfalsifiable. No conceivable evidence seems to count against it. That puts it beyond the pale as science. Empiric theories take risks. If they're really making claims about the world, there should be conceivable conditions that would refute them. Otherwise, they're not making factual claims but just spelling out the logic of their own terms; they're tautologies or nearly so. Isn't it arguing in a circle to say that species survive because they're fit, but then define fitness as differential survival?

A third line of criticism comes from the Intelligent Design movement. Eschewing the young earth doxology of Creation Science, ID advocates argue that even the tiniest organelle or the most intimate biochemical process is irreducibly complex, inoperative without the full complement of its components – and so, unreachable by natural selection: The parts would have no adaptive value without the whole.

These critiques persist. They don't succeed in unraveling the Darwinian synthesis. But they are instructive nonetheless.

Sedgwick's charges help lay bare the structure of Darwin's reasoning: The power of Darwinism rests on its capacity to explain a wide variety of seemingly unrelated phenomena. The epistemic critique, echoed by Plantinga, also reveals how powerful are the motives that lead otherwise responsible thinkers to tilt the evidentiary table when they fear the veracity of scripture and the dignity and destiny of humanity are at stake.

Turning to Popper. Plainly, what keeps evolution from collapsing into circularity are the theory's existential claims: There are heritable variations, there are helpful and unhelpful traits. Tautologies don't make existential claims. Darwin himself stated conditions that could in principle defeat his theory. Notably, he staked his all on gradualism. He also said it would "annihilate" his theory if any part of an organism "had been formed for the exclusive good of another species." That last speaks eloquently to the localization of interests so critical to natural selection. Darwin's gradualism remains controversial. Some evolutionists continue to wonder whether minute steps are enough to account for speciation.

As for Intelligent Design, I see it as a classic *reductio ad ignorantiam*, trying to make one's point by challenging adversaries to answer supposed unanswerable questions – in this case, to explain holistic systems piecemeal, without appeal to the divine designer waiting in the wings. The risk is that someone may find just the answer that was presumed impossible – may, indeed, already have one. In that sense, I think the approach is unhelpful to its exponents. It turns to a God of the gaps. That, I argue, is bad tactics for theists, because it puts God on the defensive. God shrinks as science grows. Bad strategy, too then, because theism should see God's act everywhere, not just in the seemingly uncanny.

Still, the ID critique reveals two key points about today's controversy. One is implicit in the rhetoric of the reductio, the other in the riposte to it. The rhetoric of irreducible complexity is celebratory. The ID challenge does not reveal that no natural origin can be found for phenomena like the clotting of blood or the origins of the flagellum. The impact, rather, is to highlight the intricacy and elegance of living systems – values prized by scientists and theists alike. ID advocates readily call organs, organelles, and whole organisms machines. They should hardly balk at acknowledging natural selection as a natural cause – a congeries of causes. Many of their favorite cases are even now increasingly well understood in evolutionary terms. But what rightly draws their gaze is not mechanism but something still unspoken when naturalistic explanations are complete.

This is hinted at when Phillip Johnson raises his ID critique of a dynamic common in today's scientistic polemics: They start out from a methodological naturalism entirely appropriate to natural science. Scientists, as such, should stick to natural principles and what can be studied empirically. They should not resort to pixies in explaining their results. But the polemicists push on to much stronger claims, a metaphysical or ontological naturalism: We're expected to commit to the proposition that nothing exists, no explanation can be made beyond the terms a scientist can control. That's dogmatism. Daniel Dennett typifies the claim, demanding "cranes," and not "skyhooks" as explanations – No heavy lifting without mechanism. Before inquiries have even begun, that rules out any question that would not be asked by a scientist.

Yet there are such questions. We do sometimes walk where science cannot tread, although even here science gives us food for thought. Our questions about value, and its ultimate origins, are examples. Such questions don't have mechanisms as their answers. Which brings us to our fifth chapter. Proposing that God works in and through nature, not in opposition to it, I argue that value is endemic in nature, manifest in living beings, self-aware and in some measure self-directed in the human case. Darwin does not dissolve purpose, as Sedgwick feared. He does localize it. Natural selection does not eliminate teleology. It's presumed in the Darwinian concept of adaptation, which natural selection is meant to explain. Without purposes, Darwin would have no story to tell. Evolution presumes an interest on the part of organisms – an interest in survival, one might say. But the lineages that realize that interest are not invariant. They change, and so do their interests. The purposes of an organism, what it means for it to flourish, are not those of its remote ancestors. Purposes, like species, are emergent. Autonomy and community emerge as evolution unfolds, yielding consciousness and caring. It's this kind of event that Genesis looks to.

Reductionists sometimes say that evolution is the work of chance. That's a partial truth. But there's more to nature than chance. And chance itself – randomness, more precisely – in the genetic lottery, becomes a resource, not a threat. Viewed in evolutionary perspective, sexual reproduction makes randomness a tool of adaptation and a means to adaptability. Here evolution and creation meet, allowing theists to see the hand of God, not as a tinkerer whose mind and method are just another mechanism but as a creator whose poetry is written in and between the lines of natural causes. For there is brilliant creativity not just in the crafting of living systems but also in the joyous, reckless dance of every jewel-like molecule, cell, and star.

Backgrounds

Battles over ideas can be as bitter as battles for land, and they last much longer. Frontline fighters may have long forgotten what led to the taking up of arms, or pens, or the cudgel of law. Many in today's creation–evolution battles have a pretty clear notion of their own concerns but murky images of their foes. The terrain between pitched camps, heavily mined and shrouded in battle smoke, may be hard to make out, let alone traverse. But the aim of this book is irenic, not polemical. It seeks the broad ground that separates but also links today's extremes. What are the chances for peace? What options are open, beyond mutual erasure or annoyance? A little history might help in mapping the terrain.

Creation vs. eternity

Creation has been in court before. In 529 Justinian shut down Plato's Academy, then in its tenth century. He exiled its leaders and, when a treaty with the Shah allowed their return, forbade them to teach philosophy at Athens.[1] The neoplatonic defenders of ancient pagan piety had staked philosophy itself as they saw it on their assurance that the very idea of creation was absurd. Hadn't Aristotle written, "From what is not, nothing can possibly come to be"?[2]

The Greeks lost that battle. Creation persists; pagan cosmology atrophied. But monotheists salvaged much that was precious and perennial in the old philosophy. Where some saw only enmity, they saw affinities between creation and emanation, the timeless flow of reality, truth, and goodness from an infinite Source. Without their work of synthesis, neoplatonism would have followed the fate of Stoic metaphysics, plowed into the soil of common parlance but forgotten philosophically. In philosophy, as in politics, accommodation matters.

Enlightened opinion had long opposed creation, and evolution with it. At the dawn of Western metaphysics, Parmenides argued that being could not have come to be: Nothingness had no reality to start it up.[3] Parmenides, as Aristotle saw it, boldly freed philosophy from myth, seeking the nature of being without confusing that question with questions of origins.[4] So Aristotle humors Parmenides for denying change altogether and treating any negation as an absolute negation. Parmenides may have denied time and multiplicity, but he had seen that non-being was impossible and thus ruled out a void, and creation.[5]

Absolute creation, Aristotle reasoned, would mean the becoming of becoming, initiating an infinite regress. Creation would mean effects without causes, a time with no antecedent time, a making with no matter to be made, an actuality sprung from no prior potency. Science barred creation. For science needs causes, time, matter, potentiality. Later generations, dazzled by Aristotle's brilliance, often dismissed creation in favor of ceaseless change.[6] Heaven and earth have always been as we find them, animal species neither arising, as Plato imagined, nor dying out, as Empedocles presumed. Unless the uncreated stars had always circled the earth in their indestructible spheres and species had always bred true, the fabric of the cosmos would be rent and nature's constancy would prove inconstant.[7] Well into modern times such thoughts passed for certainties. Even today there are sarcastic questions about what God was doing before creation, and demands to know who created God. As eminent an astronomer as Fred Hoyle fought the Big Bang for years, even positing the continuous, spontaneous appearance of new matter, lest the world admit of a beginning.

It was not Copernicus who sank the first deep rifts into Aristotle's celestial spheres but John Philoponus, a Christian in Justinian's empire, arguing that physical spheres cannot be the eternal motors Aristotle expected to mark the world's time. Stars shine with varied colors, so they must differ in matter, Philoponus reasoned, like fires on earth that blaze in different colors when different substances are cast into them. Hadn't Plato shown that every process has a beginning and an end? If so, the stars were not eternal, despite the fantasies that colored them divine. Nor were the heavens simple, indestructible, and uncreated. For stars must differ in substance from their settings in the transparent spheres. The cosmos was contingent. Like all things physical, it must have had an origin.[8] With all his learning and zeal, Simplicius, one of the last members of Plato's Academy, was hard pressed to answer the Christian's probing common sense.[9]

The issue smoldered long after the Academy was closed. Science seemed to side with Aristotle: Time and change had no beginning. Many scriptural monotheists read the old creation stories as allegories of the world's timeless dependence on God. Scripture could not mean that time and nature had begun, as if from nowhere. Wouldn't an origin set arbitrary bounds to God's creative act? Some did favor cosmic origins. Kindi, an Arab philosopher, added absolute creation *ex nihilo*, to the menu of changes Aristotle had allowed. The Muslim theologian Ghazali vigorously rebutted philosophical eternalists. The Jewish philosopher Moses Maimonides, declining to rest creation on scriptural authority, still saw good grounds to affirm it, although acknowledging that neither eternity nor creation could be proved.[10] Proposed proofs just trapped their makers in extreme positions: The necessity that creationists sought in proof seemed to spill over and make creation itself necessary, compromising God's freedom. Thomas Aquinas, reviewing the arguments, judged creation not impossible but an article of faith.[11] Immanuel Kant declared the problem insoluble.[12] Using tactics borrowed from the ancient Skeptics, he balanced the rival arguments: Both sides looked reasonable, but both pushed pure reason too far. Since any natural fact can be mentally denied, the world easily looks contingent. But with any such fact, one can always ask what made it so. That makes all things look necessary.

Genesis nurtures the idea of contingency: The world need not have been. But Aristotle called science a search for explanations showing why things must be as they are. Neither perspective is dispensable. We assume that things might have been otherwise when we say that without their causes they would not be as they are. But we treat things as necessary when we start from their existence and search for their causes. Generalizing such necessities evokes the image of an eternal universe. It would be nice to be able to look at things in both ways at once, as if with binocular vision. That's hard to do but not impossible, if we read necessities contextually, as givens within a causal framework, while recognizing that the entire fabric need not have existed. That approach would respect both naturalism and theism. But many demand a choice between the two. Kant did not. His brief was to restrain exalted pronouncements about ultimates. But for just that reason his modest, Solomonic ruling often goes unheeded. Exhausted adversaries battle on, little suspecting that for centuries evolution was allied with creation, against eternalism.

An historic alliance

To Ghazali, called the Proof of Islam, for his spirited arguments against the world's eternity, it seemed clear that neoplatonic eternalists could not make good on their promises of a theistic naturalism. How could God's creative act make a difference in an eternal universe? The philosophers were atheists despite themselves.[13] As a counterweight to their rationalist intellectualism Ghazali set empiricism: It seemed arbitrary to exclude creation just because the idea looked odd. Who would expect something as small as a grain to devour a town and then consume itself? But fire can do that. Expectations can be deceiving; not every seeming necessity is real. If logic is the issue, as eternalists claimed, where were the connective middle terms to sew up the proof? If the world's eternity was self-evident, why do so many disagree?

Maimonides did not brand neoplatonists atheists. He argued more mildly, that the emergence of a varied world from God's unity is better conceived in terms of will than, say, implication. Besides, thinking of a God who made a difference allows us to reason from what we know of nature back to God's creative work. If the world never lacked existence, how real was God's role – or rule?[14] Aristotle's eternalist arguments were merely persuasive, not demonstrative in force, and he knew it. It was he, after all, who taught us the difference between proof and persuasion. Aristotle telegraphs his awareness that his case is weak by resorting to persuasive language and citing the concurrence of predecessors. He lists "whether the universe is eternal or no" among the "questions on which reasonings conflict … there being convincing arguments for both views." On some matters, he writes, "we have no argument because they are so vast and we find it hard to give reasons."[15]

Arguments for eternity, Maimonides explains, sound plausible because they presume our present understanding of nature. Time, *as we know it*, does always have a past; possibility *is* grounded in matter. But these are not absolute necessities. Maimonides invokes an evolutionist analogy: A bright man, ignorant of reproduction, might readily deduce the impossibility of his own birth: He breathes air, eats food, moves about, vents bodily wastes. How could he have spent nine months inside another human being? Evidently, there's no inferring from the settled state of nature to conditions at the dawn of time.[16]

Galileo, like Ghazali and Maimonides, countered the rationalism of his adversaries with empiricism. He archly named his foil in the *Dialogues Concerning the Two Chief World Systems* Simplicio, after Philoponus' adversary.[17] The challenge he faced came not from scripture but from eternalism. Like Philoponus, Galileo naturalized the heavens. The great weakness of Copernican cosmology was in explaining what held the planets in place. Until Kepler's Laws were wedded to Newton's mechanics, heliocentrists could not say why the stars and planets don't just fall. So the eternal crystalline spheres looked too precious to discard. But Galileo boldly breached them. Sunspots and moon craters confirmed the compositeness and mutability of celestial bodies, much as star colors had for Philoponus.[18] Copernicus' elegant model must be true. Since bodies have no natural place, the planets must have been brought, like building materials, to their present positions, on a linear path that Aristotelians would have to assign a beginning. So Galileo hustled the heavens into place by way of a creationist cosmology.[19]

Galileo's creationism, like Plato's, was evolutionary. It touched biology by building on the ancient idea of adaptation. Living forms were long known to fit their environments. That thought was canonized in Aristotle's linkage of form to function. The Stoics and Galen credited an immanent providence: Organs are divine gifts, complemented by the skills to use them. The Qur'an too treats adaptations as God's gifts, and the Sincere Brethren of Basra celebrated God for equipping all creatures for the lives they lead.[20] Galileo's suggestion that any life on the moon would differ greatly from terrestrial life presumes environmental adaptation. The hint was not lost on Descartes, whose "disguisedly heliocentric and discretely evolutionary" cosmology reckons that God might have framed the planetary system in stages. Our senses fit us for survival, Descartes notes, not for discerning the true nature of things.[21]

Science does not stop at Aristotle's question about why things must be as they are. Intimately connected is the historian's question, how things came to be. Filled with the pride of the industrial revolution and the burgeoning empire that reached out to master the world, intellectually and otherwise, Darwin saw history as opening a new dimension for science:

> When we no longer look at an organic being as a savage looks at a ship ... when we regard every production of nature as one which has a history; when we contemplate every complex structure and instinct as the summing up of many contrivances, each useful to its possessor, nearly in the same way as when we look at any great mechanical invention as the summing up of the labour, the experience, the reason, and even the blunders of numerous workmen; when we thus view each organic being, how far more interesting, I speak from experience, will the study of natural history become.[22]

Biology will not just fit phenomena into patterns. It will probe the origins of living forms, just as geology asks how the earth was formed – and astronomy, how stars are born and change. Turning away from the formalism of classical biology, Darwin put the history back into natural history: Species themselves have a history. They are not just instances of a general rule. Each species is unique, in many ways contingent. The role of narrative in biological explanation makes the theory of evolution a direct descendant of the idea of creation. Yet complementarities can breed rivalries. Eager heirs may wonder why grandpa still has the family silver or still keeps the old house where he's lived so long and done so much to give the place its character.

What's at stake?

Some find it strange, so long after the Scopes trial, that debates about evolution surge recurrently back to life. True, Scopes was convicted. The Tennessee statute barring evolution from the classroom stood on the books for decades. But in the public eye Clarence Darrow scored a bruising victory. William Jennings Bryan, with all his eloquence, failed to convince even himself that evolution held no kernel of truth. Creation took a beating in the press. But John Scopes got off on a technicality, so the case was never heard by the Supreme Court, as the American Civil Liberties Union had hoped. The chilling effect, while it lasted, was less on the teaching of evolution than on efforts to pass laws like the statutes that forbade it.

Some historians see in the timing of the trial signs of a cultural lag: The spectacle, staged long after debates about evolution had cooled in Europe, was a delayed reaction to the German menace confronted in the Great War, or fear of Bolshevism, in a witches' brew with demagoguery and know-nothingism. Yet the controversy continues. New laws are tabled, school boards do battle, lawsuits are filed, textbooks tagged with warnings or filletted more closely than risqué DVDs or violent computer games. Is America still reacting to the Great War? Are there epicycles on the wheels of progress?

Some see only pigheadedness in creationism. How long, they wonder, will religious freedom, abetted by litigiousness and intellectual consumerism, bury the evidence under an impervious, imperious will to believe? Stirred by their own oratory, partisans of modernity, fighting for presumptively foregone conclusions, continue to misjudge their foes. Like their adversaries, they allay their frustration by preaching to the choir and pay little heed to the sources of resistance, except to stigmatize them. Yet to dismiss anti-evolutionists as primitives is not to understand what leads them to comb the Bible, or the science literature, for arguments to buttress what they hold sacred. The Kantian trinity of God, freedom, and immortality captures most of the issues: Darwinists seem to equate truth with science and find human dignity not in moral freedom and accountability but in liberation from revealed morality and thoughts of immortality.

Start with God. As one writer put it, laying his cards on the table, "there is a *need* for God to exist" – or the world becomes "an absurd accident that inevitably fails to honor our needs. From the point of view of atheism, all reason, love and creation is ultimately accidental, temporary, and doomed to destruction."[23] Many hail Darwin for giving theism the coup de grâce. Hume's *Dialogues Concerning Natural Religion* (published posthumously in 1779), they say, undercut the design argument, exposing the image of a watchmaker God as a weak analogy – even before William Paley published his version of the ancient argument in 1802. Darwin, once entranced by Paley, seemed to complete the Democritean project of substituting physical causes for divine intent. As Richard Dawkins put it, "Darwin made it possible to be an intellectually fulfilled atheist."[24]

Before Darwin, species fixity was often a surrogate for divine design, each type an emblem of eternal wisdom. The idea was Aristotelian. But it acquired a transcendentalist aura in nineteenth-century biology: Each species distinctively exemplified nature's plan. Biblically inclined special creationists fastened on the Hebraism affirming that God fashioned each creature *after its kind* (Genesis 1:11, 24). They still do. If cabbages cross with radishes, Frank Marsh writes, it means not that one kind can arise from another but that it was wrong to class cabbages and radishes as different kinds.[25] "Microevolution" is permissible – so long as it does not initiate or extinguish species: Natural selection prunes life's tree, correcting errors but creating nothing. Broadly defined "kinds" are expected to fit in Noah's ark; today's "varieties" will arise later. Marsh knows that *cells* can hybridize. But he cites the relative intolerance of alien genetic material, to support species discreteness: Mouse–human tissue cultures confirm the image of "man and all animals as originating from the same materials, the dust of the earth."[26] The rise of life from non-living matter is God's miracle. But it remains unasked why God wouldn't use nature toward his ends. Doesn't Exodus say God *drove back the sea with a strong east wind all through the night* (14:21)? Species fixity trumps that biblical theme: Redemption demands human discreteness.[27]

In Darwin's time, critics like the Duke of Argyll, protective of Adam and Eve, painted man as rational and mature, couth from the creation. Innocent before the Fall, chastened after it, the first humans were gentle, sensitive, language users. "Savages" were degraded humans, not grim reminders of a bestial past. The fossils, Argyll argued, conclusively exclude "any change whatever in the specific characters of Man since the oldest Human Being yet known was born." Indeed, "all scientific evidence" affirmed the origins of humanity from "a single pair."[28] Henry Morris echoes the thesis: Fossils represent "either apes or men" – nothing intermediate. No issue is more vital to the question of mankind's purpose.[29] "These ancient men are all true men, no ape-men ... Neanderthal Man, also was perfectly normal except that, as now believed, he was affected with rickets. Homo Habilis, though small, seems, to have been quite modern in every other respect."[30] Robert Kofahl chimes in:

> There is no evidence for the evolution of human intelligence. ... There is no reason to believe that non-living matter thinks, has feelings, has any sense of moral responsibility, or exercises will, or that chemical reactions can make an organism that does. Personal nature must, therefore, have come from a higher personal spiritual Source, not from an impersonal material source. This conclusion from the scientific evidence is just what the Bible teaches. We were created in the image of the infinite-personal Spirit, God the Creator.[31]

Bolton Davidheiser writes:

> The evolutionists definitely believe that early man was hardly to be distinguished from some sort of ape and made crude tools which can hardly be distinguished from naturally fractured rocks. According to the Bible the first man was created as such, talked with God, knew right from wrong, named the animals, and sinned. Early men were skillful in metalwork and the handling of musical instruments.[32]

Genesis does paint Adam and Eve as moral beings and their early progeny as artistic. But the biblical narrative is a drama of the human condition, not a history of our natural origins. Still, for many today evolution means erasing moral agency and freedom, leaving humanity tangled in our animal roots, with only the flickering lamp of evolutionary imperatives to guide our steps.[33] True, Darwin spoke of duty, courage, conscience, and love. He found animal precedents for them all. Hadn't the eminent Harvard zoologist and anti-Darwinist Louis Agassiz seen in dogs "something very like a conscience"?[34] Darwin speaks the same moral language as other Victorians. Yet evolution seemed even to him to make all moral values contingent:

> If, for instance, to take an extreme case, men were reared under precisely the same conditions as hive-bees, there can hardly be any doubt that our unmarried females would, like the worker bees, think it a sacred duty to kill their brothers, and mothers would strive to kill their fertile daughters; and no one would think of interfering.[35]

Could immortality survive if humans are mere machines, blind works of nature?

Facts and values

Clearly values were at stake in the religious responses to evolution. What critics feared most was materialism – slamming the door on a spiritual God, an autonomous mind and immortal soul. But Darwinian theory is about biological events and their causes. So critics from the start saw the need to marshal evidence. Bishop Wilberforce, in his celebrated debate with Thomas Henry Huxley, is said to have wrapped up by saying:

> I should like to ask Professor Huxley, who is sitting by me and is about to tear me to pieces when I have sat down, as to his belief in being descended from an ape, Is it on his grandfather's or his grandmother's side that the ape ancestry comes in?[36]

Huxley knew how the Oxford audience would judge that kind of low blow. Reportedly he whispered: "The Lord hath delivered him into my hand." What exactly was said in the 1860 debate may never be precisely known. But the story, as fondly reconstructed by Huxley and others, is part of Darwinian folklore. Over a century later Alvin Plantinga could still mount a baroque version of the Wilberforce ad hominem: How can Darwinians trust their scientific judgment, Plantinga asked, if they take reason to have evolved not for discovering the truth but as a survival mechanism? Cartoonists have similar fun picturing an ape at the zoo reading Darwin and Genesis, trying to decide, "Am I my brother's keeper or my keeper's brother?" No one wants to look in the mirror and see an ape smiling back at him. But Darwin had a rival iconography:

> I would as soon be descended from that heroic little monkey who braved his enemy in order to save the life of his keeper; or from that old

baboon, who, descending from the mountains carried away in triumph his young comrade from a crowd of astonished dogs – as from a savage who delights to torture his enemies, offers up bloody sacrifices, practices infanticide without remorse, treats his wives like slaves, knows no decency, and is haunted by the grossest superstitions.[37]

Addressing the perceived threat to the human image, Darwin cemented his theory to the moral ideals his readers shared. But evolution is, after all, a story of change. Its products are no less elevated, for arising through natural causes. Wilberforce, an amateur ornithologist and geologist as well as Bishop of Oxford, mounted a scientific case, not just for tactical but for principled reasons.

we are too loyal pupils of inductive philosophy to start back from any conclusion by reason of its strangeness. Newton's patient philosophy taught him to find in the falling apple the law which governs the silent movements of the stars in their courses; and if Mr. Darwin can with the same correctness of reasoning demonstrate to us our fungular descent, we shall dismiss our pride, and avow with the characteristic humility of philosophy, our unsuspected cousinship with the mushrooms.[38]

Weren't fixed species "confirmed by all observation"? Didn't science rest on the truism that things must be what they are? How could evolution pass muster without documented cases of species change or clear intermediate types? "If evolution were true," a later critic proclaimed, "we ought to find everywhere not only the fossils of endless intermediate forms … we ought to see all around us, if evolution is really a 'continuous' process, these intermediate forms of life."[39]

Darwin did have answers. The variants found in every living population are the transitional forms; variations – today called mutations – may be imperceptible but crucial, especially over the long haul. As for the fossils, Darwin reasoned, variant types are typically rare, experimental, as it were, often frangible. To the critics, early and late, such answers seemed labored, a clear sign of rationalization.

Wilberforce pledged "to scrutinize carefully every step of the argument … and demur if at any point of it we are invited to substitute unlimited hypothesis for patient observation." The starch in his commitment, his conviction that "the line between man and the lower animals was distinct."[40] Over a century later, Henry Morris will class Ramaphithecus, Dryopithecus, Oreopithecus, Limnopithecus, Kenyapithecus, and Australopithecus unequivocally as apes; Neanderthals, as humans, given their cranial capacity. "Homo erectus was a true man, but somewhat degenerate in size and culture, possibly because of inbreeding, poor diet, and a hostile environment."[41] Shades of the Duke of Argyll!

Anti-Darwinism today is grounded not in ignorance but in rejection of what many see as evolution's implications: A world without God, without immortal souls, free will, or moral spine. If Darwinism means moral relativism, if it makes survival of the strong and extinction of the weak the law affirmed in nature and confirmed by science, if fossils displace scripture and evolutionary catchwords elbow traditional morality aside, it's hardly surprising that evolution draws odium among those unwilling to give up their God and the tradition in which they find a morality of love and dignity. The more strident secularity grows, the tighter do they grip their faith and the more powerfully are newcomers drawn to its promises of peace, love, and safety from the horrors too often and too freely linked with Darwin's name.

Drawing the battle lines

Enoch Burr, Congregationalist minister, astronomer, mathematician, professor of natural theology and geology at Amherst, spelled out the issues: Evolution was awkward, implausible, ultimately irrational. Above all, it was materialist. It meant not just mutable species but spontaneous generation. It ignored the "simplest," "surest" explanation of life and the world: divine creation.[42] Charles Hodge, for nearly six decades a Princeton Bible scholar, orientalist, and Calvinist theologian, a powerful controversialist with a devoted following and a "prophetic" passion, presages the work of later anti-Darwinists. Pledged to accept scientific findings, Hodge leaned on Agassiz to bolster his conviction that fixed forms were solid science. But Darwinism, as he saw it, was corrosive. Darwin was "simply a naturalist, a careful and laborious observer." But natural selection banished divine purpose from nature. Hodge answered the question of his book *What is Darwinism?* succinctly: "It is atheism."[43] The stark choice, Darwinism or faith, sounded the classic evangelical challenge: Faith or sin, truth or error. The dramatic either/or leaves little room for graceful maneuver or retreat. But science, Hodge trusted, would not belie Scripture's testimony. Careful reading of the evidence would expose Darwin's error.

Hodge's fears persist. So essays at theistic evolution are often met with scorn. With mediating voices unheard, creation frequently falls to the lot of would be literalists and self-anointed controversialists. Hodge lived to see a handful of conciliators, whose pleas for divine immanence he branded blasphemies. Later reconcilers remained anathema to his more militant successors. Henry Ward Beecher, the Amherst-trained Congregationalist minister, ardent abolitionist and brother of Harriet Beecher Stowe, saw evolution as God's means of creation. Such proposals were predictably condemned. Beecher's sensational trial for adultery hardly helped. But what hurt theistic evolution most, perhaps, was the dethroning of a Sunday School God, leaving an apparent cosmic swirl, seeming emptiness to eyes unused to seeking God as Abraham or Kant did, in the starry heavens above or the still small

voice within. Forgotten, in the battle heat: the thought that inspired the Refor-
mation – that we all must read scripture for ourselves and make of it what we
can. Christians may view Abraham's three strangers as an apparition of the
Trinity. But a six-day creation is set high on a shelf, above interpretation.

Francis Abbot, a co-founder of the Free Religious Association, framed a
"scientific theism," with God as evolution's source and outcome. Purpose
was not abolished: "all nature and all life is one great theophany,"[44] revealing a "purely spiritual personality." But that personality did not look much
like Jesus. Nor did John Fiske's immanent God. Like many a would be evolutionist, Fiske found the spiritual (and progressive) answers he was seeking
more in Spencer's "law of universal evolution" than in Darwin's more strictly
biological account. Joseph Le Conte, a distinguished geology professor at
Berkeley, saw evolution as a continuous progress, guided by natural laws but
energized by "resident forces." Readers warmly thanked him for saving them
from "blank materialism." He showed them how to see in fossils "objectified
modes of divine thought" and "divine energy" at work throughout the
cosmos.[45] "The doctrine of Divine immanency," he wrote, "carries with it
the solution of many vexed questions" –

> Religious thought, like all else, is subject to a law of evolution ... reli-
> gion has passed from a gross anthropomorphism to a true spiritual
> theism, and the change is largely due to science and especially to the
> theory of evolution. There are three main stages ... 1) God is altogether
> such a one as ourselves, but larger and stronger. His action on Nature, like
> our own, is *direct*; his will is wholly man-like, capricious and without law.
> 2) ... God is not *altogether* like ourselves ... *king-like*. He is not present in
> Nature, but sits enthroned above Nature in solitary majesty. He acts upon
> Nature, not directly but indirectly, through physical forces and natural laws.
> He is an absentee landlord governing his estate by means of appointed
> agents, which are the natural forces and laws established in the begin-
> ning. ... God was the great *artificer*, the great *architect*, working, as it were,
> on foreign material and conditioned by its nature. ... This conception still
> lingers in the religious mind, and is in fact the prevailing one now. It is a
> great advance on the preceding, but alas! it removes God beyond the reach
> of our love ... 3) The third and last stage in this development is true spiri-
> tual theism. God is immanent, resident in Nature. ... The forces of Nature
> are different forms of his energy. ... The laws of Nature are the modes of
> operation of the omnipresent Divine energy, invariable because he is per-
> fect. ... In this view we return again to *direct* action, but in a nobler, a
> spiritual, Godlike form. He is again brought very near to every one of us
> and restored to our love, for in him we live and move and have our
> being. ... This view has been held by noble men in all times, especially by
> the early Greek fathers, but is now verified and well-nigh demonstrated
> by the theory of evolution. No other view is any longer tenable.[46]

Fiske's disciple, Minot Savage, a Unitarian minister, openly embraced pantheism and the "fire mist" that Stoics had hailed as Zeus. His book, *The Religion of Evolution*,[47] only confirmed Hodge's warnings: Evolution was a false religion. Didn't the Gospels teach: "he that entereth not by the door into the sheepfold, but climbeth up some other way, is a thief and a robber" (John 10:1)? The more welcoming words "In my Father's house are many mansions" (14:2) might find room for evolutionary theism. But they faded when alien gods threatened.

The American positivist Chauncey Wright saw the metaphysics that many evolutionists projected onto their biology. But he had seen the metaphysics even in Auguste Comte's positivism. He too had a metaphysic, of course. One can't dodge metaphysics without landing in it. But Wright bowed only to science – and thus, to evolution. Like Darwin, he did not exempt humanity from general biological laws and refused to seek some life force to guide evolution. Causality operates in biology, he held, as it does in economics, geology, or meteorology – even if complexity hampers precise predictions. Wright took C. S. Peirce's appeals to chance as just another admission of ignorance; Peirce's discovery of creativity in chance was a veiled reversion to transcendence. Wright soft-pedaled his own metaphysical riffs – reductionism and determinism.[48] Like Comte, he was an anti-metaphysical metaphysician. But his stringency carried a message: Science, being empirical, knows no purposes. Biologists should not seek them; theologians only dilute the purity of religious truth by ransacking nature for hallmarks of design.[49] Wright walled off science from religion, probably more to guard science from religious impositions than to shield religious truths. His spiritual purism was too austere even for William James; his piety, an ethical ideal.[50]

As the work of reconcilers grew more competent and confident, more technical and comprehensive, more circumspect religiously, and scientifically more thoughtful and mature, it proved no more reassuring to traditionalists fighting for their faith. Fiske and Savage had jettisoned original sin. Le Conte, Beecher, and others were inviting individuals or societies to work out their own salvation. But could notions of progress replace Christ's sacrifice? Freedom and responsibility were under threat. Hadn't Darrow himself saved Leopold and Loeb from execution just a year before the Scopes trial, his twelve-hour summation casting the privileged thrill murderers as victims, not of a morbid fascination with Nietzsche or each other but of temporary insanity and repression? Where was moral accountability? Henry Osborn and others struggled to snatch the immortal soul from the jaws of evolution.[51] But could they ensure that all thought and value would not reduce to mechanics?

C. Lloyd Morgan's idea of emergent evolution – higher order complexities defying reduction to their elements – hardly seemed to save immortality. And the moralities to be founded on evolution did not make Darwinism look lovelier. Spencer, Veblen, Dreiser, Jack London proffered strident alternatives to the Gospels, much as Edward Wilson and Daniel Dennett do today. The socialist utopianism of an H. G. Wells or John Dewey targeted Christian values. To committed Christians such men were false prophets; their pre-scriptions were perversions, symptoms of the atheist disease. The face of Jesus, unseen in nature's raw energy or the blank stare of the Commintern, was being crushed again under the boots of a brutal historicism. But comfort was precisely what Dewey meant to escape in the life of experimentalism. Science and progress became brand names of values anathema to tradition-alists, whom secularists dismissed as dinosaurs, diehards, and cranks. The bully healthy mindedness of self-styled progressives concealed a sneering, leering nihilism and masked secular idolatries rooted in vanity and pride.[52]

Religious evolutionists welcome the work of philosophers like Bergson, Whitehead, and Teilhard. But to embattled traditionalists, each conciliatory effort is another affront. Davidheiser calls Teilhard an idolator, Communist or fellow traveler, hypocrite, and heretic.[53] Rational religion seems an onion that peels down to an empty core: Scripture must be read literally to be taken seriously. The view was not primitive but reactive, seeking safety for the sacred in an elemental faith. Morris nurses Hodge's animus against deanthropomorphizing scripture:

> If we are permitted to interpret Genesis in this fashion, what is to pre-vent our interpreting any other part of Scripture in the same way? Thus the Virgin Birth may, after all, be only an allegory, the Resurrection could be only a myth of supra-history, the Ten Commandments only a liturgy, the Crucifixion only a dream. Every man may interpret Scripture as suits his own convenience and thus every man becomes his own God.[54]

Incarnation matters. What use is emblematic salvation? If liberal Christians see progress as salvation, J. Gresham Machen argues, they aren't Christians at all but humanists who wrap their unbelief in Christian trappings.[55] Creation, then, stands in for salvation.

That, of course, was part of the problem. Intellectual leaders who saw themselves as progressives often deemed religion an albatross around the neck of progress and reform. To them, Darwin's work was less important biologically than it was ideologically. Huxley, long known as Darwin's bull-dog for his vigorous championship of evolution, chose that sobriquet and that role for himself. He had his doubts about Darwin's gradualism and even about the adequacy of natural selection in accounting for speciation. But Darwin's work and the controversy it aroused raised the warrior spirit in him. He freely used the language of warfare in his writings and lectures about evolution, vehemently defended Darwin, and pursued bishops and other clergy as adversaries. He spoke of "extinguished theologians" as "strangled snakes" that "lie about the cradle of every science". He wielded the *Origin* as a club against all that he regarded as illiberal or retrograde, and above all against religion.[56]

The fight continued in much the same terms in the following century and beyond. Andrew Dickson White, co-founder of Cornell University, wrote his *History of the Warfare of Science with Theology in Christendom* (1896) as part of a lifelong campaign for secular education. Although a practicing Episcopalian, he saw religion as a foe of free inquiry and zealously spread Washington Irving's myth that the earth's sphericity was unknown before Columbus. White used that story and vivid accounts of Galileo's persecution as sticks to beat the anti-Darwinists. But hardly any geographer before Columbus thought the world flat.[57] And Galileo, as we've seen, had more in common with Genesis than with eternalism.

Proclaiming a world bereft of God, with Darwin as its prophet, loud voices still bruit relativism as the moral yield of evolution. That thought stokes the fears of fundamentalists. Small wonder, they argue, given the moral and spiritual bankruptcy of humanism, that sexual license, random violence, drug and alcohol abuse, familial disintegration, exploitation, and anomie follow in evolution's wake. The idea of natural selection, applied in social contexts, only aggravates the injury: "racism in its virulent forms is mainly a product of evolutionary thinking," Boardman, Koontz, and Morris write. Adolf Hitler, Cecil Rhodes, and Benito Mussolini were "ardent evolutionists." Beyond guilt by association, the critics see a moral link: "Karl Marx, Friedrich Engels and practically all other leaders of Communist thought, past and present, have been racists in the tradition of Charles Darwin."[58] Substituting evolutionary imperatives for divine love, modern sophists have stripped away all barriers to genocide. "It is generally believed," Davidheiser writes, "that Darwin did not condone the extrapolation of his natural selection theory into social relationships, but the fact is that he himself taught that human evolution proceeded through warfare and struggle between isolated clans."[59] True Darwin hated slavery. But he contemplates with equanimity and a sense of civilization's triumph the global "extermination" of "the savage races."[60]

Christians proudly contrast the anti-slavery witness of many churches with the shameful racism of the Smithsonian movement at the dawn of physical anthropology. Emancipation once seemed to presage the coming of the Lord. Temperance was looked to hopefully as another step toward the millennium. But as the gilt grew tarnished on lost hopes of a golden age, many blamed Darwin for godlessness, greed, license – and racism.[61] Scripture taught human unity: "God hath made of one blood all nations of men" (Acts 17:26). Darwin's talk of "favored races" seemed antithetical to that idea. Biblically, "there is one kind of flesh of men, another of beasts, another of fishes, and another of birds" (1 Corinthians 15:39). Science, a Baptist minister urged, bears that out: For "if the blood of one of these is injected into the veins of the other, death immediately follows."[62] Scripture unites mankind and divides humans from the animals. Darwin seemed to do just the opposite.

Surveying a century of genocidal horrors and contemplating the some-times self-declared moral bankruptcy of philosophy, the carnage often joined by intellectuals, today's seekers after signs are politically articulate and morally united far better than their forebears in the 1920s. When Bryan asked rhetorically, "Who says we can't bar science that deprives us of all hope of the future life to come?" a chorus of reputable thinkers could answer that evolution holds no brief against immortality – or at least its essential meaning. Today that chorus has grown fainter. Relativism and materialism are more strident, strengthening the anti-Darwinists' resolve and confirming their sense of threat: *Every* "anti-Christian system of the present day," Henry Morris wrote, is the "evil fruit" of Darwinism.[63] The socio-political aims of the Intelligent Design "Wedge Strategy" confirm the conclusion: It's not back-wardness that continually re-envigorates anti-Darwinism but the construction put on evolution by some of its most ardent advocates.

Understanding and misunderstanding

The Darwin "who lives in the collective memory of intellectuals and scien-tists," Robert Richards writes, "instituted a pervasive materialism and mechanism in the interpretation of life."[64] He "pushed back the sea of faith," replacing God with "a mechanical, materialist science," and vacated the idea of progress by making nature "morally meaningless."[65] Yet the first Darwinians drew quite different implications:

> If 'materialism' means that only matter exists, that what we call mind is simply a fixed function of matter, that ethical judgments are inescapably subjective and determined by selfish pleasure, then neither Darwin, nor his colleagues and disciples – Wallace, Haeckel, Romanes, Morgan, James, Baldwin – nor even Herbert Spencer constructed materialist theories. Darwin and Spencer found objective grounds for authentic altruism. ... If 'mechanism' implies that in the evolutionary process mind must be derivative and phantasmal, rather than directive and real, then the leading Darwinists of the later nineteenth century were the very opposite of mechanists.[66]

As James Moore writes of the early responses to the *Origin*, "Christian Anti-Darwinism was neither so anti-Darwinian nor so Christian as might be thought ... most of Darwin's critics were less opposed to what he wrote than to their misconceptions of it. ... " Yet if thoughtful critics "were as imper-ceptive as their books reveal, what must be said for the mass of lay and cle-rical anti-Darwinians who read and profited from them?"[67] Logically, loss of purpose and meaning were as far from evolution as the vulgar relativism of permissivists is from Einstein's discovery of space/time relativity. But that fact does not quiet the alarm.

The *Origin* did find support among the British clergy, often among the more conservative, whose "Christian Darwinism" markedly contrasts with the resistance of many scientists on first reading the work, and with the responses of more liberal theologians, who eagerly recast evolutionary ideas to their own Romantic purposes. Evolution complemented the conservatives' view that humans, although unique, remain kin to the rest of creation.

James McCosh, a Scottish minister, was the first Protestant theologian to endorse Darwinism. He had written on providence and naturalism and taught logic in Belfast when he came to America as president of the struggling college that would become Princeton University. Respectful of the sciences, McCosh dropped the biology of archetypes after reading the *Origin*. He admired Darwin's mastery of natural history and saw natural selection as a benign and progressive instrument of divine design. Nature, he wrote, "is travailing, but it is for a birth." Even human mental and moral capabilities may have evolved, without detriment to man's uniqueness – or to God's ultimate role in imparting the soul, by means that "cannot be known."[68]

James Iverach, a Free Church minister who served the miners outside Edinburgh and later taught at Aberdeen, welcomed natural selection as a fine description of God's immanent activity. No one, he wrote, had ever put the design argument on a better footing than Darwin had. Evolution held no danger – so long as advocates did not try to derive "the determinate from the indeterminate, intelligence from the unintelligible, something from nothing." Iverach did tend to picture selection negatively, as elimination of the unfit. But he twitted "pure Darwinians of every shade" for their adaptationism: "it is almost as if … we had a teleology run mad." The strength of Darwinism, he wrote, is that it does not rely on rare or unique divine irruptions into nature: God is always present, ruling through natural causes. Nature is freed "from the tyranny of chance." Humans too arose by evolution. Our uniqueness must not be explained in ways that will "break up the unity of human nature" – assigning the body to one set of causes, the mind to another.[69]

Aubrey Moore, a high church Oxford Anglican and accomplished amateur botanist, at home with his scientific colleagues and fellow divines, similarly took Darwinian discoveries as a revelation of God's means of creation, which was no spate of disruptions but the steady work of natural causes. Real effort was needed, he wrote, for faithful Christians to rebuild their understanding. But evolution was "the truest solution yet discovered by science of the facts open to its observation."[70] Darwin had restored natural teleology and purged biology of appeals to chance: "every adaptation, however minute, is in itself a new proof of purpose, design, and plan."[71] As for personhood, "We have, probably, as much to learn about the soul from comparative psychology, a science which as yet hardly exists, as we have learned about the body from comparative biology." But clearly, "the soul cannot be a 'special' creation." For "there is no species of soul," only individuals. We are part of nature; our souls must have gained their distinctiveness by the same processes as humankind itself.[72] Evolution was "infinitely more Christian" than special creation, since it acknowledged the immanence of God's act and "the omnipresence of his creative power." Special creation, so often invoked in defense of human uniqueness, "has neither Biblical, nor patristic, nor medieval authority." More Miltonic than biblical, its imagery has now ossified into dogma. The result: "The dead hand of an exploded theory rests upon theology."[73]

> If the theory of special creation existed in the Bible or in Christian antiquity we might bravely try and do battle for it. But it came to us some two centuries ago from the side of science, with the *imprimatur* of a Puritan poet ... it is difficult to see how the question, except by a confusion, becomes a religious question at all.[74]

There was, of course, plenty of Christian opposition to evolution:

> Conservatives and traditionalists in theology whose devotion to pre-Darwinian natural philosophies was as great as their reverence for the literal letter of the Bible certainly did resist all forms of phylogenetic evolution. And liberal theologians, typified by Beecher and Abbot, were notorious for glorying in evolution and an evolutionary faith.[75]

But "what liberals took as 'the theory of evolution' was no more Darwinism than what most conservative anti-evolutionists understood by it. Only a few far-sighted divines were saying that natural selection could, if proved true, be interpreted as part of the Divine method." Yet, "the central and regulative paradox of the post-Darwinian controversies" was probably "that it was only those who maintained a distinctly orthodox theology who could embrace Darwinism."[76] For the commitment of the orthodox to the idea of creation was infused with their openness to the immanence of God's act.[77]

Organized anti-Darwinism

By the late nineteenth century evolution seemed broadly poised for victory in America. Some Christians like Dwight Moody laughed at the thought that "old carcasses" could "testify against God." But many theologians, pursuing accommodation, posited a long gap between God's initial creative act and the six days of Genesis. John Dawson, the geologist Principal of McGill, and Arnold Guyot at Princeton read the biblical days as epochs, climaxing in man's creation. By their time almost all biologists accepted some version of evolution; many evangelicals were warming to it.[78] The twelve popular pamphlets called *The Fundamentals* (1910–15), for which Fundamentalism is named, targeted biblical criticism chiefly. They did blame Darwin for the Higher Criticism. For he had cast everything in a developmental light.

George Frederick Wright, a Congregationalist minister and serious glacial geologist, wrote an accommodationist essay on evolution, reading the opening chapters of Genesis as a polemic against paganism. The Bible, he insisted, is no scientific tract. Genesis truthfully portrayed "an orderly progress from lower to higher forms of matter and life." That left room for God's creation of life forms with "a marvelous capacity for variation" – and for the unique first couple so prominent in Christian doctrines of the fall. Although gradually growing more protective of biblical cosmology as anti-religious appropriations of Darwin became shriller, Wright retained his hopes for Christian evolutionism throughout his life.[79]

An uneasy truce between creation and evolution held, down to World War I. Some ministers and congregants grumbled, but many accepted evolution in some form. Darwinism became an object of national concern with the loss of morale occasioned by the war and the sense of rootlessness that accompanied America's great migration to the cities. Prohibition, enshrined in the Constitution in 1919, was widely flouted. Many who reveled in a newly permissive lifestyle voiced their rejection of traditional norms by reference to evolution. Conservatives saw the culture corrupting before their eyes – in music and painting, fiction, the dance halls and picture palaces. If Darwin was not the sole culprit, clearly his theory was implicated.

Bryan took up the cause. He was famous for his Cross of Gold speech at the 1896 Democratic convention, on behalf of Free Silver. Unrestrained minting of silver, it was hoped, would free America from the gold standard, the "cross of gold," on which farmers and workers were being crucified. Free Silver appealed powerfully in the agrarian west and south, but its inflationary effects were anathema in the industrial and financial east and north. Bryan lost the 1896 Presidential election to McKinley, ran against him again in 1900, and won the fight to keep Free Silver in the Democratic Party platform. But America's annexation of Hawaii and, after the Spanish American War, of the Philippines, Puerto Rico, and Guam, and the occupation of Cuba, whose independence was the nominal aim of that war, turned Bryan's attention toward combating imperialism. He controlled the Democratic platform in 1904 and ran for president a third time in 1908, losing to William Howard Taft. For helping Woodrow Wilson secure the Democratic nomination and win the presidency in 1912, Bryan was made Secretary of State. He worked tirelessly on treaties for the peaceful resolution of international disputes. But his pacifist, conciliatory bent led to a break with Wilson and he resigned.

A prophetic voice for women's suffrage, progressive taxation, direct election of senators, an end to secret ownership of newspapers, and, of course, prohibition, Bryan mounted his last great crusade against the teaching of evolution, horrified at the way natural selection was used to rationalize the notion that might makes right.[80] In Vernon Kellogg's *Headquarters Nights* (1917) he had read interviews with German officers that revealed the impact of Darwin on the German march to war. He had also read Benjamin Kidd's *Science of Power* (1918), linking Darwin to German militarism. Darwinian thinking had underwritten the atheistic Bolshevism of the newly formed Soviet Union. Marx had hailed the *Origin* as "epoch making" and had proudly sent Darwin a copy of *Capital*, seeing in evolution a scientific rationale for the theory of class struggle.[81] In Bryan's eyes, both democracy and Christianity were under fire from ideologies whose common core, as Numbers puts it, substituted "the law of the jungle for the teaching of Christ."[82] But Bryan had never ignored the log in America's eye. He had fought imperial ambitions for decades, and his battle for Free Silver, when running for president at 36, was a struggle against the rampant capitalism of the industrial and financial barons.

The great populist had long seen a ridiculous side in thoughts of simian ancestry. These now became fodder for his oratorical mill. But ridicule was just a tool. The campaign was dead serious. Accounts of the erosion of faith by Darwinism, and the attendant demoralization of young people, gave a sense of urgency to Bryan's determination to turn his eloquence and energy to his new cause: "we will drive Darwinism from our schools."[83] Confident of popular support and trusting the common sense of the common man, he toured the country, denouncing the authority of the "scientific soviet," often titling his speeches "The Menace of Darwinism."[84]

William Bateson, a founder of the new science of genetics, had argued that the mechanism of selection was far from clear. The point was a fair one at the time, although reflecting the early rivalry of genetics with evolution. Bateson had cautioned against over-interpretation of his views. But his doubts were grist for Bryan's mill. Evolution, Bryan declared, was sheer speculation; he'd rather have one verse of Genesis than all Darwin's writings. Twenty state legislatures debated a ban on teaching evolution in public schools. Arkansas, Mississippi, Oklahoma, and Tennessee enacted one.[85]

John Scopes, a popular high school teacher in Dayton, Tennessee, offered himself in 1925 to test the new law. Clarence Darrow, for the defense, was the most celebrated criminal attorney of the day. The prosecution called in Bryan in dual roles, as legal counsel and expert witness. Citizens saw the trial's carnival atmosphere as a chance of national attention for Dayton. But H. L. Mencken's acerbic reporting cast them as know-nothing yokels.[86] The scientific supporters Bryan had hoped for did not materialize, and he himself had to admit that a biblical day must be longer than twenty-four hours. After all, the sun had not shone until the fourth day. Bryan, in fact, had long tended toward accommodation with evolution. His real sticking point, like that of many an anti-Darwinist, was human uniqueness.[87]

Scopes, in the end, was convicted. He admitted violating the Tennessee statute. Victories followed for anti-Darwinism in Mississippi in 1926 and Arkansas in 1928. But in the court of public opinion, Darrow had won. He'd made fools of anti-evolution legislators, and their movement gradually lost steam, swallowed up in the election campaign of 1928 and the Market crash of 1929. Bryan, exhausted, died just days after the trial.

But anti-Darwinism lived on. Societies and publications sprang up, alliances were forged – despite deep divisions of opinion. Some held with a young earth, less than 10,000 years old. Others accepted current geology, but their Day Age and Gap accommodations offended would-be literalists. Some sought compromise. Others clung to unvarnished scripture as they saw it. Lacking a common creed, each faction viewed the others with suspicion. Accommodationists moved painfully toward theistic evolution.[88] Cut free of moderating voices, but facing a wall of scientific rejection, the critics grew more doctrinaire. They eased away from bald appeals to scripture and turned increasingly to scientific claims, as Wilberforce and Hodge had done, still hoping for support from the growing prestige of science. But they sharply rejected compromise, united by revulsion for all that seemed to seep or creep from the evolutionary Pandora's box. A literal six-day creation day became the rallying cry.[89]

Henry Morris, a Texas engineer of Baptist upbringing, had accepted evolution in his youth but spat it out as his faith deepened. Any insect, he reasoned, as a young professor at Rice, was far too intricate to arise by chance. Morris' first book, *That you Might Believe* (1946), was inspired by the work of George McCready Price, a Seventh Day Adventist and geological outsider. Fossil types, Price held, are not successive but contemporaneous: "Darwinism, or any other form of biological evolution, can have no more scientific value than the vagaries of the old Greeks." Far from advancing complexity, Price saw in the fossils only "marked degeneration." But there was evidence of "sudden, world-wide change of climate," remnants of "a great world catastrophe." Of this, "All that we can say with absolute positiveness is that *it occurred since Man appeared on earth.*" As for biology, "since modern science has forever outgrown the idea of spontaneous generation ... there is absolutely nothing on which to build a scheme of evolution." Thus, "the world to-day stands face to face with *Creation as the direct act of the infinite God.*"[90]

Heartened by Price's writing, Morris championed a worldwide deluge. Other creationists responded cooly, but Morris found an ally in John Whitcomb. In *The Genesis Flood* (1961), the two argued that most geological strata were laid down in one year, by Noah's Flood. Many creationists were horrified. Who would take them seriously if they fought the battle of the teacup against the Grand Canyon's walls? But the authors held fast. "God," Morris said, "doesn't lie."[91]

The book proved a banner to kindred spirits. Walter Lammerts, a geneticist and brilliant rose breeder, long intrigued by flood theology, found existing creationist groups far too accommodating. He joined with Morris, Whitcomb, and others to form the Creation Research Society in 1963. Determined to include only Christians committed to inerrancy, special creation, and a global flood, the group, within ten years, claimed 450 members and 1,600 supporters. They organized quests for Noah's ark, pursued fossil human footprints contemporary with dinosaurs,[92] and ransacked the science literature for evidence of a young earth.

Meanwhile, emboldened by the atheist Madalyn Murray's Supreme Court victory in shielding her child from school prayers, Nell Segraves and Jean Sumrall sued to protect their children from Darwinism. When the California Board of Education granted the plaintiffs equal rights, Morris left his academic post in 1970 and with his new allies established the Creation-Science Research Center in San Diego, aiming to meet the demand for non-Darwinian science texts, to combat "the moral decay of spiritual values," manifest in the decline of mental health and the rise of divorce, abortion, and venereal disease.[93]

Pleas for equal time and protection of children sounded much fairer than the old legislative bans. The Tennessee law had been repealed in 1967; the Arkansas statute, struck down by the Supreme Court in 1968. Clearly, religious instruction in public schools would not survive the Establishment clause. But suppressing overtly Christian references in texts for public schools seemed likely to preserve creation as a live option and allow students to draw their own conclusions about who or what was the cause. Exploiting Thomas Kuhn's idea of paradigms, the new anti-Darwinists called evolution and creation rival models.[94] The seeming relativism of such talk jars against creationists' usual insistence on objective facts. But models acquire a kind of parity, allowing entry to the moral concerns that energize anti-Darwinism: If the options are equi-balanced, wouldn't it matter which is spiritually edifying or morally degrading? The shift from credibility to costs and benefits appeals to America's pragmatic bent. But parity was an illusion.

Keenly sensitive to any chink in the Darwinian armor, creation science authors made much of human fallibility, a heritage of Adam's fall. Skepticism opened the door to faith. But a double standard tilted the floor. There was charity for favored options, but hypercritical testing of evolutionary alternatives. The presumptive scriptural message was privileged, but any alibi was enough to shoo away unwelcome evidence. Once the authority of science was shaken came an evangelical challenge to rally courage and trust, like a paratrooper ready to jump. Thus the bumper sticker: "I'm a fool for Christ, whose fool are you?"

The advocates were hardly fools, however, as critics sometimes learned to their cost. In public debates and disputations, certitude, flair, and rapport with audience values won over many. Cautiously framed evidence – or impatient dismissals – were only alienating. Creation science grew, its subtexts resonating among kindred spirits reacting to a fearsome age, eager for the reassurance of well-loved narratives. Evolution, of course, is not the source of every modern wrong. But it was a ready bogey. Secularists who made Darwinism the banner of their lifestyles only intensified the antipathy of spiritual seekers hungry for guidance and a path to the hereafter. But the guides who responded to such needs did not come unarmed with arguments.

Creation science

Advocates of creation science see a circularity in dating fossils by their strata and then dating the strata by their fossils.[95] Price had set the stage. He had read Spencer, Huxley, and Haeckel when the principal of a small high school in Canada: "for a time it really seemed to me that there must be something to general idea of organic evolution after all." But then he saw strata that would have seemed contemporaneous "were it not for fossil evidence" – and even strata overtopped by reputedly older deposits: "A great light began to break in upon my soul. I realized that no fossil form is older or younger than any others ... they may all have been living contemporaneously."[96] Following Price's lead, Morris and his colleagues urged that Noah's flood folded and mangled the earth's strata. The deluge came from high above the stratosphere:

> a vast blanket of invisible water vapor, translucent to the light from the stars but productive of a marvelous greenhouse effect which maintained mild temperatures from pole to pole ... filtering harmful radiations from space, markedly reducing the rate of somatic mutations in living cells, and, as a consequence, drastically decreasing the rate of aging and death.[97]

For many inerrantists, and their critics, the elements of such visions fuse into a litany of gambits and retorts, a ritual dance predictable enough to pinpoint the year that Menachem Mendel Schneerson, the Chabad Lubavitch leader, began to borrow Christian anti-evolutionist suasions.[98] Like his evangelical counterparts, he was bent on outreach. Darwinism was not just a threat but a marketing opportunity: The Rebbe's charisma would help him win souls away from ideas they could blame for the emptiness they hoped to escape behind walls of ritual and spirituality. The same is true in neo-traditionalist Islam.[99] The issues in the anti-Darwinist repertoire stem not from scripture but from the quest for a stable worldview and way of life.

Anti-Darwinists favor appeals to probability, finding the odds just too high for life to have emerged by chance. Morris frames in numbers the argument that first drew him in: "Assume a 'sea' of freely available components, each uniquely capable of performing a specific useful function. What is the probability that two or more of them can come together by chance to form an integrated functioning organism?"[100] If just one array is workable, Morris reckons the probability of n components falling into their proper places, at one chance in all the possible combinations: thus, 1 over n factorial or $n!$, that is, $1 \times 2 \times 3 \dots \times n$. The odds against success mount rapidly as n increases. A viable organism clearly needs numerous components. But Morris illustrates by proposing an organism with the stingy allotment of "only 100 integrated parts," stressing the "unique function" of each part, and allowing only one correct arrangement. These parts would have 10^{158} combinations, and a minuscule probability of even so simple a creature's arising by chance. For "there are only approximately 10^{80} electrons in the entire universe"! If components reshuffled and recombined a billion times per second, only 10^{78} trials would occur in 30 billion years – roughly twice the estimated age of the universe. The chances of hitting a viable combination in that time span would be just one in 10^{53}: "For all practical purposes, no chance at all!"[101] even with so spartan an organism.

The DNA to code for one enzyme, Morris adds, would need some 1,000 nucleotides of four bases each, yielding 10^{600} possible combinations. So "It seems beyond all question that such complex systems as the DNA molecule could never arise by chance, no matter how big the universe nor how long the time."[102] The talk of molecules and enzymes, DNA and nucleotides, cosmic eons, and astronomical odds dresses the argument in flashy scientific colors. But the trademark dichotomy is still sewn into the seams: Either life is a random, bumper car affair, or it's God's work, prepared for "a purpose" – shorthand for the classic drama of salvation.

William Dembski, a cohort of the Intelligent Design movement, updates the classic appeal to probability,[103] seeking to objectify the intuitions about long odds voiced in the French mathematician Emile Borel's dictum that very rare events don't occur. Dembski aims for a "filter" that can rule out chance occurrences. Rarity alone is clearly not enough. After all, any event, considered in enough detail, is not just rare but unique. Besides, highly improbable events happen all the time: The odds against winning the lottery are huge. But someone's ticket is drawn. Accidents do generally happen to other people, but it's unwise to bank on that. What can rule out chance, Dembski argues, is specification: If I *know* whose ticket will be drawn, or I regularly predict winners, the odds against my doing so just by guessing, say, or randomly picking names from the phone book, become diminishingly small. The proper rule, then: *Specified* events of very low probability do not occur. That's why we can use DNA evidence, pronounce the dice loaded, charge that stock options were backdated, or ballot boxes stuffed. Prediction speaks for regularity in a causal process, or cheating in a supposed game of chance.

Pattern, Dembski thinks, can play the same role as prediction. It's not just a coincidence if Bob and Alice's six children show up on the couple's 50th anniversary with pieces from the same, long desired china pattern: Design "sweeps the field clear of chance hypotheses." Design and chance, Dembski urges, are "competing modes of explanation." Obviously, "design prevails once chance has been exhausted." But excluding chance, Dembski insists, does not imply intelligent agency. It just makes way for it. Dembski's not just being coy here, or angling for the public school textbook market. Design, as he understands it, just means pattern. It excludes chance but says nothing about agency.

But that makes the argument circular: Pattern is proof of pattern. And what about the dichotomy of design and chance? A pattern *random enough* to impress us with its regularity might well reflect causal principles. Dembski, like other anti-Darwinists, falls in with his adversaries' assumption that natural causes diminish God's creative role. But despite the rhetoric of some polemicists, who are as eager to exclude divine design as Morris is to defend it, what Dembski rules out, that life arose by chance, is not the naturalist's claim at all.

Consider the Krebs cycle: Its nine enzymes and multiple cofactors present a daunting challenge. If evolution means that these ingredients were simply thrown together, the chances of their successful integration would be vanishingly small, perhaps one in 10^{400}, allowing for the amino acid components of all the constituent proteins. But the cycle probably arose from existing constituents. As the researchers who identified those precursors showed, "with minimal new material evolution created the most important pathway of metabolism."[104]

Scientists have long wondered about the origins of RNA, the presumed predecessor of DNA when life began. How could the nucleotides in an RNA chain have formed in nature? But John Sutherland, Matthew Powner, and Béatrice Gerland of the University of Manchester have succeeded in provoking the spontaneous compounding of ribose, base, and phosphate molecules, yielding the nucleotide ribocytidine phosphate. Adding ultraviolet light yields another nucleotide. Finding a pathway to the two remaining nucleotides will reveal how RNA could form in nature, bringing biochemists a step closer to the primal syntax and semantics of gene coding and protein synthesis, the roots of all life processes on earth.

Particles don't just join at random. Natural selection steadily picks out winning combinations. The process is highly discriminatory. Increasing complexity is spurred by selection pressure. Biodiversity is one result, as variant types find their niches. Ancient genetic tricks and biochemical pathways persist as new wrinkles emerge. Hence the survival of old types, the emergence of new, and the kinships Darwin observed: Monkeys catch cold, apes get drunk and hung over, humans host many of the parasites that plague other animals.[105] Evolution is not sheer chance. Its hallmarks, continuity and difference, point to affinities closer than our kinship with the earth.

Creation science writers do see a trend in nature. But the signposts they see point downwards. Nature cannot advance or even hold steady. The trend is toward disorder. Evolution, Morris argues, would violate the Second Law of Thermodynamics. It would increase complexity. But physics teaches entropy: Every natural system runs downhill.[106] That's an odd thought to apply to the universe at large. It's in closed systems that disorder is expected to increase, and it's hard to say if the universe is a closed system. But clearly Earth is not.

Physicists often explain entropy as loss of the ability to do useful work. Energy differentials make work possible, allowing the build up of order, won at the cost of disorder elsewhere. Increasing entropy means the equalizing of energy levels: The soup does not heat up by itself. The pot cools when the burner's off. But notice the relativity of the idea of work: What's useful depends on whether we want the soup hot for eating or cool for storage. We need energy inputs – from the stove or the fridge – in *either* case. To bacteria seeking a home, the soup's temperature needs to be just right – for them, not us. Nature is full of energy differentials. To theists that might look like a sign of grace.

Living species, over time, overall, do grow more complex. They must if they're to survive in a dynamic environment. But their advance does come at a cost. It's possible only because the earth is not a closed system. It receives huge gifts of energy daily from the sun, and smaller increments from the heat of its own molten core (still cooling from our stellar origins). Even the earth's spin and the moon's gravitation yield energy. The atmosphere and oceans respond, in the daily, monthly, and seasonal movements of the planet and flux of the tides. To organisms and potential organisms, this energy is a precious resource. Life forms proliferate at the undersea vents of newly breached volcanoes. The earth teems with life – even in the Dead Sea and the seemingly barren Antarctic; and the teeming is not static: Life forms evolve – essences change, steadily vying for a place, we might say, in the sun.

Morris, of course, recognizes the vast flood of solar energy, "certainly enough" to fuel evolutionary advance. He knows that seeds grow to trees; embryos, into adults. But that requires "a program to direct the growth," and machinery to translate ambient energy into forms that complex systems can use to order and connect their parts. Otherwise, "the environmental energy more likely will break down" any structure already formed. "A bull in a china shop does work, but he neither creates nor maintains organization." Natural selection holds no such code, Morris argues: Mutation is random, and selection "serves merely as a screen which sieves out unfit variants and defective mutants."[107]

Note the Catch-22. Both sickle and seed are providential. Design is God's signature, but entropy is the happy flaw that needs redemption. Natural selection does operate, but only to trim stray twigs from life's tree. It plays no role in speciation: "extinction is an example of decay, not development." Morris balks at making creation and destruction opposite sides of the same coin. Yet the basic fact of ecology, and chemistry, marked by Aristotle and even Anaximander, is that the build up of one thing is the break down of another. Morris sequesters development from decay – protecting species fixity, and human distinctness. The agenda drives the science.

Confronting the prodigal flow of solar energy, Morris falls back on complexity, the code needed to make energy usable. So the appeal to entropy collapses into his original claim about chance. That leaves behind the question whether nature could or God would use chance in support of creation. After all, even against the highest odds, every fair lottery has a winner.

Why aren't religious thinkers discouraged at the thought that all ordered systems run to ruin? Medieval theists took heart at thoughts of death and decay. What ends must have begun, they reasoned, and so must have a Maker, and Judge. Death was the door to immortality. To today's fundamentalists entropy is a fruit of Adam's fall: Ice ages, landslides, deviant life forms, diseases – all signify a fallen world, revealing nature's powerlessness to redeem itself.[108]

In prelapsarian nature damaging mutations were retarded by earth's primal water vapor shield. Death came only through sin (Romans 5:12, 8:20–22). Otherwise, man would have lived forever. So, apparently, would the animals (at least those possessing *nephesh* – the soul), Morris explains, using the Hebrew word. "Plant life, of course, is not conscious life, but only very complex replicating chemicals." Death, once soul was given, was a nonstarter. All that changed, with Adam's fall: "Decay and death came with the Curse, and the antediluvian environment changed to the present environmental economy at the time of the great Flood."[109] In the unexpurgated edition of *Scientific Creationism*, meant for use in Christian schools, Morris freely unfurls his theology of entropy:

> The entire world was designed for man and he was appointed by God to exercise dominion over it, as God's steward. It was a perfect environment and man was perfectly equipped to manage it. He should, by all reason, have been content and supremely happy. ... God, however, did not create man as a mere machine. God's love was voluntary, and for there to be real fellowship, man's love also must be voluntary. ... The history of over six thousand years of strife and suffering, crime and war, decay and death, is proof enough that he chose wrongly.
>
> Sin came into the world when man first doubted, then rejected the Word of God, in the Garden of Eden. And death came into the world when sin came into the world. God was forced to tell Adam " ... cursed is the ground for thy sake ... for dust thou art, and unto dust shalt thou return" (Genesis 3:17–19). The basic physical elements were placed under the Curse, and all flesh constructed of those elements was also cursed.[110]

As Morris reads Romans 8:20–22, all creation fell into vanity. Only incarnation promised freedom from the corruption in which the world still languishes. Others read the Greek quite differently. Corruption, they say, came *because of death*: Sin, through fear of death, not death through sin. Sin tarnished humanity, God's image; incarnation was not a remedy for inherited guilt but a re-burnishing of God's image, restoring human dignity and grace.[111]

Morris' thought that Adam's fall condemned the world is a cosmic case of Ruskin's pathetic fallacy, projecting human passions onto nature. Instead of stormy emotions echoed by offstage thunder, primordial sin now echoes through the cosmos and resonates in the atoms, transforming the laws of physics.

So did Adam and Eve even need to eat the fruits in Eden? Without corruption, what need was there for repletion? They were living, yet (paradoxically!) everlasting, subject to natural processes, but untouched, unthreatened by them. Carry that to its logical conclusion: Did they even breathe? Life is a constant build up and breakdown. Metabolism just is that fatal pairing. But, for Morris, chemistry and physics are only backdrops to a tale that is not about life or entropy or chance or death, but about a sense of sin that twines around the heart, molding it to a loyalty that some equate with faith.

Evolutionary fundamentalism

Polemicists fight myth with myth. Just as anti-Darwinists react against materialism and the lifestyle pegged to it, materialism too has its polemical form. Many proudly proclaim what Hodge's twentieth-century successors found obvious and odious, that evolution is not just the backbone of biology but the skeleton of thought-ways that displace religion and supplant the morality which finds its strength in religion and strengthens religion in turn. "Scientists and humanists should consider together the possibility," Edward Wilson writes, "that the time has come for ethics to be removed temporarily from the hands of the philosophers and biologicized."[112] After all, "When altruism is conceived as the mechanism by which DNA multiplies itself through a network of relatives, spirituality becomes just one more enabling device."[113] Jacques Monod frames an ethic based (solely, he insists) on respect for humans as bearers of science.[114] Dennett, Dawkins, and others idealize a world without God, where only mechanism is an explanation, and natural science is the sole source of value. Theists find such worlds unsettling. They aren't tempted to drop the golden rule, or the search for ultimacy. The outcome of Darwinism, as many see it, is moral and spiritual collapse.

Biologists know that evolution need not be progressive. Adaptation may be slow or halting but always local. Yet much of the enduring impact of Darwinism reflects the nineteenth-century enchantment with progress, still evident in Dewey's debt to Spencer: his lambent faith in change *as* progress. Many self-styled naturalists today are not students of nature but deniers of anything that can't be measured and controlled. Like their creationist bugbears, they have an agenda: minimally, perhaps, the Epicurean program of disrobing natural mysteries and dethroning the divine in the cosmos and the transcendent in morals. Science will replace ignorance and fear with a command of natural causes and complaisance toward down-to-earth desires, discreetly renamed reason to mask the gap between inquiry and a social platform. Some seek sodality, or tax relief, under the name Brights – painting all rival views as dim or befuddled. Why shouldn't naturalism enjoy the standing (but avoid the obloquy) of a creed?

Many who see scientism as the wholesome fruit of cultural evolution are troubled at the persistence of theism, creationism, and traditional moralities. But armed camps preserve each other. The value freighted idea of creation is roused repeatedly by the spectre of its presumed alternatives. Over a quarter century of Gallup Polls (1982–2008) find more than two in five Americans agreeing that "God created man pretty much in his present form at one time within the last 10,000 years or so." More than a third affirm divinely guided human evolution. Only one in seven or eight bar God from the story of human origins.[115] The stable numbers and focus on the human case suggest abiding concerns remote from biology. Few respondents were scientists. But far more who identified as political conservatives rather than liberals upheld creation – as did 80% of those who reported attending religious services weekly, versus 47% of those who attended less often. Plainly creation carries a valence beyond biology.

Today's anti-creationists rarely reaffirm Chauncey Wright's protectiveness toward the purity of religion. Some, like their adversaries, press for legislative or judicial vindication. A secular minded mother wonders if her child must be taught that God "programmed the spider" to build a perfect web.[116] Dennett wants to protect children from religious instruction, even by their parents. But politicizing questions about ultimates harms both science and religion. It creates sanctions that institutionalize dogma and oversimplify the alternatives. The parties, being parties, seek unity and discipline, slogans, fighting songs, banners, and creeds. Polemics breed enmities, not understanding. The wounded and stigmatized withdraw from the field – from public schools and public fora. Intellectual diversity is diminished, discussion disabled. Complacency holds the ground, and hometown victors lose the art of self-criticism. So science stagnates; religion grows torpid and smug. Dogma breeds schism, heresy, and hermeticism, stifling curiosity, and spiritual and intellectual growth. Talent is wasted framing passable platitudes. Discovery suffers along with freedom, which is precious even apart from its historic service to the sciences and arts.

The Catholic Church tried and failed to squelch Teilhard's writings, as it failed to quash Galileo's thinking, or his impact, when it silenced the man. Detractors can't smother evolution. But even Fundamentalists have rights. Activists often confuse education with indoctrination. But today's issue is not whether but how evolution shall be taught. It's a rich, well-founded biological truth. Reckoning with its implications is an intellectual obligation. Teaching it is a constitutionally protected right that I for one have exercised for years. Yet it troubles the educator in me to see evolution made a dogma or the vehicle of cheap ideologies. The would be defenders of biology, alarmed by creationism, often say that something must be done. But it's bad pedagogy to use intellectual authority to impress any catechism on untutored minds. Myths and striking imagery, soundbites and banners, trump evidence and argument, as the advertising people know well. Associative thinking is their mace. Public relations campaigns may call themselves educational, but they rarely heighten intellectual sensitivity. What they call sophistication is typically cynical, parochial, and dismissive.

Years ago Carl Sagan published a popular book, *The Dragons of Eden*. The cover bore an M. C. Escher image: Dragonlike reptiles emerged from a sketchbook and marched, breathing fire, over a volume about nature and back into the page. Nearby lay a miniature Book of Job; two cacti struggled for space in one small pot. Escher, a favorite of the mathematical games school of aesthetics, loved visual paradoxes, his art simpatico to their notion of creativity as a quirkiness sprung from cerebral symmetries.[117] But here Escher was made the iconographer of a heavier hypothesis:

> We are descended from reptiles and mammals both. In the daytime repression of the R-complex and in the nighttime stirring of the dream dragons, we may each of us be replaying the hundred-million-year-old warfare between the reptiles and the mammals.[118]

We are risen not just from primates but from lizards – in a fraught sense, not risen at all. We remain mere things, or worse, creatures, nonmoral yet somehow loathsome – just the inference anti-Darwinists warned against. But science can do worse than call us bad names. It can lose its own dignity vested in its differences from dogma, swamped by the images conjured up in its defense. The twist is worthy of an Escher.

Truth and facticity

Northrop Frye tells an interesting story about stories. Certain narratives, he wrote, are powerful enough to absorb others as their subplots or variants.[119] *There-and-back-again* is one such plot, typified, say, in the *Odyssey*, or Tolkien's *Hobbit*. Creation is another. Its power comes from imaging our world against the backdrop of eternity. Like any mythically framed idea, creation can be misunderstood, most readily, perhaps, when sucked into the space of a rival myth – the myth, say, of facticity. Eric Voegelin calls efforts to reduce primordial truths to mere events, "historiogenesis" – as when Clement of Alexandria tries to prove that biblical figures antedate the pagan pantheon:

> Isis and Demeter, Dionysius and Apollo become historical personages with a definite date in time ... Clement can let his inquiry concerning the gods be followed, without a break of method, by the arguments

concerning the date of Christ ... all are pored over and bound together
by the pseudo-reality of "history." They are petrified into "facts" by a
fundamentalism or literalism that had been alien to the free mythopo-
esis, be it of the Memphite Theology, or the creations of a Homer,
Hesiod, Aeschylus, or Plato. The symbols of the myth have their truth as
an analogy of being; if this consciousness of analogical truth is now
destroyed, one of the principal causes (there were others) must be seen in
the "historization" of myth through historiogenesis. The tone peculiar to
the arguments of Clement, half comic, half embarrassing, stems from
this grossness of destruction. The problem is still with us today in the
debates on Biblicism and demythicization, as well as in the discussion on
the "historicity" of Christ.[120]

Creation, revelation, incarnation lose their power when made mere incidents.
If a Christian believes that God became a man, that mystery does not boil
down to sheer facticity. Likewise with Genesis, as Leon Kass writes: "Like
every truly great story, it seeks to show us not what happened (once) but
what always happens. ... its truth may lie not so much in its historical or
even philosophical veracity as in its effects on the soul of the reader."[121]

A thoughtful essay in a popular science magazine makes a similar point
about the Shroud of Turin: "the resurrection was not a circus trick."[122] If the
fabric said, miraculously, to bear the visage of Jesus, is to have the meaning
claimed for it, it can't be the sort of meaning that would rest in a piece of
cloth – despite natural yearnings to bring transcendence down to earth. To
make God or the soul depend on photographs of auras or recordings of
bumps in the night, is not to find more things in heaven and earth than are
dreamed of in mechanistic philosophies but to succumb to the crabbed
standards of a mechanistic metaphysics. Hence the wisdom of Saadiah
Gaon: In seeking an ultimate cause one must expect a transcendent Author.
We defeat our purpose if we make the ultimate just another object to
explain.[123] Pious souls, eager to vindicate scripture, strip creation of its place
as an epiphany even as they proclaim their faith. Taken seriously, creation is
a truth, indeed is a fact. But never a *mere* fact.

So creationists face more than legal difficulties in trying to inject creation
into biology. And when they press on school curricula alternatives to evolution
that are not openly theistic they risk deracinating their thesis. For creation is
vacuous without the transcendent. Hence Judge Overton's focus, in striking
down the Arkansas creation science law in 1982, not on academic freedom for
biology teachers, or on the credibility of creation science, but on the evidence
that the statute promoted a particular religious view. Citing Justice Black's
reasoning, that "a union of government and religion tends to destroy government and to degrade religion" (*Everson v. Board of Education*), he labeled Act
590 "a religious crusade, coupled with a desire to conceal this fact." He saw
"no evidentiary or rational support" for separating creation from theism.[124]

It's logically possible, of course, that the world had no primal cause – let alone a divine one. Hume entertains that possibility. But the drafters of Act 590 expected students to think causally and hoped they would credit life – especially human life – to a being great enough to create a world. Creation, in our cultural milieu, is inevitably a religious doctrine. Genesis shapes that milieu, presenting heaven and earth not as eternal fixtures but as objects of creation; and human lives, not as toys of fate but as works too, governed in part by human choices. Causal thinking leads naturally to thoughts of a universal cause. As Judge Overton saw, you can take the creation out of religion, but you can't take the religion out of creation.

Morris admits as much when he labels secular humanism a religious view, founded, like his own, on faith in unseen powers, if only those of "omniscient chance."[125] That barb oversimplifies, as barbs will. But secularists do have views about religion. They do gather around shared hopes, not just in what they want to debar but also in what they want to establish. Naturalism slips into the chair of metaphysics once it affirms that only what responds to scientific methods is real. It touches religion when it denies God. It poses for a prophetic role when it tries to draw a moral from its suppositions about nature. In proposing evolution as the ultimate paradigm and creation as a spent fable, secularists promote a mythology of their own, centered on images of science and progress. Such myths, like creation narratives, take many forms. Their visions of natural necessity, like the rival visions of contingency, are found in every age and culture. For both schematizations rest on core categories of human thought.

The idea of creation, as we've seen, springs from the primal abstraction – *What if things were otherwise?* That question reaches peerless simplicity when asked not of tobacco, dogs, or painting, rites or prohibitions, but reality at large: The universe is not a *fait accompli* but a contingent possibility. That picture leaves room for change, including progress. Contingency, of course, is not science. But it is presupposed by science: The contingent is what we seek to understand when we see that things need not have been as they are and try to discover what made them so. We explain by finding the necessity in what need not have been. So both necessity and contingency are presumed in causal thinking. One fosters determinism, even eternalism, if stressed; the other nourishes thoughts of freedom and creation. Human understanding cannot abandon either. Like the relative and absolute, they gain meaning from each other. Making all things contingent absolutely would render thought impossible. But to hold all things necessary absolutely is to deny time and change. We see the necessary through the contingent, just as we see the contingent in the factitious. Causality shuttles between the two perspectives.

Evolution, like all of science, rests on contingency, seeking causes for what might not have been. Living species are not immutable figures on a cosmic merry-go-round but temporal products of natural events. In an evolutionary world, as in Genesis, the future is open and unlike its past. Yet special creationists champion species fixity, a tenet of eternalism. In an ironic twist, evolutionists defend nature's transformation in the name of immutable natural laws; creationists uphold eternal types, on behalf of radical transformations in the past.

Both creation and evolution presume essential change. So both were once allied against eternalism. Today, when the two are often at loggerheads, miscues are easy. Creationists fear that evolution usurps God's role. That looks like a loss of faith or nerve. Evolutionists of scientistic stamp lampoon creation as an atavistic superstition that ignores science and fetters humanity. They forget the creationist backgrounds of the idea of evolution and the biblical roots that have long sustained the idea of history and the ideal of freedom. Both parties pin their values to their cosmologies and paint derisive caricatures of their opponents.

Myths are stories that speak of ultimates – ultimate values, ultimate causes, possibilities, necessities. So Aristotle was right to call myth-making poets the primal philosophers. But myths do their work by narrative, not syllogistic argument. Their incidents need not be empiric for the narrative to be veracious. Indeed, one function of mythic discourse is to protect from reduction to mere facticity our deepest truths and insights.[126] Creation is an idea borne in many narratives that have long absorbed their rivals. Having gained the scope that signals power in ideas, creation signifies far too much to be cast aside. But evolution belongs to the story of creation. It does not threaten scripture. Efforts to substitute it for creation will fail, as surely as efforts to rewrite scientific findings in hopes of proving that evolution never took place.

Evolution, Dennett believes, may or may not endure in biology, but its larger impact permanently disables all explanatory appeals to the divine. I'm dubious about both ends of that claim. Natural selection is far too well confirmed to be dislodged. Like Darwin, I doubt that it explains every biological fact. New principles doubtless await discovery. But natural selection, I expect, will remain as vital to biology as the idea of function, on which it is built. Theism too, I think, is here to stay. If I had to place a wager on the long-term outcomes, I'd favor creation as the survivor in a contest against all-pervasive naturalist reductionism. Sheer mechanism doesn't address the questions that creation answers. The story we began with, about the fate of emanation, may help show why creation is as robust as it is.

Emanation is the idea that all beings radiate from a divine, eternal source by an intellectual process, much as theorems flow from axioms. Neoplatonists expected the idea of emanation to displace creation stories, the myths from which they thought philosophy had rescued thinking. The divine Plato, salamander like, could frolic in those poetic worlds, conjure creatively with mythic fires, and emerge philosophically unscathed. But neoplatonists, using Plato's insights and his vivid, poetic language, enlivened by a spiritualized version of Stoic physics, structured by a re-forged Aristotelian metaphysics, and burnished with traces of Philonic theology, thought they could turn myth to marble, a temple of the mind.

Emanation was a powerful idea. But it did not absorb creation. It was absorbed by it, becoming a variant on the monotheistic theme – not because hysteria breeds insight but because the creation idea holds values and truths not captured by any other. Neoplatonists called creation a myth. Emanation was the truth behind the story. For eternalism bespoke God's impassivity and nature's constancy. But for many a monotheist, emanation was the poetic symbol. Platonic images of a flowing spring, or light flooding from the sun, caught fragments of the truth, captured too in scriptural imagery. In the Psalmist's figure, the spring was God's fount of life. The light by which we see light was more than an epiphany. It was a way of life, a call to emulate God's transcendence, not by quitting nature, "cutting away everything," as Plotinus thought, but by sanctifying life within this world.

The neoplatonists were committed to philosophy, and to pagan piety, perched on as high a plane as they could set it. But monotheism triumphed, not through Justinian's dogmatic policies but largely because pagan theology withered under the moral and intellectual scrutiny of thinkers like Philo, Origen, Augustine, and Philoponus. Emanation outlasted Plato's Academy, partly because monotheists adopted it, as a metaphor of creation. Pagan purists found the cosmology of Genesis crude. To others it seemed profound. They wove their thoughts around and into it, not for any astronomy, physics, or biology they found in Genesis, but for scripture's oblique introduction of a God never reduced to lesser terms.

With that history as evidence, I can venture a prediction or two beyond my twin claims that Darwinism in biology and creation in religious thought are here to stay. I think the relations of evolution with militant secularism, value relativism, and scientistic ethics – like its past flirtations and affairs with Marx and Spencer, with the anthropological racism of the quondam Smithsonian movement, and many other lovers – will pass. That claim might surprise some ardent exponents and detractors of evolution today, whose eyes are on the valence, not the core of Darwinian biology. But only time will tell.

I have another prediction to make meanwhile: A time may come (especially if the real enemies of science have their way – superstition and the notion that truth is just a power struggle) when creation again becomes the ally, and perhaps the best protector of evolution. That Darwinism might be harbored through some dark future by virtue of its sacredness to conciliators like Bergson, Whitehead, or Teilhard is no real irony, if we consider how Platonic metaphysics, Stoic ethics, and Peripatetic logic were preserved and cultivated in the past – the pre-Socratic *physikoi* by Eusebius; the neoplatonists by Christians, Muslims, and Jews. But my prediction assumes that the champions of creation learn how to accommodate theism and evolution to one another. This, I think, they can do, more readily than those who have made creationism a stalking horse or evolution a hobby horse for personal or political agendas. The wise always chose houses with more than one window on the neighborhood.

2

Leaving Eden

What does Genesis actually say about creation? Can we learn from a message sprung from so deep in antiquity?

> *In the beginning, God created heaven and earth. The earth was formless and void, darkness on the face of the deep, God's spirit brooding over the face of the water. God said: "Let there be light," and there was light. God saw the light, that it was good. God divided the light from the darkness. God called the light day and the darkness he called night. Evening, and morning. One day.*

Painted in somber grays, the scene is suddenly lit up, then wanes into evening. The procession of days and nights begins. God remains unseen, beyond the light and dark, the earth and watery abyss. He is called *Elohim* here. The noun is in plural form but takes verbs in the singular. This opening gives a freshness to the God idea: The Creator is no familiar deity but unknown, unique.[1] The plural form, says Abraham Ibn Ezra, is honorific. It sounds generic, abstract, setting a courtly distance, sidestepping deep personification. God here is not the hero of some saga; creation is not a literary fiction.

The word for heaven too (*ha-shamayim*) is not singular in form, but dual, perhaps reflecting some long dead cosmic architecture, yet already no more portentous than our speaking of the sunrise. The definite article (ha-*sha-mayim*), Ibn Ezra explains, shows that the familiar sky is meant. The plain intent: to account for the world we live in. *Heaven and earth* means everything natural: God made the world – earth, sky, and all they contain.[2] The vision of a unified cosmos shines through in a homely ancient gloss: God made heaven and earth together, "pot and lid."

Ultimate causality

The Torah assigns God neither lineaments nor lineage. There is no backstory. Other creation accounts, some familiar to ancient Hebrews, tell of battles subduing the Sea or River. But here the writhing coils of Leviathan or

Tanin, the turbulence of Rahab are stilled.[3] The Mosaic Law, Philo writes, is no mere fiat. It has a cosmological preface. The legislator is the Creator. But the Law is not tricked out with mythologies, as if to bare God's motives. This is no aftermath but *the* beginning. That speaks powerfully, if obliquely, of God's goodness. The only face here is the surface of the deep. Brooding over it, with a rustling hinted in the sound of the word (*merahefet*), is a wind or spirit said to be of God. In the bold whimsy of one ancient reader, that rustling presence is the human soul.[4] The rare word for brooding, a participle, feminine, to match the gender of *ru'ah*, wind or spirit, recurs when the song of Moses recalls God's finding Israel in a howling waste, brooding over them as an eagle stirs his young (Deuteronomy 32:11), *no alien god beside him* (32:12). The fierce, protective presence that brooded over the waters still sustains God's beloved.

In the Talmud (B. Hagiga 15A) Ben Zoma will say that this spirit was hovering like a dove over its young. An eagle, Rashi explains (at Deuteronomy 32:11), does not just burst into its nest but flutters overhead, not settling its weight on the fledglings but hovering, "touching but not touching." Neoplatonists visualize God's immediacy in geometrical language: Plotinus' word, *aphe*, describes the weightless contact of a tangent with a circle, or a wrestler's touch[5] – thus, Jacob's contact with the angel (32:25) – not union but communion. On the Sistine Chapel ceiling Adam's finger all but touches God's outstretched hand: Our being is our own; we are of God, yet apart.

Genesis does not detail God's creative methods. The implied metaphor is of a monarch, who has only to speak for his will to be done (Ibn Ezra at 1:3; Rashi at 1:6). God commands, nature obeys; both object and instrument of creation. The Gospel of John will hypostatize God's word. For a word embodies thoughts, and can seemingly demystify creation. But the reification, prefigured in Philo and the Jerusalem Targum, is perhaps too graphic. Genesis, humbler in its metaphysics and hardly intellectualist in its poetics, does not analyze the act. Its focus is on creation itself, and light, the primal fact.

God called the light day. There was, as yet, no human to do the naming. Scripture looks ahead, Ibn Ezra observes (at 1:8; cf. Nahmanides at 1:10). "But God sets the boundaries, as if telling the light, 'Day shall be your province'; and the darkness, 'Night shall be yours'" (Genesis Rabbah 3.7; Nahmanides at 1:5; cf. Rashbam at 1:14). Day followed night, and night day. The division of light from darkness set nature's rhythms, lest all remain in murk – or conflict, as Philo says, dawn "gently restraining darkness," and evening "gently welcoming" the dark.[6] "We are being alerted to the invention of time," Sasson remarks,[7] "a medium forged out of darkness, decidedly the least promising element available to the universe" – until God assigns its role.

So darkness too is good. But light's goodness is worthy of remark – first for its beauty, falsifying the cliché about Hebrew moral sense missing the aesthetic. The first command was an artist's. Light shone before it had a name, just as a virgin is lovely before she's loved. God didn't just find the light and call it good. He gave it being and *saw* that it was good.[8] Light was good not just because it served God's purpose. It had no use as yet. It was good in itself. The old commentators compare Pharaoh's daughter, examining the infant Moses and seeing *that he was good* (Exodus 2:2) – well formed, full of vitality.[9] Nature too is a good. "Reality," Sarna writes (at Genesis 1:4), "is imbued with God's goodness. The pagan notion of inherent, primordial evil is banished. Henceforth, evil is to be apprehended on the moral and not the mythological plane."

Nahmanides finds a commitment to preservation implicit in God's seeing *it was good*. That hardly makes natural kinds changeless, as he (at 1:10, 12, 1:31) and Ibn Ezra (at 2:4) urge. Unchanging species are foreign to Genesis. As Maimonides explains, stiffly fixed natures yield an unchanging universe (*Guide* II 19). The Talmud (B. Hullin 60A) does deny that nature changes. But that means the causal order, not species: God does not capriciously alter nature's course. Preservation matters because nature deserves sustenance. God's free act of creation, Hermann Cohen argued, like any act of love, entrains commitment. And, like law, God's creativity enriches the freedom it imparts. Need and vulnerability are present from the start, Kass writes: But hunger is met with blessings. Indeed, even appetites are blessings: "From this germ of appetition ... emerge desire, feeling, and a rich inner life, a badge of distinction for the higher animals and man. Life, precisely because it is perishable, has aspiration for what is eternal."[10]

Creatures, Genesis assumes, will pursue their interests. Nature (as Aristotle saw) recycles its materials. But that means more than Aristotle knew. For natures, as we now know, are dynamic: God delegates creative responsibilities. Individuals grow; species evolve. Biblically, light will stand for all the blessings of life, and insight: *For with Thee is the fountain of life; by thy light do we see light* (Psalms 36:10).

> God said, "Let there be a vault (rakia) amid the waters, dividing water from water." God made the vault to separate the water below it from the water above it, and it did. God called the vault the sky. Evening, and morning: A second day.

The verses suggest an artisan at work. The curtains part a bit as we follow his glance: God himself made the vault of heaven. Genesis, unlike Plato, is not queasy about ascribing work to the Highest. God's face remains unseen, but a product of his art comes into view: a barrier to keep the waters above from flooding earth below. The rare word *rakia*, the so-called firmament, suggests hammered metal (cf. Exodus 39:3; 2 Samuel 22:43), dome-like, dividing the waters much as darkness divides the days.

In the Babylonian *Enuma Elish* fresh water (Apsu), commingling with the surrounding Sea (Tiamat), engenders the gods. But biblical chastity fosters naturalism: The waters are not powers. They are naturalized under God's control.

In ancient texts rainwater pours from cisterns in the sky (Psalms 104:13; Genesis Rabbah 4.2, 4.5). But no one need take that literally. If hailstones are missiles, their storehouses would be armories. God asks Job if he has seen such armories. The point is that we mortals don't control the hail (38:22). God challenges Job again, asking if it's he who binds the Pleiades or loosens Orion's cords, or if he knows the womb from which ice issues (vv. 29, 31). Is it faith to think frost comes from a womb, or that stars are reined with leather traces? In the Psalms (104:3) God's upper rooms house waters. Is it piety to miss a metaphor?

Ecclesiastes knows the source of rain: *When clouds are full, they pour down rain on earth* (11:3). In Job too rain comes from clouds (37:11). R. Eliezer, a Talmudic sage, knew that clouds are replenished from the sea; he cites Job (36:28) to confirm that clouds distill the water they yield as rain.[11] Saadiah sought no cisterns in the sky. Didn't Job pair them poetically with clouds? "The substance of rain is the moist vapor that rises into the air by a force of its own. Once it reaches the limit of its power to rise it falls back upon the earth by its own nature."[12] Ibn Ezra, similarly, cites Amos (5:8): *God calls the waters of the sea and pours them on the face of the earth.* God acts through nature here. Literalism would only dilute the message: That God made the world, marked the seasons, and set limits to all natural forces.

> *God said, "Let the waters beneath the sky be gathered up, and dry land appear." And it was so. God called the dry land earth; the gathered waters, he called seas. God saw that this was good. God said, "Let the earth sprout herbage – grass bearing seed, fruit trees on earth, yielding fruits of their kind with their seeds in them." And it was so. The earth brought forth herbage – grass, bearing the seeds of its kind, and fruit trees yielding fruits with the seeds of their kind within. God saw that this was good. Evening, and morning. A third day.*

It's good that the earth shows above the water. Philo pictures the alternative: water everywhere, "as if soaking a sponge."[13] Land makes room for plants. Their creation is good in itself. But it also portends opportunity. And nature joins in God's plan, Ibn Ezra stresses: It is the waters that teem with life, the earth that puts forth grass and living creatures (Genesis 1:11, 20, 24). The fecundity is nature's, but still God's blessing, cheered on by God's *be fruitful and multiply* (1:22), ending the earth's barrenness. All life on earth, says Ibn Ezra, comes from the natural elements (at 1:24). But even a fertile earth does not yield plants without seeds.[14]

The ancient word for gathering here connotes boundary setting (Genesis Rabbah 5.1) – limits once again. So was the earth once wholly under water? That again would miss the point. We're asked to imagine how things might have been – no light, no division of day from night. The Torah acknowledges dry land, grasses, trees, not to preach a fantasy history but in the vein of those modern authors who urge that without tiny differences in the quantities of matter and anti-matter nothing would have survived the Big Bang. Genesis is explanatory in a way, pointing to the work of a transcendent God – but also celebratory: Without God's act there would be no natural order to explain.

Biblical naturalism

Genesis does not say that land was made for plants but only that the waters were gathered up, so land showed above the water. For terrestrial plants that's marvelous. But the plants are not immortal, nor continuously created. They have seeds inside, yielding others of their kind. No organism literally reproduces. Living beings produce others of their kind, just as the Hebrew says. But *of its kind* just means "of all sorts," as the parallels show in God's charge to Noah (6:20) and in the dietary laws (Leviticus 11:14–16, 19, 22; Deuteronomy 14:15). Species do breed true: "Baboons don't produce peacocks," as one polemicist put it.[15] But here the focus is on profusion and variety, not reproductive isolation. The Bible knows about hybridization. It tends to disapprove (Leviticus 19:19, Deuteronomy 22:9). But mules are well known (Genesis 36:24, 1 Kings 10:25, 18:5, 1 Chronicles 12:40, 2 Chronicles 9:24, etc.). "Fixity of species," as Shai Cherry remarks, "never became a Jewish doctrine."

The old exegetes readily imagine species changing, crossing, disappearing.[16] In the Midrash the snake loses not only his feet but his guile. Even his scales, molting, and forked tongue alter his original condition (Genesis Rabbah 19.1, 20.4). The mole lost its eyesight; frogs, their teeth – lest they destroy everything (Psalms Rabbah 58, 300; cf. B. Moed Katan 6B). The mouse's mouth and raven's gait and courtship changed after the Flood; the steer's nose lost its hair when Joshua kissed it for bearing him into battle at Jericho (Alphabet of Ben Sirah 25–26). The enmity of cats and dogs, midrashically, like cats' mousing, is acquired. The homilies, like any fables, accept species change – quite innocent of the notion that creation, being perfect, must hold constant, or can only decline from its primordial state.

Dolphins, in midrashic legend, are half man, half fish and can gender with humans. Noah, on God's instructions, is said to have selected for the ark only submissive beasts. He excluded dogs that bred with wolves, and roosters that mounted peahens.[17] He chose for purity and obedience, just as God chose him for probity, not hardihood. God created many worlds before ours, says the Midrash, and other humans before Adam – all discarded (Genesis Rabbah 3.7; Psalms Rabbah 90:13; cf. B. Shabbat 88B). Moral worth was the test, not sheer survivability.

> God said, "Let there be lights in the vault of heaven, dividing day from night, marking the seasons, days, and years, as lamps in the vault of

heaven, lighting the earth." And it was so. God made the two great lights,
the greater light to preside by day, and the lesser light to preside by night;
and the stars. God set them in the vault of heaven to light the earth and
preside by day and night and divide light from darkness. And God saw
that it was good. Evening, and morning. A fourth day.

Genesis does not say that plants were made for human use. It cites their
enjoyment (2:9), prospectively, not to delimit their purposes.[18] But fruit trees
are delightful. One midrash remarks: The whole world was like a table set
for man, yet he came last, like a latecomer to a feast[19] – a lesson in humility:
Even the gnat predates us. Maimonides, in this spirit, calls it the height of
arrogance to imagine that celestial bodies exist for us alone: "The right view,
in my judgment, religiously and rationally, is not that all beings should be
taken to exist for man's sake but that they too exist for their own sakes. ...
Don't be misled when it says of the stars, *to light the earth, and preside by*
day and night (Genesis 1:17–18) ... this only discloses their nature. ... as
when it says of man, *rule over the fish of the sea* (1:28) – which does not
mean that's why we were created but only describes the nature God was
pleased to bestow on us" (*Guide* III 13). Celestial bodies do mark the seasons. But that's not their purpose. Starlight and sunlight spread in all direc-
tions. Only a fraction comes our way. The inference Genesis invites is simply
this: Without God's act, none of this would have been. Like the first light,
heaven's lamps are as precious for their beauty as for their later uses. Their
sublimity betokens fealty to God (Ben Sirah 9:17, Genesis Rabbah 6.2).
Their beauty is God's hallmark. So the Psalms say they praise God (19:2,
148:1–6). But the sun was not made to ripen crops.

Ancient commentators often wondered about the light created before the
sun. Nahmanides suggests (at 1:12) that the vault of heaven blocked the
primal light, so the earth needed lamps of its own. A fanciful expedient.
Plainly not all light came from the sun. But Genesis does not make light the
first object of creation so as to teach astronomy. Nor should readers be
troubled, Ibn Ezra explains (at 1:17), that it says God set the stars in the
firmament. They're far above the sky, but scripture puts them there just as it
speaks of God's setting the rainbow in the clouds (9:13): where it's seen, not
where it is. Genesis aims to situate us in the world, but it's not a map.

Some ancient exegetes have the sun and moon created on the first day but
situated on the fourth (B. Hagigah 12A). Maimonides generalizes the
approach, to vindicate biblical naturalism: The whole cosmos was created as
an integrated system – the laws of nature, the heavenly bodies, time itself –
nature's history, typified (as in Galileo) by the placement of the stars (*Guide* II
17, 19, 30; cf. III 32). The Malbim thus envisions the progressive development
of the Godgiven potentials of things, bringing nature to the state we know.[20]

Modern apologists sometimes make background radiation the light that
antedates the stars. But the Bible's disenchanting of nature affords a better

explanation: When Genesis dethrones the pagan gods it naturalizes their emblems. The polemic is muted but powerful: The sun is a created thing. Genesis tells of vegetation before the sun shone, Philo explains, precisely to exclude the sun's divinity. It too is created. It is not life's ultimate source.[21] The greater and lesser lights preside. They do not fix our destiny. Indeed, as Kass notes, the heavenly dome or vault is the first created thing not marked as good by God:[22] The sky is not divine. It's just a hunk of metal, as it were. Compare the scandal to Athenian piety when Socrates was calumnied as having called the sun a rock.[23]

The sun and moon give light, but they're not alive, or even named.[24] The planets get no separate mention, although, as Ibn Ezra notes (at 1:16), Jupiter is far larger than the moon. The great lights, he explains, are so called for their brilliance, not their size. Genesis mentions the stars almost as an afterthought, slighting their supposed powers. Jeremiah inveighs against awe at celestial portents (10:2); other texts find star worship revolting (Deuteronomy 17:3, 2 Kings 21:3, 2 Chronicles 33:3–9). To curb its hubris, the moon, midrashically, is diminished, and made to wax and wane (B. Hullin 60B). In the eighth-century hymn *El Adon*, the planets are beneficial, but created servitors – not dreadful gods but cheerful ministers of God's intent, acclaiming his sovereignty by spreading their light, exercising a delegated power and no arbitrary dominion,[25] their procession, calming, like the regular changing of the guard at a royal palace.

> *God said, "Let the waters teem with living things, let birds fly over the earth, across the vault of heaven." God created the great sea creatures and every kind of crawling animals that teem in the waters, and all sorts of winged fowl. God saw that it was good, and God blessed them, saying: "Be fruitful and multiply and fill the waters of the seas, and let the birds increase on earth." Evening, and morning. A fifth day.*

God's creativity is compounded in his *be fruitful and multiply*. Life itself flourishes, on land and in the seas – the plural in that last word forestalling confusion with any sea god. The *Tanin*, too, ancient ally of the Sea, defeated in its theomachy with Baal, is now just another creaturely kind, blessed by God with all the rest (Sarna, at 1:21). Again there's delegation. Nature's call to living beings to thrive in their diverse ways is God's command, but also a blessing, the Torah's first such pairing. Plants, Nahmanides writes (at 1:22), need no special blessing; their proliferation is seen to in their seeds. But animals procreate more actively. The mandate, Rashi notes, is to be fruitful, and to multiply. But the mandate, as Ibn Ezra writes, is no guarantee of fecundity. There's little worry that life will overrun the earth or overfill the seas. Creatures have their work cut out for them staying alive and sustaining their kinds. Animals need special blessings, in fact, since humans will decimate them (Genesis Rabbah 11.2). But God seeks their preservation. For life is a blessing; its profusion shows God's bounty:

God said, "Let the earth bring forth every sort of living being: beasts, creeping things, all sorts of land animals." And so it was. God made land animals of all kinds, beasts of all sorts, and every kind of creature that crawls in the soil. And God saw that it was good.

The Hebrew table benediction blesses God for bringing forth bread from the earth. Everyone knows that people bake bread. Loaves don't just spring from the soil. But the prayer echoes the Psalmist's allusion to our partnership with God (104:14), focusing on God's role since He imparts the powers by which all ends are won. The natural progression from seed to wheat, to harvesting, threshing, milling, kneading, and baking, holds miracles at every stage. Similarly here: The earth brings forth living beings – at God's command, with many intermediate stages.

Again Genesis celebrates the variety of living kinds, not their invariance: The living creatures are good. As with first light, the standard is intrinsic worth, not utility. Hence, as Ibn Ezra notes, the inclusion of wild beasts – even predators (cf. Nahmanides at 1:24). The wild ass, as God reminds Job, laughs at city traffic; the wild ox ploughs no furrow, seeks no manger, and scorns the threshing floor (Job 39:5–7, 9–11). God feeds the badger, wild goats, storks, and lions; dolphins serve him by their play (Psalms 104:17–27). Nature's exuberance is God's glory.

God said, "Let us make man in our own image and likeness. Let him rule over the fish of the sea, birds of the sky, beasts of the earth, and every creeping thing that crawls upon the earth." And God created man in his own image. In the image of God did he create him: Male and female created he them. God blessed them, and God said to them: "Be fruitful and multiply, fill the land and master it. Rule over the fish of the sea, the birds of the sky, and every living creature that crawls upon the earth."

Saadiah reads *Let us make* as a plural of majesty. Nahmanides sees a hint of the earth's collaboration, providing Adam's matter (at 1:26). God addresses the angels, Ibn Ezra suggests. For humans, unlike the rest, are no mere compound of the elements. They have a higher destiny. *Image and likeness*, Nahmanides writes, announces man's affinity to God: "In bodily dispositions he will be like the earth from which he was taken; in spirit, like the supernal beings. For the spirit is not a body and will not die."

God, Sarna notes (at 1:26), does not just command man into existence, like the light and all the rest, with an impersonal jussive verb. The hortative *let us make* suggests deliberation – as if God were musing, R. Hila says, as when we say to ourselves 'Lets see … ' But the Midrash finds a springboard here (cf. 11:7): God consulted, as it were, with his retinue. So should we, in determining any great matter (Sanhedrin 38b, Genesis Rabbah 8.8). God needed no help, Rashi explains (at 1:26–27). He was modeling deference, even to one's inferiors. Maimonides takes the heavenly host more cosmologically: Angels are the natural forms and forces God deploys – just as Plato's craftsman god, the Demiurge, *consults* an ideal pattern (*Guide* II 6, alluding to *Timaeus* 29–30). But matter too is God's creation. So is energy. As Elijah Benamozegh writes (citing Nahmanides and Genesis Rabbah 8.3), "The words, *Let us make man*, addressed all the forces in the universe."[26] Nature's created powers were God's medium and vehicle.

The human image

God's *image and likeness*, Maimonides reasons, is the human mind (*Guide* I 1).[27] For God has no physical likeness. As Ibn Ezra writes, "Scripture clearly rejects such notions, saying, *To whom will you liken me?* (Isaiah 40:25)." Indeed, Genesis deconstructs its own anthropomorphism; for both man and woman are created in God's image (1:27). Yet humans, like God, speak, command, name, bless, and hallow, work creatively, behold and assay their work, care for its goodness, and sustain other beings. All traits, Kass notes, that "lift us above the plane of merely animal existence."[28]

Does Genesis make God in the human image? Not quite. True it uses anthropomorphic terms, but only for traits we esteem and can hope to emulate – not God's absoluteness but his goodness and mercy; not rapacity or violence but God's holiness, which the Torah finds in love (Leviticus 19:2, 19:18).

Like other animals, humans are mandated/blessed with procreation, but separately (B. Kiddushin 35A) – not vegetatively like plants, or even actively like animals, but more consciously and conscientiously. The blessing, Nahmanides notes (at 1:28), is introduced by *said* rather than *saying*: It's no longer implicit in the procreative act, *as if* pronounced by God. For humans are articulate: We grasp commands and can recognize blessings. "Here," Sarna writes, "God directly addresses man and woman. The transcendent God of Creation becomes the immanent, personal God, who enters into unmediated communion with human beings." God, the Rabbis say, taught mankind how to bless when he blessed Adam and Eve.[29]

Humans hold dominion not by dint of language or culture but by God's command. Our talents, like every facet of creation, are God's gift. But human supremacy is the premise, not the thesis here. Responsibility is the implication. God's mandate legitimates man's rule, but Genesis aims not to warrant the gift but to prize it and acknowledge its obligations.

> God said, "Behold, I have given you every seed bearing plant on the face of all the earth, and every tree with seed-bearing fruit. These are yours to eat. To all the animals of the land, birds of the sky, and all living creatures that creep on the earth, I give every green plant for food." And so it was. God saw all that he had done, and lo, it was very good. Evening, and morning. A sixth day.

Once again God saw the goodness of his work, critic as well as creator. Creation now, as every commentator notes, was not just good but very good. What was very good, Ibn Ezra reasons (at 4:1), was the totality. By themselves nature's constituents were only good. Indeed, their deficiencies and oppositions could make them just the opposite. But each had its role in the panoply. "Even things that you may think utterly superfluous to the world's creation, like fleas, gnats, and flies, are included. God achieves his purpose in all things, even snakes, scorpions, gnats, and frogs" (Genesis Rabbah 10.7). Moses Almosnino, a Renaissance exegete, wrote: "when God saw the sum of all created things, duly arranged and interacting, he saw a special goodness in the whole beyond the worth of each separate thing. The rabbis allude to this, saying God was called complete when the world was complete (Genesis Rabbah 13.3)."[30]

What made the world complete was humankind: *me'od*, very, is a Hebrew anagram of *adam*, man – the crowning touch (Genesis Rabbah 9.12, 14). Yet humans were not the be-all and end-all. They were given all manner of fruits to eat. But so were the animals. Meat, it seems, was not yet allowed (Genesis 9:3, B. Sanhedrin 59b). Dominion was not carte blanche.

Some take human dominion to signify *intellectual* mastery. Hertz goes further. Quoting Lyman Abbott, he learns from the verse of mind's governance of matter. Others see a charge of stewardship. For the Torah protects the land and ordains that even in a siege fruit trees must be spared (Exodus 23:10–11; Leviticus 19:23; Deuteronomy 20:19–20). The Midrash embroiders: "When the Holy One, blessed be He, created the first man, He took him and led him 'round all the trees of the Garden of Eden, saying, 'Behold my works, how fair and lovely they are. All that I created, I created for your benefit. Take care not to spoil or destroy my world. If you ruin it, there's no one to repair it after you'" (Ecclesiastes Rabbah 7.13). Even when God seems to dedicate everything to human usufruct, nature's uniqueness, beauty, and fragility ordain responsibilities. Adam must work the garden and preserve it.

The world was created with ten sayings, the Rabbis say, to show how precious it is! (Avot 5.1). But God's work is not toil (Genesis Rabbah 27.1). Rather, each command marks a stage in nature's history. The labor was done at God's behest: His creativity, nature's work. Noting that the chronicle of the world's history is labeled *toldot*, a genealogy,[31] Ibn Ezra takes *the generations (toldot) of heaven and earth* (2:4) to include all that they generated: all that God made through nature's instrumentality.

The ancient rabbis often thought of nature as preformed (Genesis Rabbah 12.4), but unfurled, developmentally. Along with heaven and earth, Maimonides reasons, God created all that they contain: "The universe was created at one fell swoop, and then things differentiated gradually. The Sages compared this to the simultaneous sowing of various grains: Some sprout after a day, some after two days, or three, although all were planted at once" (*Guide* II 30). The accounts jibe with the naturalism of Genesis itself: Nature is given scope to develop. Following an elegant schematization by Umberto Cassuto and Leo Strauss, Kass sees Genesis as setting nature's constituents "in order of progressively greater freedom of movement." Humans outrank the stars, not by outshining them but by exercising freedom. Like the sky, humans are not called good, although the world that includes them is "very good." Freedom, Kass infers, makes man good potentially. Adam, as created, is not *yet* good.[32]

> *Heaven and earth were finished, and all their array. On the seventh day God completed the work he had done. So, on the seventh day God ceased all his work. God blessed the seventh day and hallowed it, since it was then that he ceased all the work he had done to create. Such is the history of heaven and earth at their creation–*

The world was finished on the sixth day. But then we read that God completed his work on the seventh. "What did the world still lack?" Rashi asks. "Rest," he answers, dissolving the apparent paradox by answering the riddle: What could be done in which nothing was done? "With the Sabbath came rest. Only then was the work complete!"(at 2:2). Glossing further, the Rabbis see the Sabbath as marking the boundary between nature as we know it and God's setting out the laws under which nature is governed. Sabbaths signal the harmony of nature's laws with God's will and gain a cosmic sanction by their institution at the creation.

By sanctifying the Sabbath, God models the holiness humans must seek, lest workaday needs overwhelm all else. God is not reduced to his creative work; and human dignity mirrors God's, as befits the human image. Unceasing efforts to control nature enslave us. A halt makes us free and becomes the emblem of our freedom. Understanding the linkage of this emblem historically to Israel's redemption from slavery and cosmically to God's freedom, as celebrated in the creation narrative and constantly retold, is the key to grasping the prominence of the six days of creation in the Torah's cosmogony. Special creation in the vexed sense that concerned Darwin's critics was not the issue.

Sarna (at 2:3) contrasts our passage with the Babylonian myth, "which culminates in the erection of a temple to Marduk by the gods."[33] The first biblical mention of holiness, Heschel notes, sanctifies not a place but a time.[34] Even slaves, even animals, share in Sabbath rest (Exodus 20:10). Humans are dehumanized, Aristotle will argue, without leisure to think or freedom to choose our ends. Yet he justifies enslaving some, to give leisure to a few, and fulfillment to those wise enough to seek it and fortunate enough to find it. Tacitus sneers at Israel's indolence: They give servants the ease of gentlefolk. But the Torah secures leisure not through slavery but through sabbaths, marking, mandating, and guarding the holiness of each person. Scripture mandates six days of work (Exodus 20:9), crowned by the Sabbath.

No astral rhythm inscribes the pattern. Rather, it projects a law imparting dignity and allowing humans to reach toward God. Sabbaths, the ancient homilists will say, make kings of all who keep them.

Laboring to revere the words, *For in six days did the Lord make heaven and earth, the sea and all that is in them, and he rested on the seventh day*, would be inerrantists slight the normative cap: *Therefore did the Lord bless the Sabbath day and make it holy* (Exodus 20:11). They freely shift the protected day to the first of the week and compromise its safeguards but vehemently defend a six day creation. Philo found such literalism "utterly foolish," since there was no sun until the fourth day. God, he reasons, transcends time, which must have begun with the heavens that mark its measure.[35] God's week, Nahmanides reasons, might outlast the world. The hexaemeron poetically parses the cosmos. It is not a timetable of God's creativity.

Is Genesis just the story of a spectacular construction project? Would creation be less awesome if it took billions of years? The Midrash, spurning literalism, asks: "Does he tire? Does it not say, *He faints not, nor does he grow weary. … He gives strength to the weary* (Isaiah 40:28, 29). … Yet he let it be written of him that he created his world in six days and rested on the seventh"[36] – to demonstrate in practice what it means for humans to be made in God's image.

Alluding to the creation, scripture says: *He ceased and was refreshed* (Exodus 31:17).The rare word *va-yinaffash* etymologically suggests a breather, as in *that your ox and your ass may rest and your bondman and the stranger be refreshed* (Exodus 23:12). How is that if God neither sleeps nor slumbers? Homilists, taking *va-yinaffash* transitively, as the causative verb form seems to invite, find a hint of God's breathing life and spirit into Adam's form. Stacking midrash upon midrash, they see Sabbaths imparting a second soul (*nefesh*) to all who keep them, lifting spirits to a higher plane. The poetic wordplay strikes home, since sacred rest opens a window on transcendence. That theme is lost if creation is just a conjuring trick, making a world appear in six days and nights.

The human condition

Having sketched the origins of the cosmos, Genesis backtracks to detail the human story. The narrative, as Kass notes, differs in sequence:

> The first creation story focuses on heaven and earth … the second focuses on human beings. … The first story ends with man; the second begins with him. … In the first, man is to be the master of life on earth (1:28); in the second, he is to be the servant of the earth (2:5, 15). In the first male and female are created together; in the second they are created sequentially. … In the first story, man is made directly in the image of

God (1:27); in the second he is made of earthly dust and divine breath (2:7) and becomes godlike only at the end – 'now man is become like one of us' (3:22) – and only in transgressing.[37]

Still, the large themes hold steady.

> *The day the Lord God made earth and heaven, before there was any shrub of the field on earth, before any grass of the field had sprouted, since the Lord God had not yet caused rain to fall on earth, and there was no man to work the soil, but mist rose from the soil and watered all the face of the earth, the Lord God formed man of clods of earth and blew into his nostrils the breath of life, and man became a living soul.*

God works directly here, forming a man from the soil. Puffed alive by God's breath, Adam is hardly exalted, shaped from the clods he will one day work. Rabbi Meir, chief architect of the Mishnah, glosses *clods of earth* as hinting that Adam's clay came from the whole earth, presaging the common origins of all nations.[38]

Adam's name reflects his origins. He came from the soil (*adamah*). Our word *human* and the Latin *homo* similarly connect with *humus*, soil, and *humilis*, humble. Indeed the Hebrew root *a-d-m* may also connect with *homo*, as suggested by the Akkadian *a-m-l*, and the Arabic *a-n-m*, both meaning human.[39] Darwin affirms a *less* humble origin:

> The Simiadae then branched into two great stems, the New World and Old World monkeys; and from the latter, at a remote period, Man, the wonder and glory of the Universe, proceeded. Thus we have given to man a pedigree of prodigious length, but not, it may be said, of noble quality. ... Unless we close our eyes, we may, with our present knowledge, approximately recognise our parentage; nor need we feel ashamed of it. The most humble organism is something much higher than the inorganic dust under our feet; and no one with an unbiased mind can study any living creature, however humble, without being struck with enthusiasm at its marvelous structure and properties.[40]

Darwin's point is rhetorical, of course. His humans too stem ultimately from non-living matter. But he focuses on the many steps preceding our present state. That does not obviate the miracle that both he and scripture address: the rise of living, conscious beings.

Humans, midrashically, were not God's first creatures. That distinction goes to the behemoth mentioned in Job (40:15, echoing Genesis 1:24). The rabbis love such humbling notes. In Hebrew *living soul* can also mean animal, as Ibn Ezra notes (at 2:7, citing 1:20, 1:21, 9:10). Rabbi Yehudah, long before, had inferred that man at first had a tail, removed by God, to spare our dignity (Genesis Rabbah 14.10). To Naftali Halevi, a rabbi of the Jewish Enlightenment, such accounts seem to anticipate Darwin: Eden was a state of nature, thousands of years of struggle and competition, in fact, before humans arose from the beasts.[41]

Despite our earthly origins, humans consummate God's work. His face remains unseen, but the breath enlivening our clay is his. Genesis is silent about immortality. *Nefesh* here, as Orlinsky explains, means breath – life by synecdoche. It will come to mean a creature (Numbers 6:6, 19:13). But disembodied souls await the Maccabean interest in resurrection; "even then it is not *nefesh* but *neshamah* that becomes the term for 'soul'."[42] Still, Genesis sees more in life than its components; and human life is unique: *The spirit* (neshamah) *of man is God's candle* (Proverbs 20:27). Matter too is a gift, Philo writes, but Adam's breath links him with divinity.[43]

Genesis harks back to a barren, untilled earth, not because two disparate stories are rudely stitched together but because this image, like the earlier vision of emptiness, sets off the richness of God's bounty. Would be literalists clash with Bible critics here, who oddly share their literalism. But traditional exegetes, more open to the biblical idiom, have no such difficulties. The Torah, Rashi writes here, heeds no strict chronology. "Scripture, you must see," the Rabbis say, "teaches nothing whatever about what came first or later" (Genesis Rabbah 2.7). Adam is the type and figure of humanity. To miss that is to miss everything.

God did not make two bodies in one, as Plato, satirically, has Aristophanes propose (*Symposium* 189D–193E), and some midrashim, in Plato's wake, imagine, playing on *male and female created he them* (1:27).[44] Philo thinks the pre-physical human Form governed both sexes.[45] Justin Martyr (*Cohortatio ad Gent.* 30) and Clement of Alexandria (*Instructor* 3) follow Philo. Tertullian sees the first mention of mankind's creation as a general summary, followed by details (*Adversus Hermogenem* 26).[46]

Rabbinically and liturgically, every raindrop brings special grace.[47] Genesis dramatizes the coming of rain, suggesting complementary responsibilities: God waters; humans till the soil. Accordingly, Ibn Ezra and David Kimhi gloss *asher bara' elohim la-'asot* (2:3), literally, *which God had created to make*, as a call for reciprocity – "which God had created (for creatures) to make." Creation remains to be completed (Genesis Rabbah 11.6). Paradigmatically: "God rooted procreative powers in all species" (Ibn Ezra at Genesis 2:3).

The Lord God planted a garden to the east, in Eden. There he placed the man he had formed. The Lord God caused all sorts of trees to sprout from the ground, lovely to see and good to eat; the tree of life in the midst of the garden, and the tree of knowledge of good and evil. ... The Lord God took the man and settled him in the garden of Eden, to work it and tend it. The Lord God commanded the man: "Of every tree in the garden you

may eat. But of the tree of knowledge of good and evil you shall not eat.
For the day you eat of it you shall die."

Human needs came easily in God's orchard (cf. Ezekiel 31:3–9) – including
the needs for work and caring. The tree of life was not forbidden. Indeed,
since Adam typifies the human condition, Maimonides says this tree is still
at hand! It is emblematic, Benamozegh will say, of humanity's struggle for
regeneration.[48]

Genesis Rabbah identifies the forbidden fruit variously (15.7): Some say it
was wheat, since a naif is said never to have tasted wheat. Others blame the
vine, a source of sorrow and folly. Some, noting God's command not to eat
of the tree, name the citron, whose wood, like its fruit, is edible! Others
specify the fig tree, which showed contrition for abetting the couple's disobedience by affording their first coverings. In one tradition the offending
tree was a pomegranate, holding a seed or two of trouble for everyone. But
Joshua ben Levi says the tree remains unnamed, lest it be shamed for the ills
it brought. In all these homilies the tree is symbolic. As Ibn Ezra remarks (at
2:9), only in Eden do life and knowledge grow on trees. But the symbolism
remains for the narrative to reveal.

> *The Lord God said: "It is not good for the man to be alone. I will make*
> *him a helpmeet." Having formed from the earth each beast of the field*
> *and bird of the sky, the Lord God brought it to the man to see what he*
> *would call it. Whatever the man called each animal was its name. The*
> *man named all the beasts, birds of the sky, and every wild animal. But for*
> *Adam no helpmeet could be found. So the Lord God cast the man into a*
> *deep slumber and while he slept took one of his ribs and closed up the flesh*
> *again. From the rib he had taken from the man the Lord God fashioned a*
> *woman. He brought her to the man, and the man said: "This time, bone of*
> *my bones and flesh of my flesh! She shall be called woman* (ishah) *because*
> *she was taken from man* (ish).*" Therefore does a man leave his father and*
> *his mother and cleave to his wife* (ishto), *to become one flesh. The two*
> *were naked, the man and his wife, but unashamed.*

Until now Adam has been "the man" (*ha-adam*), named for his origin,
strikingly reversing mythic linkages of woman with earth. Now he is Adam,
a person, not a type – although hitherto, as Philo says, "ignorant of himself
and his own nature."[49] He acquires an identity only when he finds his mate.

Adam is articulate, Ibn Ezra notes (at 2:7, 2:17), ready to invent names.
There is no story of his maturation. That would only open a pointless
regress. Darwin will follow the roots of the human tree into non-human soil.
But scripture is not seeking the headwaters of the human stream in a pre-
human past. In a way Genesis is less mythic than many a museum diorama:
It does not try to picture quasi-humans. Adam and Eve are naive but never

crude. Humanity begins with the birth of consciousness. Where evolution asks how we came to be, Genesis probes what it is to be human. It answers in terms of thought and moral agency. These are personal. They need embodiment, but also a social matrix. This Scripture finds not in some primal clan or pack. That would both presume and ignore too much. Genesis looks to a dyadic relation – not Freud's mother and infant, or Hegel's master and slave, or even Aristotle's friend with friend, but the couple: woman and man. *Three things*, Proverbs says (30:18–19), *are too marvelous for me, four I cannot fathom: the way of an eagle in the sky, the way of a snake on the rock, the way of a ship in the sea, and the way of a man with a maid.*

Language is human. Just as God gives things their energies and penchants, he lets Adam name the animals. "Only one species," Peter Lawler says, "is composed of beings who name."[50] Gardening, evidently, not prostitution, was the oldest profession; biology, the first science. Taxonomy will be objective: Although naming is conventional, there are natural kinds. So in finding his counterpart Adam faces objective constraints. He can name his mate but cannot make her in his image. Still she is uniquely apt to him, answering his incompleteness. The Midrash warns misogynists: "He who is without a wife lives without good, without help, without joy, without blessing, without atonement" (Genesis Rabbah 17.2).

'Helpmeet' is Tyndale's coinage, following the Hebrew *'ezer ke-negdo*, sometimes rendered a "fitting helper." Genesis hushes ancient fears of women by choosing a word of unmarked gender: *ᶜEzer*, like 'mate', entails support. But God is too often called help, Sarna writes, for the word to be demeaning. *Two are better than one* (Ecclesiastes 4:9), Ibn Ezra explains (at 2:18). Nahmanides concurs: Reality is good, and Eve enhances reality: "Man cannot be called good when alone. He cannot even exist" (at 2:18).

Eve and Adam are one flesh. Yet she is as much God's work as he. Their partnership stands against all notions of some inveterate battle between the sexes. The moral textually drawn from their affinity is a command, conveyed, Rashi says, by the Holy Spirit: *Therefore does a man leave his father and his mother and cleave unto his wife, to become one flesh.* Social fact, natural norm, and blessing merge here: Blood is not thicker than water. Our first loyalty, even above parents, is to our spouse. As David Hartman explains, we are linked to our parents (and God) existentially: They give us being. But commitment to a spouse, like every covenant, is freely chosen. It needs continual care and renewal.[51]

There are young men alive today who have incinerated their brides at the kitchen fire for failing to bring to the parental household sufficient bridal gifts – electronics, consumer goods. Many cultures countenance, even celebrate sexual adventurism, yet demand "honor killings." The Torah stands forcefully against all this, finding in created nature the proper precedence of human attachments. Its moral message here is too easily obscured by wilful literalism about Eve's origins, if not by misogyny and an ambivalence about sexuality and eros that is radically unbiblical. The stunning biblical symbolism of a man, just this once, giving birth to a woman, is glossed in Genesis itself: Woman is not of alien flesh but an ally and kindred spirit, herself in the image of God. Imagine bandaging that thought in some feat of faith affirming that once a woman was made from a man's rib! God, at least, closed up Adam's flesh and left no gaping hole where the moral once stood. Dogma, like midrash, will always find a hook. But a faithful midrash takes its cue from larger textual themes, not from some extraneous enterprise.

Celsus knows that both Jews and Christians take Adam's rib allegorically.[52] Philo says: "The language is mythic. How could anyone assume that a woman or any human, came from a man's side?"[53] But two millennia of wiser readings don't hold truculent literalism in bounds. A medieval case study offers a fitting object lesson: Seeking strictly to obey God's words *they shall become one flesh*, Karaite exegetes treated the kin of brides and grooms as relations in the same degree – spawning a tangle of consanguinities: A bride's sister became the groom's sister, her daughter by a previous marriage became his daughter, relations of a second wife became her new husband's kin. The resulting marital restrictions, dating to the eighth-century origins of the sect, wreaked havoc, especially in small communities, binding virtually everyone, in time, in chains of forbidden relations. By the late tenth century vigorous opposition arose; by the eleventh it was accepted that *they shall be one flesh* had no bearing on the laws of incest. The resulting reform, Leon Nemoy notes, was "the only one in the history of Karaite law."[54]

The birth of morals

Why was the Tree of Knowledge of Good and Evil forbidden? Was God protecting humankind (cf. Ibn Ezra, at 2:18)? "Some people," Maimonides remarks, "are horrified when grounds are given for any of God's laws. They would rather no sense were found in any injunction or prohibition." Such readers see God's first ban as a test of faith – as if bald authority were the theme and sheer obedience had worth without any determinate content. That kind of submission, Maimonides argues, discipline for its own sake, would make God's commandments vain or idle. God does not need human deference. All of his commands seek our good, as the Torah declares (*Guide* III 31, citing Deuteronomy 6:24). The real question was, and remains, whether we humans would judge goods objectively, using our Godgiven reason, or choose selfishly, subjectively, driven by appetite, passion, or convention (*Guide* I 2).

> Now the serpent was the subtlest of the wild beasts the Lord God had made. Said he to the woman, "Did God really tell you to eat of no tree in the garden?"

The woman said to the serpent, "We may eat of the fruit of any tree in the garden, but of the fruit of the tree in the middle of the garden God said, 'Do not eat of it, do not touch it, lest ye die'."

Said the serpent to the woman, "You shall not die actually. God knows, in fact, that the day you eat of it, your eyes will be opened. You will be like gods, knowing good and evil."

Seeing that the tree was good to eat and delightful to the eyes, and a wonderful source of wisdom, the woman took some of its fruit and ate it. She gave some to her husband too, who ate it. Their eyes were opened, and they knew that they were naked. So they stitched up fig leaves and made themselves loincloths.

There's much wordplay here. The Hebrew for *subtle* echoes the word for naked. The word for *serpent* also means copper – perhaps because copper veins may have a serpentine form.

No one, we might suppose, would expect to gain wisdom from a piece of fruit. Yet I vividly recall how Leary and Alpert drew my Harvard classmates to experiment with LSD, to expand their consciousness. Bearing no hint of danger, the invitations appealed to romantic notions that inhibitions stifle creativity and shutter the portals of the mind. Many pursued quick, drug-mediated insight. I still encounter the casualties of that deception. The Midrash, however, says the serpent told the truth (*Pirka d'Rabbeinu ha-Kadosh*, § 3), and God admits that the humans became godlike in knowing good and evil (3:22). Evidently the serpent's subtlety held a deeper deception than a simple lie.

Adam, Ibn Ezra argues (at 2:17), must have had discernment already, when he named the animals. Indeed, he must have had moral discernment to receive divine commands. So what came from the tree? Plainly Genesis is reflecting on responsibility. But that too does not grow on trees. Besides, Adam and Eve had duties from the start – tending the garden and avoiding one tree while enjoying the rest. Was it conscience they acquired?

Answering a questioner who worried that moral knowledge seems a reward, not a punishment – as with those mythic figures "whose sins and crimes were so great that they were made stars in the heavens" – Maimonides argues (*Guide* I 2) that the forbidden fruit brought not moral wisdom but the opposite. For its first effect was that Adam and Eve suddenly felt naked (3:7). Such embarrassment, Maimonides reasons, reveals no great moral truth. Modesty is a matter of convention. What the two acquired was not conscience but a rude sense of propriety. In place of moral knowledge, derived from living in God's presence, they had gained subjectivity. Their shame represents all the biases and conventions that tincture our moral judgment with promptings of interest and desire. We become godlike, in our own eyes, creators of our own values. But our appetites and passions set us, in fact, on all fours with the beasts.

Autonomy does make us like gods in one way. But we lack the calm wisdom we might need for its exercise. Independent judgment comes with fallibility and bias. Eve's choice to eat what seemed attractive, harmless, even enlightening, signals the weld of freedom with fallibility that marks every human choice. Sexuality is not the great theme here. Like reason, that was present from the start, presumed with typical biblical earthiness – Adam and Eve were man and wife. The muddling of sex with guilt is a Hellenistic pre-occupation. Nor was death the price of disobedience. Science, Nahmanides (at 2:17) notes, declares Adam mortal from the start, since he was com-pounded of diverse elements. Hadn't Maimonides cited Galen (*De Usu Par-tium* III 10, at *Guide* III 12), to quiet unreasonable expectations about the body? Likewise Ibn Ezra (at 3:6): "A Greek physician has proved beyond doubt that it is impossible for a man to live forever." Thus: "As animals are destined to die, so too must man. Man's superiority to the beasts lies in our gift from on high."

Adam and Eve did not die the day they ate the fruit. So there are numer-ous glosses of God's warning. Some make the day last a thousand years, Adam's lifespan, less 70 years reserved for his descendants (Genesis Rabbah 19.8, citing Psalms 90:10). Some say Adam died the same day of the week; others, that when the couple tasted the fruit they *began* to die. But, far from dying, Philo notes, Eve conceived a child: The couple died morally, he rea-sons, by succumbing to the passions.[55] Many assume that human mortality began at Adam's lapse. But what crime did Adam's offspring commit, Ibn Ezra asks. The notion of inherited sin is incoherent and morally repugnant. Adam repented, Ibn Ezra concludes, and God relented. For the ancient rabbis say: "Wisdom said, *Evil pursues sinners* (Proverbs 13:2); prophecy said, *The soul that sins shall die* (Ezekiel 18:4); but the Holy One, blessed be he, said, *Let them repent and be forgiven. ... Therefore does he show sinners the way* (Psalms 25:8) – of repentance."[56] Death did not enter the world with a single sin. As Adam says in a trenchant midrash: "You die on your own account, not mine" (Ammi ben Nathan in *Midrash Tanhuma*, Hukkat).

The Talmud does link death with sin (B. Bava Batra 16ʙ). But the Hebrew for sin means misstep. And overreaching, all too human, is found in every living being. Eve, whom scripture calls the mother of all that live, typifies life's assertiveness in her thirst for wisdom. All creatures reach for life and light. But finitude is of the essence in creation. Death, in that sense, is life's counterpart, not sin's consequence. Genesis is not the first canto of a saga of redemption by a dying god but the tale of the human condition, each of us repeating Adam's choice, overreaching (and redressing) in our own way.

Existentialists, drawing on Pascal's sense of creatureliness, see both earthy and godlike sides to our humanity. The tension between our need to frame universal moral judgments and our weakness in doing so lies at the heart of the biblical narrative: A human couple naively confront the serpent's subtle nakedness, the tempting fruit, the threat of death and promise of immortality,

a tree of life, and another of earthly wisdom, bought at the price of subjectivity. Exile from Eden is no punishment but the emblem of our situation.
As Kass writes:

> the prototypical human being gets precisely what he reached for, only to
> discover that it is not exactly what he wanted. He learns, through the
> revealing conversation with God, that his choice for humanization,
> wisdom, knowledge of good and bad, or autonomy really means at the
> same time also estrangement from the world, self-division, division of
> labor, toil, fearful knowledge of death.[57]

Eve erred, the Midrash says, in adding to God's words a warning against
touching the tree. That gave the serpent an opening: She had already
touched the tree unscathed, so the serpent could wheedle: "See, that didn't
kill you." Tasting came next (Genesis Rabbah 19.3). The tree of life is forgotten for the moment. Genesis, Sarna remarks (at 2:9), drops the pagan
thirst for immortality, prominent in Gilgamesh or the story of Adapa,
focusing on our relationship with God. Acceptance of life, even with
mortality, is scripture's greater theme.

> *Hearing the sound of the Lord God walking in the garden in the afternoon*
> *breeze, the man and his wife hid from the Lord God in the garden woods.*
> *The Lord God called to the man, "Where are you?"*
> *He answered, "I heard you in the garden and was afraid, since I was*
> *naked, so I hid."*
> *He answered, "Who told you you were naked? Have you eaten of the*
> *tree I commanded you not to eat?"*
> *The man answered, "The woman you gave to be with me gave me of the*
> *tree, and I ate."*
> *The Lord God said to the woman, "What have you done?"*
> *The woman replied, "The serpent beguiled me and I ate."*

Adam's sin, the Rabbis say, was ingratitude (B. Avodah Zarah 5ʙ). Trapped
in a lie, he blames Eve, as if God were at fault for giving him his mate.
Adam was not banished, Rabbi Abba says, until he had thus dishonored
God (Genesis Rabbah 19.12).

Adam did not sin unwittingly, Ibn Ezra notes. Eve had reported the serpent's words. Indeed, Sarna argues, Adam heard the whole exchange with
the snake (at 2:6). For the serpent consistently used the plural. "The woman
is not a temptress. She does not say a word but simply hands her husband
the fruit, which he accepts and eats." One midrash has him freely share Eve's
fate, refusing to give up his beloved companion even for a chance of
remaining in the garden. That lovely patch of embroidery assigns Adam a
romantic nobility, gentling the bruise of his petulant finger pointing when
found out by the garden's owner.

Ancient and medieval commentators alike (Genesis Rabbah 19.12; Maimonides, *Guide* I 24) balk at thoughts of God's strolling in the afternoon breeze. What Adam heard, they stress, as the Hebrew has it, was God's voice, not his tread. But God had not yet called when the couple hid, and Scripture, Nahmanides observes (at 3:8), often has God walking among humans (e.g., Leviticus 26:12). The anthropomorphism signals that the story is not meant literally: It's not that God couldn't find Adam. He calls him, as he will summon Cain, baring the face of evasion.

> *The Lord God said to the serpent: "Because you did this, accursed shall you be beyond all cattle and wild beasts. You shall go on your belly and eat dirt all your life, and I will set enmity between you and the woman, and between your seed and hers. They shall strike your head, and you shall strike their heel."*

So, reading literally, animal forms were not fixed from the creation. Only now does the serpent slither on its belly. The anti-pagan undertow, Sarna notes, would be plainer to the original audience: Serpents, divinized in Canaan and Egypt, are humbled. They were already naturalized, as just another of God's creatures, albeit the subtlest. God's *all your life* (3:14) stresses their mortality. Midrashically, the serpent once had not just speech and cunning but legs and upright stature (Genesis Rabbah 20.5). All these now are lost. Snakes become mere vermin. Swatting the detested worm, Eve's offspring attack the head; snakes bite back, pathetically, at the heel. In divine reproofs (Deuteronomy 28:13, 44), success is the head, failure the tail: The serpent is all tail, and no god.

> *To the woman he said: "I will sharply increase your labor pangs. In travail shall you bear children. You will long for your husband, but he shall rule you."*

Biologists ascribe women's labor pains to the size of the fetal brain case, a concomitant of humanity. For Genesis this is women's lot, a consequence of the disobedience that marks the human condition. The serpent is cursed, but Eve's fate is not called a curse. Benno Jacob glosses homiletically: She needed no punishment. Biology gives women enough trouble. The Midrash likes the parataxis of birth pangs with longing: Fear of pain might discourage love making. Pregnancy makes a woman a nursemaid, Nahmanides writes. But desire draws her back (Genesis Rabbah 20.7). Rashi (at 3:16), rejecting male domination, completes the sense thus: "*You will long for your husband* (sexually, but lack the face to assert your demands), *but he shall rule you.* (He will take the lead, not you. The longing here is sexual desire.)" As the Talmud says, a woman may court with her eyes, but only men, typically, do so verbally (B. Eruvin 100b).

To Adam he said: "Because you heeded your wife and ate of the tree I commanded you not to eat of, cursed is the ground for you. By toil shall you eat of it all your life. Thorns and thistles shall it sprout for you, and you shall eat of the grasses of the field. By the sweat of your brow shall you eat your bread, until you return to the earth, for from it were you taken. You are dust and to dust you will return."

Adam's fate is a life of toil. His labor, *ᶜitzavon*, matches Eve's, *ᶜetzev* (Genesis Rabbah 20.9); his food, not far from the dirt the serpent crawls in. Tilled soil, says Ibn Ezra, is no Eden. But nature is not condemned, as Morris imagines. The irony strikes humankind: We cultivate yet seem to see more weeds than crops. Fruits become luxuries. Grains become the staff of life. But "Unlike cattle," Ibn Ezra writes, "you will have to labor at winnowing, grinding, kneading and baking, before you can eat." The earth that gave our bodies grudges their sustenance and reclaims them in the end. Even our handful of earth, the Rabbis say, is not ours to keep (Genesis Rabbah 20.10).

The man named his wife Eve (Ḥava). For she was the mother of all that live. And the Lord God made Adam and his wife tunics of skins and clothed them.

Eve too now has a name. She was the mother of humans, not literally of all life, as Onkelos and Saadiah note. Her name plays on the idea of life. But this mother figure, Sarna writes, is "demythologized and naturalized," testifying to human unity.[58] Motherhood, given the Torah's powerful pronatalism, was hardly a punishment. Abraham's promised offspring, numerous as the stars or the sand at the sea (Genesis 22:17), are but a fraction of Eve's progeny.

God models charity, respecting his creatures' needs and new notions of dignity. The skins are rough, since weaving is not yet known, but better than leaf-wraps. Gender-marked garments come later (Deuteronomy 22:5), but the tunic (*ketonet*) God fashions, Sarna notes (at 3:21), reflects late Bronze and Iron Age styles. God did not neglect appearances.

The Lord God said, "Now that the man is like one of us, knowing good and evil, he might put out his hand and take of the tree of life too, and live forever." So the Lord God sent him from the garden of Eden, to work the soil from which he was taken. He banished the man and set the cherubs east of the garden of Eden, and a flaming, whirling sword, guarding the way to the tree of life.

Cherubim are familiar figures (see Exodus 25:18–22, 26:1, 31; 36:8, 35; 37:7–9). So they are not described. But Eden's signage is clear: The road is closed. Eternal life is a virtuality; the unreachable tree bespeaks mortality. Man is estranged. Moral choice does make us gods in a way, but it robs us of the intimacy with God that nature still enjoys. Subjecthood completes the work of creation but sunders our connectedness. It makes us both free and fallible.

We are not told whom God meant in saying *like one of us*. Again an angelic court is suggested. The Rabbis embroider: Some angels, they say, plead for mercy, and their pleas were not unanswered. Repentance brought humans back to God, closer in exile than in Eden. Adam and Eve face moral adulthood. Relations with God are harder now, and more precious.

> *The man knew Eve his wife. She conceived and bore Cain, saying: "I have gotten* (kaniti) *a man with the Lord." She went on to bear his brother Abel.*

Much has been written about knowing in the biblical sense – a metaphor, not a metaphysic. As Owen Barfield taught in *Poetic Diction*, any exotic idiom may sound poetic if read too literally. Still, connotations count. 'Coitus' is clinical; 'intercourse,' abstract, missing the rich resonance of intimacy in the Hebrew: Not just erotic play (cf. Genesis 26:8) or experiment but discovery is meant, hinting at the cognitive depth of eros and the creative power of knowing. Guilt is absent. Sexuality is not Adam's crime or Eve's punishment. The Midrash assumes it even in Eden. But children arrive outside the Garden, softening the blow of exile, despite Eve's birth pangs and the grief awaiting both parents as their offspring grow.

Sexuality is the key to individuality. Budding and mitosis yield no such clear identities. Death grows sharper as individuality grows more pronounced. But personhood arises too, setting our humanity apart from its matter. For little parental matter reaches offspring. Chiefly conveyed is a message, opening potentials that underscore the ancient recognition that there is more to our humanity than the embodiment that makes it possible. That thought gives special poignancy to Maimonides' bold claim that the tree of life, in no crude sense, is still at hand, the spinning sword glittering with flashes of insight.[59]

Procreation is a more immediate response to death, offering an immortality quite distinct from personal persistence. The Torah rejects afterworlds. It accepts both the weakness and the power of our embodiment. Here progeny are the blessing that fulfills our strength and redresses our weakness. That stance anchors the mission biblically assigned to Israel, to become a nation by which all families of the earth will be blessed (Genesis 12:2–3, 15:5, Exodus 19:5–6, Leviticus 19:2, Deuteronomy 7:6, 14:2). Adam in exile, the Midrash imagines, had no wish for offspring, until his despond was met by visions of Israel's accepting the Torah: The human project still had meaning; life, despite the loss of Eden, was not in vain (Genesis Rabbah 21.9). That thought, a homily not a dogma, points to grounds for hope: Sufferings find their answer in moral and spiritual futurity. Life is not absurd.

Grasping the miracle she has shared, Eve freely credits God. He is as much the author of the second man as the first. But God is not the father. Adam knew Eve, she conceived and bore her child. Parents are proximate causes. God's is the ultimate agency. The Torah sees no conflict in setting the two kinds of explanation side by side: God acted through nature, just as he used the wind to gather the waters or caused flowers to spring from seeds (Rashbam at Genesis 1:1). The causal doubling is critical: Creation would mean nothing unless it energized the natural causes that animate the world: "Neither man without woman, nor woman without man, nor the two together without God's immanence (*shekhinah*)" (Genesis Rabbah 22.2; cf. 8.9). The Talmud (B. Niddah 31) paraphrases Eve's thought: "When God created me and my husband, he acted alone; now we are partners." At Abel's birth the process is familiar – still miraculous, and still natural.

My brother's keeper

Abel became a shepherd; Cain, a tiller of the soil. In time, Cain brought an offering to the Lord from the soil's fruits, and Abel too brought one of the finest firstlings of his flock. The Lord favored Abel and his offering. But Cain and his offering he favored not. Cain was enraged and crestfallen. The Lord said to Cain, "Why are you so incensed and discouraged? If you do what is good you can recover. If not, sin lurks at the door. It ravens for you. Yet you can master it."

Sin is a beast licking its chops. To avoid a tragic misstep, Cain must overcome his resentment. Grudges provoke deadly extremes (Leviticus 19:17–18). Indeed, a prior grudge distinguishes murder from manslaughter (Numbers 35:20–23). God heeds his own law by warning Cain against the crime he contemplates (Sifre 173 at Deuteronomy 18:12; B. Sanhedrin 56в). But Cain, free and thus responsible, fails to master his feelings.

Exegetes have long scratched their heads over God's preference for Abel's sacrifice. It was his best, and the Midrash fancifully disparages Cain's offering. But the story is less about the offerings than about the birth of crime, typified in a dreadful fratricide – since Adam's fatherhood makes all men brothers (Malachi 2:10).

Cain spoke to Abel his brother. When they were out in the field, Cain attacked his brother Abel and killed him. The Lord said to Cain, "Where is Abel your brother?"

He answered, "I don't know. Am I my brother's keeper?"

He said, "What have you done? The voice of your brother's blood cries out to me from the ground!"

Cain had words with Abel, their content unstated. The Septuagint and other versions fill in with some empty challenge or an invitation to step outside, but the added words add little. They look conjectural and leave the issue looking insubstantial. The textual weight falls on the repeated word brother:

Cain has killed his brother. The enormity does not strike him until God calls him. Even as he denies responsibility, his sarcastic *Am I my brother's keeper?* betrays him. We eavesdroppers catch the dramatic irony: We *are* each other's keepers.

Sarna doubts that the brothers' quarrel prefigures a pastoral-agrarian rivalry. For the two ecologies and economies were complementary. Nor does Genesis disparage Cain's vocation, although God was not pleased with his offering. God himself planted a garden, which Adam tended. Humanity faces agrarian labors, and Cain's descendants figure prominently in the rise of craftsmanship and culture (Genesis 4:20–22). It matters biblically, I think, that Cain's crime looks arbitrary; the irritant, trivial, as in the ballad: "What fell ye out about? Little son pray come tell me. / Twas over a withy-withy wand, that never could be a tree."[60] The brothers quarrel not for their father's favor, or their mother's favors. Abel dies, but it is Cain who falls prey to the beast skulking at the door. Sin looks for an opening. Still, we can master it, despite its fatality.

The figures are archetypal: a killer ducks responsibility. His victim need not be pure, regal or heroic. Even a simple shepherd's blood cries out to God. Each human life matters, cosmically. Thus the Mishnah, noting the poetic plural:

> It is written *the bloods of thy brother cry out* … his and his posterity's … just one man was created – to teach us that whoever causes the death of a single soul is seen biblically as if he'd caused a world to perish; and whoever saves one life, as if he'd saved a world – also, for peace among mankind, lest anyone say to another, "My ancestor was greater than yours." … And to proclaim the greatness of the Holy One blessed be he. For a mortal stamps many coins with a single die, and all are alike. But the King of kings, the Holy One blessed be he, stamped every human with the type of the first. Yet not one is like another. (Sanhedrin 4.5)

These famous homilies, framed to caution witnesses in a capital case, pin the sanctity of human life to irreplaceability. They reject all claims to noble birth and celebrate uniqueness as God's hallmark: Where Plato and Aristotle prize unity of type, the Torah finds inestimable value in the individual. To make an act of faith out of the facticity of Abel's murder while neglecting the story's moral charge, the imperative to cherish each human life and accept responsibility for one another, is completely to miss the point.

> *"Now are you cursed from the soil that gaped to take your brother's blood at your hand. When you work the soil, no longer will it give you its strength. A restless wanderer shall you be on earth."*

The earth that witnessed Cain's crime now executes his sentence. But, again, the earth was not literally cursed, as Ibn Ezra and Nahmanides stress. Nor does soil literally gulp blood. Cain violated nature not by watering the soil with Abel's blood but by his murder. The earth remains God's dominion;

nature, personified, cries out against the crime. Murder will out, as Chaucer and Cervantes will say. *The earth will expose the blood she has drunk and disclose the slain she has immured* (Isaiah 26:21). Cain is exiled, not just from Eden but from any fixed abode. The earth still gives its strength to others. But Cain has become a stranger there (Genesis Rabbah 22.10).

> *Then Cain said to the Lord, "My sin is too great to bear. You have exiled me today from the face of the earth. Banished from your face, I'll be a restless wanderer on earth. Anyone who finds me will kill me."*

Cain repeats God's words *restless wanderer* – outlaw and fugitive. His fears anticipate the cities of refuge, where homicides other than murderers find sanctuary (Numbers 35:6–29, Deuteronomy 4:41–43, 19:1–13). The world Cain pictures, populated perhaps with Abel's kin, seems ready to avenge him. God moves swiftly to mitigate those fears:

> *The Lord said to him: "Wherefore, whoever kills Cain shall suffer vengeance sevenfold." The Lord set a mark on Cain, lest anyone who found him smite him, and Cain left the Lord's presence and dwelt in the land of Nod east of Eden.*

Nod is not a place. The word is symbolic, Sarna notes, playing on *restless wanderer (na' ve-nod)* – Wanderland. God's "wherefore," Sarna adds, is formulaic, evoking a legal context: Cain is said to leave God's presence, as if a trial had ended.

Cain's mark, vulgarly confounded with his curse, has been fantastically identified with the melanin of black races, a thought utterly unfounded biblically. The mark is protective and is not inherited. Only Cain needs it, since Abel's murder is his crime alone. Cain owns his act when he calls his sin too great to bear. He does not ask for mitigation of his punishment, Nahmanides explains (at 4:13) – only that it not be compounded, by vigilante zeal.

The ancient rabbis differ about Cain's mark or sign. God made the sun shine on him, one says; another, that God gave him a dog. God *showed* Cain a sign, says Ibn Ezra, to help him face the world (at 4:15). Nahmanides concurs. Two ancient exegetes see Cain himself as the sign: an object lesson, says R. Hanina; a sign to penitents, says Rav. Both are right, of course. In one midrash (Genesis Rabbah 22.13) Adam meets Cain and asks the outcome of his case. Cain tells of his repentance and reconciliation, and Adam claps his hands to his face, exclaiming: "So great is the power of penitence, and I did not know!"

The rise of culture

Now begin the begats. They support the biblical theme of human unity. Genesis, Sarna notes (at 1:27), does not say "of every kind" when it comes to human beings. The genealogy, like Homer's catalogue of ships, will matter deeply to seekers of roots and ancestral eponyms. But, for us, the ancient equation of history with pedigree has faded in the constellation of human values. So I skip over these verses here. I've written elsewhere about their impact on the idea of universal history, first stitched together with the sinews of genealogy.[61] I've also noted how Lamech's boast to his wives – *If Cain is avenged seven-fold, then Lamech seventy-seven fold* – sets off his spiteful machismo against Mosaic norms, which fit the punishment to the crime and not, like Hammurabi, to the parties' status.[62] The text records the emergence of music, agriculture, the pastoral life of *those who dwell in tents* (4:20). There is no steady state world here but a progression climaxing in the revelation of God's law.

Many of the names in Genesis bear meanings. Enoch, for instance, connotes learning and culture. But Ibn Ezra (at 4:19) warns against making too much of ancient names: "even if we knew Hebrew perfectly, how could we tell the events they commemorate?" Lamech, the first polygamist, is Cain's descendant. Does that suggest disparagement, Sarna wonders. Clearly, the patriarchs were polygamous, although their stories also hint at matriarchal norms and matrilineal conventions. But the model of Adam and the linkage of natural with divine law in the expectation that a man *cleave unto his wife* sets biblical norms apart from biblical history. Many actions of the patriarchs are hardly made exemplary: Abraham's ruse in twice calling Sarah his sister, Rachel's theft of her father's household gods, Judah's resort to a presumed prostitute and subsequent readiness to put his widowed daughter-in-law to the flames for harlotry, Joseph's sale into slavery, the treacherous vengeance of Dinah's brothers after her rape by Shechem. So patriarchal practice does not make polygamy a norm. The practice was long tolerated but ultimately, like slavery, extruded by the Torah's higher values.[63]

The names of Lamech's wives, Adah and Zillah, may mean dawn and dusk. The Midrash reflects: In those days men took two wives, one for procreation, one for recreation. The former was kept like a widow; the latter, given a contraceptive drug and encouraged to act seductively (Genesis Rabbah 23.2). Lamech, midrashically the best of the generation lost in the Flood, is no ideal. But to Nahmanides (at 4:23) he is a skillful craftsman who taught his sons their animal husbandry, metal working, and music. Tubal-Cain is apparently the eponym of his people. His sister Naamah, the fair or lovely, seems to be a lady of distinction. Her story is lost in the mists, but Genesis Rabbah (23.4) honors her goodness by making her Noah's wife. Nahmanides, however, balks at the suggestion that any of Cain's seed survived the Flood, perhaps fearing lest efforts to name them aggravate group enmities.

All the culture heroes named are mortal. None has supernatural powers. Egyptian and Mesopotamian mythologies credit each new tool and art to some deity. But the Torah demythologizes culture along with nature: Just as all heaven and earth are the work of one God, using the natures he imparts, human crafts and artifacts are the work of human hands. Unlike Noah's ark or Bezalel's art (Exodus 35:31), they are not ascribed to inspiration.

Bible readers have long worried that Genesis seems to commit Eve's progeny to incest. Jubilees (4:9) and the Talmud (B. Sanhedrin 58B) bite the bullet: If Cain did not sleep with his mother, his spouse must have been his sister. But I think the silence about Cain's mate reveals something rather different: Scripture's concern is its teachings. Cain may model contrition or redemption, or crime and uncaring, or of all of these. But unlike Adam and Eve he is not a model of marital relations, so nothing is written of how he found a mate. Relevance to Mosaic norms is what casts light or shadow in the Torah's chiaroscuro. The drama lies in humanity's unfolding relationship with God. So biblical narratives remain episodic.

Adam knows Eve again, and Seth is born, his name suggesting a new beginning. Eve says God has given her Seth *in Abel's place, because Cain slew him* (4:25). Why should she state the obvious, the Midrash asks. Does Eve hint at something beyond her grief? The syntax allows her words, counterintuitively, to mean that Abel killed Cain: Cain died, ultimately because of his crime – "as if two trees stood near each other, and the wind uprooted one, whose fall brought down the other" (Genesis Rabbah 23.5).

Glossing *Adam knew his wife more* (4:25) Genesis Rabbah (23.5) takes *more* to mean more deeply: Previously he desired her only when he saw her; now, even out of sight – "a tip to seafarers to remember their families and come directly home." Ibn Ezra reasons: Since Cain's progeny perished in the Flood, his name was effaced. If progeny are the ultimate blessing, their loss is the ultimate punishment. Seth's son is Enosh, another name for humankind. Religion began in his time: *It was then that the name of the Lord was first invoked* (4:26). Ibn Ezra refutes the rabbinic innuendos about pagan profanations of God's name. Genesis welcomes piety, however oblique its intent. As the Psalmist writes: *From the rising of the sun to its setting praised is the Lord's name* (113:3).

Genealogy steams ahead with the ages of key figures at death and the begetting of their firstborn. The lifespans are immense – if modest beside the millennia of some monarchs in Babylonian king lists. Sasson sees an effort to round out history's epochs. But change is coming:

> *As humans began to increase on the face of the earth and daughters were born to them, sons of the gods saw how goodly human women were and espoused those they chose. Said the Lord, "My spirit will not lodge in man forever. For he too is flesh. Let his days be one hundred twenty years."* The nephilim *were on earth in those days, and later, when the gods' sons consorted with the daughters of men, who bore them offspring, the heroes and famed men of old.*

Sarna writes: "humans strove to rise to the level of divine beings, and God intervened. Humankind cannot be immortal." Spurning the man-god idea is one way of affirming this life.

Mortals still dream of congress with extraterrestrials. But Scripture sequesters the offspring in antiquity. The word *nephilim* sets an ironic tone. It recurs only in the alarmist majority report of Moses' spies (Numbers 13:33). Alert to the disparagement but with one eye cocked to his own day's ills and the monarchy that would martyr him, Tyndale renders *nephilim* tyrants. Genesis Rabbah (26.5) similarly spurns demigods: The *sons of the gods* were oppressive nobles exercising *droit de seigneur*. Still, Genesis does not tap the problematic matings to provide spouses for Cain or Seth. It simply reassures the credulous by calling the spawn of the putative unions heroes of yore, much as Greek myth banishes disused gods as vanquished titans. But the specters of antediluvian decadence mark the segue to visions of a humanity depraved.

A sentence suspended

> *The Lord saw how very evil man was on earth, how every plan formed in his heart was evil all the day. He regretted making man on earth, grieved at heart. The Lord said, "I will blot out man, whom I created, from the face of the earth – man and beast alike, and the creeping things and birds of the sky. I'm sorry I made them." But Noah found favor with the Lord.*

The Midrash notes the heavy anthropomorphism: "How bold of the prophets to liken the Creator to his creature" (Genesis Rabbah 27.1). Ibn Ezra invokes the rabbinic dictum: "Torah speaks in human language" (B. Yevamot 71A). For "If a human did as God did, destroying his own creation, he'd be called sorry he'd made it" (at Genesis 6:6).

The Lord saw again suggests court proceedings, Sarna remarks. But the juridical persona slips as God passes judgment even on the animals. Human evil provoked God's sorrow.[64] But disappointment wearies God as the work of creation never had. Man was to have been the crown jewel. It's as if a king had built his son a bridal chamber but slew him in a fit of rage and then turned on the lovely room, rending its draperies and partitions (Genesis Rabbah 28.6). For any flaws in the design God could blame only himself. But man's failing lay not in the nature God gave him but in not living up to it. Reducing the world to its elements meant havoc. But at least the elements would never flout God's law (Genesis Rabbah 27.4, 28.2). Where the creation narrative celebrates God's work, the Flood story attests to the destructive impact of decadence, eclipsing nature's beauty and delight.

Noah was Lamech's son, named for the respite Lamech expected from him. But Genesis (5:28) links his name with consolation (*n-ḥ-m*), not rest (*n-w-ḥ*) – strikingly, Sarna notes, since *niḥamti* is the word for God's regret over his unhappy experiment (6:6–7). Noah's merit is a consolation weighed against that sorrow. Some commentators have God favor Noah for his descendants' sake (Genesis Rabbah 29.5). But, textually, Noah was chosen for his own sake, being upright where others were not (7:1), as Nahmanides insists (at 6:8). For others too might have been spared for their descendants' sake.

> *This is Noah's history. Noah was a righteous man, perfect in his generation. With God did Noah walk. Noah begot three sons: Shem, Ham, and Japhet. For God, the earth was ruined now, filled with outrage. God saw the earth: ruined. All flesh on earth, on a path of ruin. God said to Noah: The time has come for me to put an end to all flesh. For the whole earth is filled with their outrage. I'll ruin them, and the earth.*

Righteous and *perfect*, Ibn Ezra writes, mean that Noah's acts were just and his heart pure. *In his generation*, sparks a famous debate. Rabbi Yehudah sees hints of a reservation: Yes, in those corrupt times, Noah was saintly; but he would hardly shine alongside Moses or Samuel. Rabbi Nehemiah reads more generously: If Noah remained pure even in those dark days, imagine his virtues had he lived in Moses' time (B. Sanhedrin 108; Genesis Rabbah 30.9).

The word ruin re-echoes in God's promise to spoil the spoilers. But the devastation they have wrought is moral, not physical: Violations of right and justice ruined the world. Still, God's sentence was not passed in the heat of passion. He bore with the world until outrages and violence had become pervasive. In ancient Mesopotamian flood stories, what brings the deluge was a clamor disturbing the gods' sleep. Here it is corruption – just as vicious mores are later said to pollute the land, rendering the evildoers unworthy and incapable of continued tenure (Numbers 35:31–34, Deuteronomy 21:22–23, cf. 24:1–4).

The outrage, *hamas*, that provoked the Flood, the Rabbis say, was lawlessness, larceny too petty for prosecution but too general to endure (Genesis Rabbah 31.5). Nahmanides (at 6:13) specifies robbery and oppression. Ibn Ezra adds rape and perversion. Genesis Rabbah (31.6) finds overtones of murder, idolatry, and incest. Rabbi Huna (Genesis Rabbah 26.5) elaborates: "The generation of the Flood were not eradicated from the world until they wrote nuptial songs celebrating pederasty and bestiality." Citing contexts where *hamas* means falsehood, deceit, and bloodshed, Sarna understands "flagrant subversion of the ordered processes of law. From the divine enactments for the regulation of society after the Flood, detailed in Chapter 9, it may be deduced that *hamas* here refers predominantly to the arrogant disregard for the sanctity and inviolability of human life." What was ruined was the world's ethos.

Custom may condone a practice or make it seem insignificant. But actions are accountable. Long before Sinai there were standards people should have known. The Torah is sparing with abstract language, but the underlying idea broached here is what later thinkers will call natural law, with its counterpart, natural rights.

Warning Noah of the coming flood, God instructs him to build an ark of gopher wood – cedar according to the Targums and the Rabbis (B. Sanhedrin 108A, Genesis Rabbah 31.8); cypress, say some moderns – and seal it with pitch. The Midrash envisions the number and layout of its chambers, its provisions and portholes for shoveling out wastes (Genesis Rabbah 31.10–11, 14). The ark is a *tevah*, like the ark for the infant Moses (Exodus 2:3–5). In Mesopotamian flood stories, Sarna remarks, a real ship is built, seaworthy and crewed. Noah's craft is boxlike and crewless, adrift before God's will. With the ark complete, God is ready to act:

> *I will bring the flood now – water on earth – effacing from under the heavens all flesh with the breath of life. Everything on earth shall perish. But I establish my covenant with you. Enter the ark, you, and your sons, your wife and your sons' wives with you. Bring with you into the ark two of each animal, a male and female of all flesh, to preserve alive with you. Two of each – of the birds of every kind, beasts of every kind, creatures that creep upon the earth of every kind – shall accompany you to survive. Take every sort of food and stow it with you, for you and them to eat. All this Noah did, as God commanded. Then the Lord said to Noah, Enter the ark, with all your house. For you have I found righteous before me in this generation.*

God makes Noah his partner, not in the destruction but in preserving humanity and the animals. Notice the words *of every kind* (*le-minehu*), confirming that *after its kind* in the creation narrative indicates comprehensiveness and variety. Discreteness and fixity are not at issue.

God's pact with Noah, the first biblical covenant, like any contract, involves reciprocity. God preserves Noah's household, but Noah must save the animals – just as Adam tended the garden. The earth is laid waste, but life must be preserved (Ibn Ezra at 6:19). The creatures find Noah; he need not hunt them down (Genesis Rabbah 32.8; Ibn Ezra at 6:20): Just as seeds propagate plants, animals fend for themselves. Noah's obedience typifies his virtue. Similar language will describe adherence to God's law (Deuteronomy 31:5).

God's instructions are now enlarged: Noah will need seven pairs of clean animals and birds – allowing for later sacrifices (8:20). Genesis and its early audience are innocent of what genetics finds about the critical size of breeding populations. But the moral case is clear: Noah must preserve each species (7:3) lest nature be diminished (Genesis Rabbah 32.4). The ark bespeaks life's value and man's responsibility. Noah need not love the animals. But he must save them, whether or not they seem useful or attractive.

God brings 40 days and nights of rain, *to wipe from the face of the earth every being I created* (7:4). All the fountains of the abyss and floodgates of heaven burst open. Noah's family, with their menagerie, rest safe in the ark, which God himself has sealed behind them. Borne up by the flood, the ark floats free. Even mountain tops are submerged fifteen cubits deep. No breath of life remains on earth. But God remembers Noah and the animals. After 150 days, he sweeps the earth with wind. The waters subside. Mountain tops are seen. Noah sends out a raven, then a dove, which returns, as doves do, bearing an olive leaf on its second visit: Branches appear above the surface. The raven, an accomplished forager, might have fed on carrion and not needed to return; but when the dove stays away, land has clearly emerged from its watery confinement, as at the first creation. Opening a hatch, Noah sees dry land. The earth dries, and God invites the survivors into the open air, to release their charges to teem again on earth.

Noah builds an altar and sacrifices specimens of each clean kind, a sweet savor (*re'ah niho'ah*) to the Lord, the phrase later applied to fitting offerings (Leviticus 1:9, 26:31, etc.) – and another play on Noah's name (Genesis Rabbah 33.3). The absence of a libation, Sarna adds, may signify that God needs no sacrifices. The Mesopotamian gods have a disquieting appetite for beer. In Gilgamesh they crowd the altar "like flies."

> *Smelling the sweet savor, the Lord said to himself: No more will I curse the ground on man's account. For the bent of man's heart is evil from his youth. No more will I smite every living thing as I have done.*

A seeming non sequitur. Is this the vengeful God so often made a foil of Christian love? Why does a bad bent win promises of survival? A parallel is God's command, *Do not hate the Egyptian. For you were a slave in his land* (Deuteronomy 23:8). The move is moral. Pace Nietzsche, *Thou shalt* projects no vengeance morality but empathy for the stranger, the oppressed, even appreciation for the Egyptian (Exodus 23:9, Deuteronomy 10:19). Scripture does not say, like Hannah Arendt, "We too might have been oppressors." Clichés about the banality of evil might readily rationalize new crimes. But the Torah recalls a happier side of the Egyptian sojourn. Even in bondage, Israelites were in some ways the Egyptians' guests (cf. Numbers 11:5). That must be recalled on meeting their descendants. Here the moral turnabout takes another route: As Lyman Abbott wrote, "The Hebrew myth of the deluge embodied the truth that destruction of sinners can never cure the world of sin."[65] God knows human weaknesses. The heavens don't open up and strike down the wicked. God is forbearing, as Jonah knows (4:2). Nature is stable. That too is part of Noah's covenant:

> *So long as earth endure, seedtime and harvest, heat and cold, summer and winter, day and night, shall not cease.*

The rainbow, emblem of God's covenant with life and nature (9:12–17), is a sign of hope poised against any omen drawn from storms and floods. Man may now eat meat. But murder becomes a capital crime, and even animals' blood must be respected. Limbs must not be savagely devoured from the living creature.[66] The rhythm of the seasons and the interplay of nature with culture will continue. Human weaknesses, recognized in the narrative as if newly discovered, mark the autonomy we enjoy or abuse. Nature's constancy is freedom's matrix, not its straitjacket, just as the constancy of the law is no constraint but the enabling condition by which freedom flourishes.

What, then, do we learn from the biblical creation story? Beyond the rumbling undertones of its ancient polemic against paganism, we hear moral messages: Woman and man are partners, not of alien flesh. Human life is irreplaceable. We are indeed our brothers' keepers, and stewards of nature, even beyond God's garden. There are spiritual messages too: Life and light are good, gifts in fact, pointing to a caring Source. Time itself can be sanctified, a day set apart from labor, not at any astral signal but in testimony to our links with the Transcendent. At the interface of the spiritual and moral: God, well aware of human weakness, forbears to disrupt nature's course. But moral choice, a point of human pride, comes at a price, the risk of its suborning by our seeming interests, appetites and passions, usages and prejudices. Evolution is the story of our origins and the natural causes that brought us to the plateau on which we stand. Genesis addresses what it means to stand there, empowered to think and choose, act and care, *little less than divine*, the psalmist says (8:5), but with more than a world to win or lose.

All this drops out of sight in the flurry of defensive literalism: God's love of life in its rich diversity is masked by dogmas of species fixity, uninteresting to Genesis and ill fitted to its tracing of all flesh to the dust of the earth. Even the rainbow is eclipsed by searchlights scanning the skies for the source of Noah's floodwaters. Biblical naturalism and human dignity, never breached in Genesis, are crusted over with alien and incongruous dogmas. The would be defenders of inerrancy and inspiration seem to assume (along with their foes) that the sacred text will lose its dignity and profundity once its poetic workings are understood. The refusal of would be literalists to see poetry in scripture, although it is poetry that gives scripture its beauty and truth, is not a way of taking revelation seriously but a side-gutter diminishing scripture's seriousness and making its text a caricature of all that is imagined primitive and crude.

Centrally for us, literalism loses sight of the biblical idea that God works through nature. Anti-Darwinists remove God from nature yet expect him to manipulate it. They underrate the local agency and purpose of all creatures, whose ultimate source we biblical monotheists infer must be divine, of infinite reality and goodness, not reducible to the phenomena its act and

presence were invoked to explain. For the core message of biblical monotheism is this: that the wind or spirit that is of God still hovers over the
waters, not denaturing them but imparting the nature by which they flow
and ripple in the wind – touching, but not touching, as Rashi has it – ever
present, in and beside all things, imparting the agency and freedom that
allow all things, actively, to be what they are. Genesis sees God's governance
enacted, his creativity expressed, in the liveliness of all that he creates; his
purpose, realized in the life and consciousness of his creatures, each seeking,
not always with insight or success, a good that is its own.

3

The case for evolution

When Darwin published the *Origin* in 1859, his thesis was straightforward: Plants and animals vary in their abilities to survive. The fittest pass on key traits to more offspring than the rest. So even slight advantages spread. As variations accrue, useful traits are elaborated and accentuated, and new species arise: "If a variety were to flourish so as to exceed in numbers the parent species, it would then rank as the species, and the species as the variety; or it might come to supplant and exterminate the parent species; or both might co-exist, and both rank as independent species."[1]

Species, then, are not immutable, inviolate, or discrete. They differ not in some unseen essence but because their members share traits through inheritance. Variations long dismissed as too rare to matter are not negligible – not if they confer advantage, or disadvantage, measured in differential fertility. "Species," as Diderot had urged, "are only tendencies."[2] The continuum of natural variation leaves many gray areas. Even the most exacting taxonomists face tough judgment calls. As Buffon had written, responding to Linnaeus' pathbreaking schematization: "Nature proceeds by unknown gradations and so does not lend herself wholly to these divisions but moves from one species to the next and often from one genus to the next by imperceptible shadings."[3]

The natural continuum was an old idea, nursed by neoplatonists like the tenth-century Sincere Brethren of Basra.[4] The inspired metaphysics of the full universe supported the idea. But species mutability temporalized the Great Chain of Being, as Arthur Lovejoy put it. Natural selection afforded a powerful explanation of the birth of species.

Darwin's premises

The entire text of the *Origin*, Darwin wrote, forms "one long argument."[5] That argument rests on four premises: 1) All organisms face challenges. They need habitat and nourishment. They must cope with heat and cold, predators and parasites. They compete, even with members of their own kind, for place, sustenance, reproductive opportunities. 2) Organisms inherit at least some of their capabilities and disabilities. 3) Natural variations can make a difference in survival and reproduction. 4) Life has lasted long enough on earth for less effective species to die out and new ones, as Darwin put it, to supplant them.

Darwin's assumptions found support in the work of Charles Lyell, Thomas Malthus, and Jean Baptiste Lamarck. The experience of breeders, hobbyists, and sportsmen showed the extent of variation within species. So did Darwin's own observations and the communications he received from colonial officials, travelers, and naturalists, including Alfred Russel Wallace, whose findings closely paralleled his own.[6] Lamarck had championed the idea of species change, a notion long fascinating to Enlightenment thinkers including Darwin's grandfather Erasmus. Lyell's geological uniformitarianism reassured Darwin that the earth was old enough for natural selection to shape living species. But it was Malthus' modeling of the critical checks on population increase that showed Darwin how disease, climate, competition, violence, and sheer limits of space render critical even the slightest natural advantage.

Variants

Darwin opens the *Origin* with thoughts about variation. It is absurd, he argues, to trace each race of domestic cattle to a separate wild prototype. That would assume a vast, unevidenced, variety of ancestral species.[7] Domestic dogs, Darwin allows, might have ancestors in more than one species. But the birds bred by English pigeon fanciers reveal natural variation as the leading edge of evolution, not the trailing hem of mere crossbreeding.[8] Joining two London pigeon clubs, Darwin saw an astounding range of breeds – carriers, tumblers, barbs, pouters, runts, jacobins, fantails. Some differed so strikingly in form, size, and plumage that naturalists might readily have called them separate species had they turned up in the wild. But all seemed to stem from a single type, *Columba livia*, the rock pigeon, found in nature but widely domesticated. The show birds and racing pigeons could not be bred by crossing geographically diverse races of rock pigeon; nothing like them was found in the wild – or would survive there in many cases. Yet, despite striking differences at the extremes, domestic types formed "an almost perfect series." The variants led, like points of a star, back to the rock pigeon. Their crossbred offspring were fertile and often bore markings typical of *Columba livia* but absent in their parents.[9]

The fuller's teasel, a thistle long used in brushing fabrics, differed from the wild type. Evidently it was a product of selective breeding. So were draft horses, racehorses, and the bloodhounds and greyhounds familiar in England. The fighting cock, turnspit dog, and many a garden plant and orchard tree had plainly been bred for desired traits.[10] Stock breeding, Darwin argued, as old as civilization, had doubtless altered many breeds.

Victorian readers knew that selective breeding can establish distinctive breeds of dogs or horses. Keepers pursued useful or interesting traits – warmer, softer wool in sheep, richer milk in cattle. There were dogs that could take down a stag, hold off a bear, scurry down a rat warren, scent game, or retrieve ducks. Breeders might prize a curiosity or a specialized work animal. But nature too breeds selectively, Darwin argued, singling out types more capable of surviving and reproducing. So varieties shade into new species, much as speech patterns shift gradually from dialect to dialect.[11]

Naturalists often took for granted individual differences in size, coloration, or even fecundity that might matter to breeders but couldn't count as species differences. Still, Darwin argued, even tiny causes can have large effects. Unseen changes, well within the range of natural variation in a species, can confer vital advantages, or disadvantages:

> These individual differences are of the highest importance for us, for they are often inherited, as must be familiar to everyone; and they thus afford materials for natural selection to act on and accumulate in the same manner as man accumulates in any given direction individual differences in his domesticated productions.[12]

Taxonomists often minimized seemingly inessential differences. They even disparaged the organs in which such differences appeared. So their reasoning spiraled into circularity: Features that seemed to blur species boundaries were dismissed as insignificant. But the firmness or crispness of species divisions was just the point at issue. Seemingly non-essential traits, Darwin argued, might prove vital. Peach fuzz may seem unimportant, but "smooth-skinned fruits suffer far more from a beetle, a Curculio, than those with down."[13] Swatting flies may seem a trivial use for a giraffe's tail, but only by ignoring the exhaustion harassment can bring[14] – not to mention insect-borne diseases. Recent studies of the tiny fossils preserved in Cretaceous amber suggest that insects and other pests furthered the decline of dinosaur populations well before the K-T event gave the great beasts the coup de grâce sixty-five million years ago.[15] But even useless traits, Darwin argued, are telling markers of common ancestry, preserved where the variations were tolerable.[16] Learned specialists on oaks grew more hesitant about species boundaries as their knowledge grew. The stricter the criteria, the more dubious hard and fast lines became.[17] The lesson: not that taxonomy is arbitrary but that species are related – distinct, but not discrete.

Malthus

Variants would matter little if nature were infinitely commodious. But earth is not Eden. Hence Darwin's redefinition of essential traits not as placards marking archetypes but as tools in life's struggle. Every organism must contend with climate and scarcity, competitors and predators. Nothing, Darwin remarks, is easier to admit than the reality of the struggle, or harder to bear constantly in mind: Only the constancy of struggle makes sense of "the whole economy of nature, with every fact of distribution, rarity, abundance, extinction and variation."[18]

> We behold the face of nature bright with gladness, we often see super-abundance of food; we do not see or we forget, that the birds which are idly singing round us mostly live on insects or seeds, and are thus constantly destroying life ... we do not always bear in mind, that, though food may be now superabundant, it is not so at all seasons of each recurring year.[19]

Darwinian struggle is not typically a frontal battle. There is conflict and competition, notably over mates. Darwin speaks of "the law of battle" and of "teeth and claws," echoing Tennyson's phrase, "nature red in tooth and claw."[20] There is predation. But more typical is the struggle of a plant at the desert's edge, or the germination of just one seed from a thousand that a plant produces.[21] Fecundity itself is an evolutionary response.

Populations, Malthus had argued, would increase geometrically if unchecked. Darwin pressed the point: "There is no exception to the rule that every organic being naturally increases at so high a rate, that, if not destroyed, the earth would soon be covered by the progeny of a single pair."[22] Limitations of resources block population growth decisively. But the same assaults that increase fecundity give impetus and direction to evolution. Darwin tells in his autobiography of discovering Malthus over 20 years before publishing the *Origin*:

> In October 1838, that is, fifteen months after I had begun my systematic inquiry, I happened to read for amusement Malthus on *Population*, and being well prepared to appreciate the struggle for existence, which everywhere goes on, from long-continued observation of the habits of animals and plants, it at once struck me that under these circumstances favorable variations would tend to be preserved and unfavorable ones to be destroyed. The result of this would be the formation of new species. Here, then, I had at last got a theory by which to work.[23]

Malthus built a theodicy of famine, plague and war from his recognition that death kept human populations from outstripping their resources.[24] "Misery and vice" were inevitable consequences of overpopulation; poverty was nature's retribution for profligate reproduction. Malthus urged delaying marriage until a family was practical. Neomalthusians urged population control, typically by means that Malthus condemned.

Darwin agreed about the prudence of delaying marriage. But he went much further: Population pressure, he reasoned, forges the struggle for survival into a sharp, incessant chisel, shaping the course of evolution. Seeds and seedlings are destroyed by slugs and insects; eggs, birds, and mammals are devoured by predators. Drought and cold, dearth and disease decimate living populations; milder conditions often favor predators and parasites. Grasses, shrubs, and trees compete for sunlight and rooting; flowering plants, for pollinators. Cattle cropping a hillside prevent a forest from arising.[25]

Natural selection, Darwin argues, yields the organs used in mating and in breaking free from the egg or chrysalis. It sets the patterns of growth and maturation, shapes the instincts of animals and the flowers of plants, providing nectar that rewards insect vectors, and forming the proboscis that reaches that reward.[26] Steady as Newton's laws of gravity or motion, nature's rule is survival of the fittest,[27] the phrase Darwin adopted from Herbert Spencer in the fifth (1869) edition of the *Origin*. Variation may be random, but selection ruthlessly prunes nature's tree. And variety is not infinite; for any type has limited potentials, and not every variant survives. Large populations thrive and constantly produce new variants, but without some distinctive advantage, rare types stay rare or disappear.[28]

Lyell

Given natural variation and the checks on increase, evolution needs time. That makes Lyell's geology critical to Darwin's case. Lyell founded modern geology by championing uniformitarianism. Present formations, he argued, reveal the earth's history. The underlying processes don't change dramatically. Lyell's three-volume *Principles of Geology* (1830–33), constantly revised and throwing off ever more imposing "handbooks," went through twelve editions in his lifetime. Lyell probed the causes of earthquakes and volcanic eruptions, explained how glaciers shifted ancient boulders. He named the pliocene, miocene, and eocene epochs, based on the marine invertebrate fossils preserved in French and Italian strata.

Lyell's first volume, a gift from Captain FitzRoy, was Darwin's constant companion on the voyage of the *Beagle*, heavily used to interpret what he saw. Volume 2, which reached him in South America, rejected Lamarck's transmutationism, well before Darwin had settled his own evolutionary thinking. Indeed, Lyell thought the progression of fossils was an illusion, prompted by wishful thinking. Lyell was at bottom an eternalist: The rise and fall of landmasses was an ever-ongoing equilibrium, almost as if the earth were breathing. Still, Lyell's geology was steadfastly naturalistic. It had no truck with Noah's flood, or with any unseen agency pressing, between catastrophes, for the advance of life. Lyell's steady state geology painted the backdrop for Darwin's theory and inspired his vision of the role and method of the independent naturalist. Uniformitarianism made the earth itself evolution's clock. Reading Lyell as he contemplated coral reefs, the Andes, and the pampas, Darwin amplified Lyell's thinking in ways that made Lyell an admirer and supporter even before the two men met. They would become fast friends. Lyell had his qualms about evolution. Only in his tenth edition did he publicly endorse natural selection. But he was early convinced of the power of Darwin's theory. Despite his reservations, it was he who organized the joint presentation of Darwin's and Wallace's work in 1858, saving Darwin's claims to ownership and originality. He was among the first to hail the *Origin* – even if he did irk Darwin by treating the theory as a variant of Lamarck's. And it was Lyell who first spoke to John Murray about publishing the *Origin*.[29]

As Darwin's thoughts matured, he grew less dependent on Lyell, outgrowing his early expectation that evolution depends on sports of nature, themselves stimulated by geological changes like the rise and fall, joining and parting, of land masses. The variations that mattered most were not the occasional extra limb or digit but the constant, scarcely perceptible, variance of individuals in many, many traits. Here, although the source of variance remained unknown, was the raw material of evolution. Darwin's shift from gross to fine anatomy parallels the shift in ancient evolutionary ideas from Empedocles' imagined (clearly unviable) "man-faced ox-progeny" to the finer grained, Epicurean model.[30] Schooled by eight years studying the barnacles, Darwin no longer needed movements of the earth's crust to provoke variation. It was a natural consequence of reproduction. Evolution, moreover, did not require geographical isolation, as Darwin had initially supposed.[31] But Lyell's gradualism remained rock solid in Darwin's thought, the hallmark of his naturalism and key to the time scale that evolution required.

Darwin knew that erosion and sedimentation, rain, wind and tide, frost, and organic growth alter the face of the earth. He knew that carbonic acid in rainwater etches away rock.[32] In the first edition of the *Origin*, he calculated that it would take over 300 million years to erode the Weald chalk deposit near his home in southern England – not to mention the time needed for its deposition. At exposed fault lines he saw suppressed and upthrust strata and sedimentary arrays thousands of feet deep. He quoted one estimate that a river would take six million years to cut a thousand foot gorge.[33] Borrowing an illustration, he asks readers to picture the time scale: Graphing ten centuries to the inch, it would take over 83 feet of paper to chart a million years. Until we think, or calculate in millions, Darwin wrote, we have no idea of evolutionary time.

Lamarck

In deriving new species from old, Lamarck drew on his own exhaustive studies of French flora and invertebrates. He coined the term *invertebrata*[34] and marked out the classes still recognized today: annelids, crustaceans, arachnids, infusoria – and the tunicates, which he classed as invertebrates. His fossil findings made him the founder of invertebrate paleontology and sparked his evolutionary thinking:

Since all living bodies are productions of nature, she must herself have organized the simplest of them and endowed them directly with life and the faculties distinctive to living bodies; and from these first generations, formed at the start of the plant and animal series, nature has gone on to confer existence on all other living bodies in turn.[35]

Lamarck began from traditional definitions: "Any collection of like individuals produced by others similar to them is called a species." But he went on to brand species fixity a myth:

to this definition is added the claim that the individuals constituting a species never vary in their specific characters, and consequently that species have an absolute constancy in nature. It is just this claim that I propose to attack, since clear proofs drawn from observation show that it is ill-founded.[36]

Lamarck died blind and impoverished, his arguments widely ignored. But his theory was not unknown, and his claim that acquired traits could be inherited, disputed even in his day by Georges Cuvier, remained attractive to many.

Ambiguities often mask damaging confusions. Risky in Lamarck's case was the notion of habit: Are habits patterns of behavior, or growth, like the difference between shrubs and trees? Are adaptations rightly described in the language of challenge and response? Today evolutionists sharply distinguish individual responses from heritable changes. But we have the benefit of hindsight and a clear grasp of genetics. For Lamarck species change was the issue. He could only speculate as to how it comes about. The fossil array showed him that species "over time have changed their characters and shape."[37] But was this something species had undergone, or something they had *done*?

great alterations in the environment of animals lead to great alterations in their needs, and these alterations in their needs necessarily lead to others in their activities. If the new needs become permanent, the animals adopt new habits which last as long as the needs that evoked them.[38]

'Habit' here might refer to behavior. Or it might signify a pattern of fur, or a new organ:

Every new need, necessitating new activities for its satisfaction, requires the animal either to make more frequent use of some of its parts, which it had previously used less, and thus greatly to enlarge them; or else to make use of entirely new parts, which the needs have imperceptibly engendered, by efforts of its inner feeling.

So need, effort, even feeling can engender organs. Webbed feet in ducks and geese, the stork's long legs, the swan's neck and anteater's tongue, all result from effort[39] – and are inherited:

> All the acquisitions or losses wrought by nature on individuals, through the influence of the environment ... are preserved by reproduction ... provided the acquired modifications are common to both sexes, or at least to the individuals that produce the young.[40]

When Darwin relaxes his usual discipline of hewing close to the evidence, he often tracks Lamarck. Fifteen years before the *Origin*, he wrote:

> We have every reason to believe that every part and organ in an individual becomes fully developed only with exercise of its functions; that it becomes developed in a somewhat lesser degree with less exercise; and if forcibly precluded from all action, such part will often become atrophied. Every peculiarity, let it be remembered, tends, especially where both parents have it, to be inherited. The less power of flight in the common duck compared with the wild, must be partly attributed to disuse during successive generations. ... Some naturalists have attributed (and possibly with truth) the falling ears so characteristic of most domestic dogs, some rabbits, oxen, cats, goats, horses, etc., as the effects of the lesser use of the muscles of these flexible parts during successive generations of inactive life. ... When the eye is blinded in early life the optic nerve sometimes becomes atrophied; may we not believe that where this organ, as is the case with the subterranean mole-like Tuco-tuco (*Ctenomys*), is frequently impaired and lost, that in the course of generations the whole organ might become abortive, as it normally is in some burrowing quadrupeds having nearly similar habits with the Tuco-tuco?[41]

Fortified with further evidence, Darwin writes with greater confidence in the *Origin*:

> Habit also has a decided influence, as in the period of flowering with plants when transported from one climate to another. In animals it has a more marked effect; for instance, I find in the domestic duck that the bones of the wing weigh less and the bones of the leg more, in proportion to the whole skeleton, than do the same bones in the wild-duck; and I presume that this change may be safely attributed to the domestic duck flying much less, and walking more, than its wild parent. The great and inherited development of the udders in cows and goats in countries where they are habitually milked, in comparison with the state of these organs in other countries, is another instance of the effect of use. Not a single domestic animal can be named which has not in some country

drooping ears; and the view suggested by some authors, that the drooping is due to the disuse of the muscles of the ear, from the animals not
being much alarmed by danger, seems probable.[42]

Darwin warms to the subject further on:

> I think there can be little doubt that use in our domestic animals
> strengthens and enlarges certain parts, and disuse diminishes them; and
> that such modifications are inherited. Under free nature, we can have no
> standard of comparison, by which to judge of the effects of long con-
> tinued use or disuse, for we know not the parent forms; but many ani-
> mals have structures which can be explained by the effects of disuse. As
> Professor Owen has remarked, there is no greater anomaly in nature
> than a bird that cannot fly; yet there are several in this state. The logger-
> headed duck of South America can only flap along the surface of the
> water, and has its wings in nearly the same condition as the domestic
> Aylesbury duck. As the larger ground-feeding birds seldom take flight
> except to escape danger, I believe that the nearly wingless condition of
> several birds, which now inhabit or have lately inhabited several oceanic
> islands, tenanted by no beast of prey, has been caused by disuse. The
> ostrich indeed inhabits continents and is exposed to danger from which
> it cannot escape by flight, but by kicking it can defend itself from ene-
> mies, as well as any of the smaller quadrupeds. We may imagine that the
> early progenitor of the ostrich had habits like those of a bustard, and
> that as Natural Selection increased in successive generations the size and
> weight of its body, its legs were used more, and its wings less, until they
> became incapable of flight.
>
> Kirby has remarked (and I have observed the same fact) that the
> anterior tarsi, or feet, of many male dung-feeding beetles are very often
> broken off. ... In the *Onites apelles* the tarsi are so habitually lost, that
> the insect has been described as not having them. In some other genera
> they are present, but in a rudimentary condition. In the Ateuchus or
> sacred beetle of the Egyptians, they are totally deficient. There is not
> sufficient evidence to induce us to believe that mutilations are ever
> inherited; and I should prefer explaining the entire absence of the ante-
> rior tarsi in Ateuchus, and their rudimentary condition in some other
> genera, by the long continued effects of disuse in their progenitors; for as
> the tarsi are almost always lost in many dung-feeding beetles, they must
> be lost early in life, and therefore cannot be much used by these
> insects.[43]

Today biologists say that milk cows have larger udders than their wild cousins because they were bred, through the ages, for milk production; break-
away limbs would be products of genetic changes that proved useful. Floppy

ears do reflect a lack of use, but not because ears went limp from disuse. Hormonal shifts, we now think, were involved; but inheritance is governed by the genes. So if floppy ears are inborn it's because some once critical genes are otiose after the shift to domesticity. But Darwin was innocent of genetics. "The laws governing inheritance," he wrote, "are for the most part unknown."[44]

Darwin's argument

Lyell's earth affords time for evolutionary change. Malthus' somber ruminations demonstrate the need. Breeders' experience shows how natural selection might have worked. But none of this shows that evolution actually occurred. Geology shows that it could; Malthus, perhaps, that it should. But breeders' experience offers only an analogy. Paley had as much when he compared the world to a watch. In the later chapters of the *Origin*, Darwin argues his brief. He does appeal to fossils, but more largely to the affinities among species – in morphology, embryology, vestigial organs, and patterns of distribution.

Morphology and taxonomy

Anatomy makes Darwin's clearest case.

> What can be more curious than that the hand of a man, formed for grasping, that of a mole for digging, the leg of the horse, the paddle of the porpoise, and the wing of the bat, should all be constructed on the same pattern, should contain the same bones, in the same relative positions? How curious it is, to give a subordinate though striking instance, that the hind-feet of the kangaroo, which are so well fitted for bounding over the open plains, those of the climbing, leaf eating koala, equally well fitted for grasping the branches of trees, those of the ground-dwelling, insect or root-eating bandicoots, and those of some other Australian marsupials, should all be constructed on the same extraordinary type, namely with the bones of the second and third digits extremely slender and enveloped within the same skin, so that they appear like a single toe furnished with two claws. ... We see the same great law in the construction of the mouths of insects: What can be more different than the immensely long spiral proboscis of the sphinx-moth, the curious folded one of a bee or bug, and the great jaws of a beetle? – yet all these organs, serving for such different purposes, are formed by infinitely numerous modifications of an upper lip, mandibles, and two pairs of maxillae. The same laws govern the construction of the mouths and limbs of crustaceans. So it is with the flowers of plants.[45]

Why should there be five digits in a bat's wing or a whale's fin, if not through common descent? Why should whales suckle their young, unless they descend from other mammals? Congruence of body plans and strategies silhouettes the Linnaean scheme as a family tree: "if our collections were nearly perfect," Darwin writes, representing life's full diversity, "the only possible arrangement would be genealogical."[46]

Bodily form has grounded classification since living species first were named. So Linnaeus anchored his taxonomy firmly in anatomy. But that leaves much to judgment: Which similarities matter, which are incidental? Lamarck distinguished essential differences, homologies, from functional analogies. Richard Owen, the great anatomist who identified key specimens and fossils from the *Beagle* expedition, a founder of the British Museum and coiner of the term dinosaur, defined homology developmentally: Its criteria lay in embryology, regardless of the functions organs acquire or lose. Homology, Darwin wrote, is the "very soul" of natural history. Without it we might as well have classed the greyhound with the racehorse, or called the whale a fish. But homologies, Darwin argued, are not just anatomic affinities or developmental parallels. They are clear roadsigns revealing a common heritage.[47]

The array of species, Darwin argued, is "not arbitrary like the groupings of the stars in the constellations."[48] Varieties branch out within a species, and species within a genus, just as the sun has its planets, the planets have their moons.[49]

> Why, on the theory of Creation, should there be so much variety and so little real novelty? Why should all the parts and organs of many independent beings, each supposed to have been separately created for its proper place in nature, be so commonly linked together by graduated steps?[50]

Evolution gives classification its basis in nature. Types cluster, not by chance but by ancestry. What Linnaeus saw, then, *was* a family tree. Sketching the "tree of life," Darwin finds it far fetched to ascribe the pattern to chance, uninformative to lay it simply to God's plan.[51] Evolution explains it perspicuously: The clustering of kinds reflects inheritance and selection. Species may have ragged edges or fuzzy boundaries. But taxonomy is not "an inextricable chaos." Shared descent makes species "tolerably well-defined objects."[52] Birds have feathers, fish have scales, mammals have fur or hair, because their ancestors did: "Nothing can be more hopeless than to attempt to explain this similarity of pattern in members of the same class, by utility or by the doctrine of final causes."[53] Organs are useful, but each in its own way. Utility underdetermines its means, and utility alone causes nothing. Utility is nature's test. But until we can trace the origins of a living structure or process we cannot say why it serves these ends in just this way. History sharpens to a keen point the broad idea of purpose. Genesis took history seriously, but Aristotle had handled adaptation with the gloved hands of *as-if*: Some organs seem adjusted to new functions – but to Aristotle, that language is an expository trope not a historic fact. "All the parts," he wrote, "are first marked out in outline and later get their color and softness or hardness, just as if nature were a painter making a work of art."[54] Aristotelian species don't change. Darwin saw that they do. Natural selection explains how.

In formalism pattern displaces history, focusing on nature's aesthetics. But the lovely volute and cone shells of the Eocene, Darwin writes, were not created so that "man might ages afterwards admire them in his cabinet."[55] It's "wanting in due reverence," to have God pursue variety solely for his own pleasure, creating species whimsically, for their beauty or variety, "almost like toys in a shop."[56] Yet even Kant, a proud exponent of the Enlightenment, reduces biological purposes to aesthetic terms and blankets design in the language of as-if, unable to reconcile mechanism with purpose. "Our reflective judgments," he wrote, seem constrained to regard all life structures and processes "as if produced by an ideal plan" – like works of art.[57] Goethe, Coleridge, Schelling, and dozens of academic naturalists, followed Kant here. Darwin too found beauty in natural forms. But, like Aristotle, he found it, above all, in comprehending their causes. Purpose remains. But natural selection is now the locomotive.

Sheer formal values like symmetry or completeness, Darwin insists, would never do in explaining planetary orbits. Why accept that in biology? Descent with modification does explain the phenomena. "Monstrous plants" plainly show that sepals, petals, stamens and pistils are modified leaves, "arranged in a spire."[58] The array of a mammal's skull parts mark their origin as vertebrae. "Why should one crustacean, which has an extremely complex mouth, formed of many parts, consequently always have fewer legs; or conversely, those with many legs have simpler mouths?"[59] The missing legs have become mouth parts. Darwin challenges his critics to find a better explanation. Their repertoire is typically too general to reach such specifics.

Development and rudiments

Embryology came early in Darwin's thinking, as his notebooks of the 1830s and 1840s reveal. He was fascinated by the idea that "the birth of the species & individuals in their present forms are closely related."[60] His grandfather had expected the spurs to adaptation to differ in the womb and the world. The grandson held onto the idea that embryos differ from adult forms because they face different environments. "Embryology," he wrote, "is my pet bit in my book."[61] Accordingly, Darwin acknowledged as a predecessor Karl von Baer,[62] the Estonian embryologist who taught at Königsberg and later St Petersburg and discovered the notochord and the mammalian ovum: von Baer denied species change. But he had seen the affinities of embryos to a more general type, and embryology held the key to evolution.

In its earliest biological uses, 'evolution' meant the embryological unfolding of mature forms, a notion critical to the preformationism of Jan Swammerdam.

Epigenesis, championed by William Harvey, had seemed not mechanistic enough, as if awaiting some occult power to draw an organism from formless liquid. Albrecht von Haller posited unseen structures in an egg and abandoned epigenesis for preformation. His friend Charles Bonnet agreed. He had discovered parthenogenesis in aphids, and his microscope revealed the imago of the adult in the grub. Bonnet pictured seedlike germs from the first creation spawning every life form. Ever more perfect species spring from the germs that survive nature's recurrent catastrophes. So life could advance without divine interference or essential (hence unnatural) change. But Caspar Wolff scored Haller's mechanism. Chicks, he insisted, are formed in homogeneous matter by an "essential force." Bonnet's germs were prefabricated miracles. Nothing was gained by pushing back creation to the start of time. Living nature changes ceaselessly "by its own power."[63]

In 1824 Etienne Serres wrote that each embryo must "traverse a multitude of fugitive forms," starting from creatures of "inferior classes." Cuvier's student Friedrich Tiedemann went further: "Just as each individual begins with the simplest formation and during its metamorphosis becomes more evolved," so life itself "seems to have begun its evolution with the simplest animal forms, the animals of the lowest orders."[64]

Among biologists before Darwin, the chief rival to evolution was the idea of archetypes, broad structural plans that settle each species into its own life pattern. Cuvier pioneered the scheme, dividing all animals into four classes, based on their body plans: radiata (starfish, jellyfish), mollusca (oysters, squids), articulata (insects, crabs), and vertebrata (fish, mammals). The types were static. But the lacing of each type into its métier anticipates the idea of an econiche, and the stable body plans survive in Darwin's recognition of inherited structural features. Although hardly evolutionary, Cuvier's paradigm did unify each of his four classes. Lamarck's ally and Serres' teacher Etienne Geoffrey Saint-Hilaire, finding affinities between molluscs and radiata and between articulata and vertebrata, took the unification further. By 1830 he saw a broad unity of type in all animals. Cuvier was incensed, but his own unities had opened the door. Saint-Hilaire went on to draw transformist inferences, vaulting the boundaries of Cuvier's types. Von Baer, loyal to Cuvier, kept archetypes discrete. Yet, within each type, he saw the earliest developmental stages as closest to the simplest taxonomic forms.

Richard Owen judged recapitulation nonsense. Transmutation was "still more objectionable."[65] The language is telling: Transmutation was the alchemists' term for changing the essential natures of things. The alchemist's magnum opus was not the counterfeiter's trick of turning base metal to gold but the ancient dream of bringing inert matter to life. Transmutation meant magic, superstition, spontaneous generation. Still, von Baer had supported recapitulation, and Owen had defined homology developmentally. Even Agassiz had seen that embryos often resemble fossil types. Biologists like Tiedemann saw recapitulation as proof that a single law governs the emergence of species and individuals. Robert Grant, who taught Darwin his marine invertebrates at Edinburgh, was thinking on similar lines. A materialist and transformist friend of Saint-Hilaire's, he was a firm believer in recapitulation. Darwin, in his *Autobiography*, recalls Grant's rhapsodizing about Lamarck's transformism. At the time, he confesses, such thoughts made little impression. But in 1837 he read an article by Serres calling molluscs "the permanent embryos of the vertebrates and of man." In August, 1838, he speculated in his notebooks that embryology somehow consolidates past gains, giving species a platform for further development. A month later he read Malthus and found in natural selection the mechanism that could shape that development:

> One may say there is a force like a hundred thousand wedges trying to force every kind of adapted structure into the gaps in the oeconomy of nature, or rather forming gaps by thrusting out weaker ones. The final cause of all this wedgings [sic], must be to sort out proper structure & adapt it to change.[66]

But utility was no wedge. Natural selection drove evolution. Adaptation was the outcome. Darwin had married mechanism to purpose.

Rather than tilt headlong at the archetype idea, he absorbed it into his growing conceptual toolbox. Writing on the back flyleaf of Owen's 1849 book *On the Nature of Limbs*, Darwin transformed von Baer and Owen's thinking: The generalized forms visible in embryos must represent real ancestral types, modified in the descendants by real forces.[67] Descent was "the hidden bond of connection which naturalists have been seeking."[68] Individual development and species evolution came together not because they were so commonly linked already but because natural selection could explain unity of type in both taxonomy and embryology. The broad notion that nature follows common patterns in shaping individuals and species gave way to Darwin's pointed naming of an underlying cause: the struggle for existence.

Special creation offered no perspicuous explanation of why there are species at all. Talk of archetypes offered to explain why living beings cluster into types but only rhapsodized about the symmetries. The idea of a full universe failed more gravely. It was untrue. Life forms do not form a perfect continuum. Some whole genera, as we now know, survive in just one species. *Gingko biloba* is an example: the only living deciduous gymnosperm, sole survivor of a type that flourished 248 to 65 million years ago. But natural selection explains both continuities and gaps: The clustered types are kin. The gaps are failed experiments – and possibilities never tried.

Once Darwin saw species developmentally, the affinities that had entranced transcendental naturalists, from Goethe's musings to the careful dissections of von Baer and Owen, became phenomena that kinship could explain. The metamorphoses of individuals were not just parallels but evidence;

the embryo, "a sort of picture, preserved by nature, of the former and less modified condition of the species"[69] – "even more important for classification" than the adult.[70] Likewise with disused organs:

> As we have no written pedigrees ... we choose those characters which, as far as we can judge, are the least likely to have been modified in relation to the conditions of life to which each species has been recently exposed. Rudimentary structures on this view are as good as, or even sometimes better than, other parts of the organization.[71]

Rudiments, "bearing the stamp of inutility," hold evidence of common descent: The "bastard wing" of birds was once a digit; the undeveloped second lung in many snakes survives from a once paired organ. The tiny, useless wings of flightless insects, often "firmly soldered together" beneath the wing case, mark a descent from forms that flew:[72]

> the same reasoning power which tells us that most parts and organs are exquisitely adapted for certain purposes, tells us with equal plainness that these rudimentary or atrophied organs are imperfect or useless. In works on natural history, rudimentary organs are generally said to have been created 'for the sake of symmetry,'or in order 'to complete the scheme of nature.' But this is not an explanation, merely a restatement of the fact. Nor is it consistent with itself; thus the boa constrictor has the rudiments of a pelvis, and if it be said that these bones have been retained 'to complete the scheme of nature,' why, as Professor Weismann asks, have they not been retained by other snakes, which do not possess even a vestige of these same bones?[73]

The bones mark the site where limbs once grew. A dugong and a mouse, Darwin writes, are most alike in their reproductive systems, where environment matters least and inheritance holds most constant.[74]

Ernst Haeckel, a fervent follower and popularizer of Darwin's, who coined the terms 'ecology' and 'phylum,' canonized the tracking of evolution by development as the "phylogenetic law": Ontogeny recapitulates phylogeny. A human embryo starts out as a single cell, then looks like a colony, then an invertebrate, an amphioxus, and a fish, then very like a fetal dog or pig. Darwin, in the *Descent of Man*, bolstered his case for human origins with woodcuts showing the likeness of dog and human embryos. The similarity is imperfect, of course. A human embryo remains distinctively human; it will never become a dog, and there is no actual phylogenetic law. But Darwin's explanation for the parallels is robust: Embryonic and adult forms face different selection pressures. A barnacle, anchored to its rock, has lost the traits of its ancestral type. Yet the free living larva reveal it as a crustacean. The shrimplike appendages did not atrophy from disuse. But sessile adults don't need them, and the cost of keeping them was never offset by sufficient reproductive advantage.

In a brilliant 1866 paper sent to Darwin from Russia, A. Kowalevsky showed that larval ascidia, then classed as invertebrates, had what are now called chordate characteristics. The sessile adult form had lost them.[75] Darwin saw the implications:

> at an extremely remote period a group of animals existed, resembling in many respects the larvae of our present Ascidians, which diverged into two great branches – the one retrograding in development and producing the present class of Ascidians, the other rising to the crown and summit of the animal kingdom by giving birth to the Vertebrata.[76]

Development, then, told an evolutionary story. Tadpoles have gills that disappear when they begin to use their lungs as frogs. Reptiles, birds, and mammals, as early embryos, have gill slits, aortic arches, and two-chambered hearts, like fish – although, unlike amphibians, they have no aquatic larva. Their hearts will become three chambered – later, four, in birds and mammals, where warm bloodedness makes its demands. Special creation does not explain these features, "but under a theory of evolution they are obviously ancestral relics."[77]

The dorsal stripe in some horses harks back to a time when horses needed camouflage.[78] The human appendix, long seen as useless, even detrimental, is now thought to survive as a reservoir of valuable digestive flora sometimes decimated by illness. But it still seems to be vestigial, a small reminder of abandoned digestive pathways. The tailbone too may still have uses, anchoring minor muscles or supporting pelvic organs; but its presence and the occasional tail of newborns point to simian ancestors. Overlooking no scrap of evidence, Darwin reads the little bump near the top of some people's ears, and the ability of some people to wiggle their ears, as relics of ancestors whose ability to prick up their ears could be a matter of survival.[79]

Fossils and extinction

The affinities of living types to fossil counterparts cement Darwin's case: Dugongs may lack even rudimentary hind limbs, but the extinct Halitherium has well-defined thigh bones. The Zeuglodon and Squalodon connect living cetaceans with aquatic carnivores; the Archeopteryx connects the birds with reptiles.[80] Moralists sometimes ask how God could countenance the destruction of whole species. But to Darwin, extinction was evolution's cutting edge. The fossil record discredits the notion of eternal species and tracks the emergence of new kinds. Gottfried Treviranus had noted the increasing complexity of organisms in each higher geological stratum: fish far below amphibians, reptiles above them, then birds, then mammals. New players emerge on new stages, each with new strengths.

New types arise at varying rates. So Darwin sees no evidence for a steady drive toward improvement. The stop-and-go traffic confirms the role of natural selection: Evolution accelerates when types compete.[81] But Darwin discounts catastrophe. Confirmed evidence of rapid evolutionary change, he writes, "would be fatal to my views."[82] Extinctions would be gradual, as populations thin and succumb to "hostile agencies." Still, once extinct, no species returns. The thread of descent is broken.[83] New forms might fill a vacant niche. But continuance depends on heredity – and prosaic factors like disease resistance. Size, Darwin reminds unwary critics, can be a detriment. For food supplies often fail.[84]

During the voyage of the *Beagle*, Darwin saw fossil mastodons and remains later identified as Megatherium, a five-ton sloth some 20 feet tall. There were Glyptodons, rhinoceros-sized armadillo-like creatures weighing a ton, perhaps a fifth of it armor. He shipped back to England the fossil head of a Toxodon, an ungulate not unlike a hippopotamus. The vanished mammals lived as long as two million years ago. But these specimens were recent. The types died out some 16,000 years ago, in the last Ice Age. A striking find was a horse's tooth.

> No one I think can have marveled more at the extinction of species than I have done. When I found in La Plata the tooth of a horse embedded with the remains of Mastodon, Megatherium, Toxodon, and other extinct monsters, which all co-existed with still living shells at a very late geological period, I was filled with astonishment; for seeing that the horse, since its introduction by the Spaniards into South America, has run wild over the whole country and has increased in numbers at an unparalleled rate, I asked myself what could so recently have exterminated the former horse under conditions of life apparently so favourable. But how utterly groundless was my astonishment! Professor Owen soon perceived that the tooth, though so like that of the existing horse, belonged to an extinct species. Had this horse been still living, but in some degree rare, no naturalist would have felt the least surprise at its rarity; for rarity is the attribute of a vast number of species of all classes, in all countries. If we ask ourselves why this or that species is rare, we answer that something is unfavorable in its conditions of life; but what that something is, we can hardly ever tell. On the supposition of the fossil horse still existing as a rare species, we might have felt certain from the analogy of all other mammals, even of the slow-breeding elephant, and from the history of the naturalization of the domestic horse in South America, that under more favorable conditions it would in a very few years have stocked the whole continent. But we could not have told what the unfavorable conditions were which checked its increase, whether some one or several contingencies, and at what period of the horse's life, and in what degree, they severally acted. If the conditions had gone on,

however slowly, becoming less and less favorable, we assuredly should not have perceived the fact, yet the fossil horse would certainly have become rarer and rarer, and finally extinct; its place being seized on by some more successful competitor.[85]

Horses, Darwin knew, were unknown in America until brought by the Conquistadores. The tooth made sense when he learned that it came from an extinct New World species. Species are fragile. Ancient horses had died out where mustangs would flourish in historical times.

Fossils help bridge the gaps in the evolutionary continuum. But fossils too fall into definite species. So Darwin's picture was still drawn in dotted lines. Evolution could connect the dots. But the lines, critics complained, remained broken. More fossils would be found, Darwin promised: "Every year tends to fill up the blanks between the stages."[86] History has answered that hope year by year. As Donald Prothero notes, fossil remains of Archaeopteryx, marking the transition from reptiles to birds, were first unearthed just a year after the *Origin* appeared. *Homo erectus*, once called Java man, came to light by 1900. Today we have a precious sequence of hominid fossils, a new fossil that may mark the transition from lemurs and lorises to higher primates like monkeys and apes,[87] and fossils that mark the return of land mammals to the seas as whales, manatees, and seals. We can chart the evolution of elephants, rhinos, and a host of smaller creatures that early paleontologists often overlooked – "an embarrassment of riches."[88]

Full as the fossil sequence gets, it never provides a perfect continuum. Too much depends on the vagaries of migration and the luck of discovery.[89] Surviving species may point to an extinct common ancestor but rarely announce a chain of lineal descent. Transitional types are naturally rare. For intermediate forms were often mediocrities, experimental prototypes, as it were. Only variants with just the right combination of adaptations proliferate.[90] Darwin's explanations sounded apologetic, so they didn't settle much. Still, the fossils told a story: The toxodon was an ungulate of a vanished genus. The giant sloth and armadillo, despite their exotic traits, were clearly of familiar types. Kinship explains the resemblances: Insects have six legs and spiders eight, not because either number confers some magical advantage but because creatures inherit their basic body plan. Changes yield new forms, but always from the old. Adaptiveness may explain why one form supplants another, but nature must work with the given. And location matters: The extinction of horses on the pampas leaves a niche. Rheas browse where horses once grazed. They prosper without the competition. But rheas will never become horses.

Horses, in fact, fulfill Darwin's promise of a tighter fossil sequence. No fossil series is more continuous. Othniel Marsh turned up the key specimens in North America in the 1870s. Huxley made them famous, and later paleontologists added tesserae to the mosaic. The fox-sized Hyracotherium, or Eohippus, lived in New World forests about 52 million years ago. Its nearest relatives, the tapir and rhinoceros, like it had an odd number of toes and a flexible upper lip. An agile runner, Eohippus, like other mammals, had five digits, but one toe on the front legs and two on the rear were off the ground. The padded toes were tipped with tiny hooves. Over some 20 million years, the creature's diet, as the teeth reveal, shifted gradually from leaves and fruits more strictly toward foliage. But Eohippus fossils, found by the thousands in Wyoming's Wind River basin, yield gradually, some 50 million years ago, to Orohippus, a slimmer beast with longer head, leaner forelegs, and the hind legs of a fine jumper. The footpads remain, but each foreleg now has four toes, and each hind leg three. The toes already vestigial in Eohippus are gone. The first premolars are much smaller; the last, now a molar. There are pronounced tooth crests, and the molars are more prominent, a trend continued in Epihippus, which appears some 47 million years ago.

As North America grew drier, 32 million to 24 million years ago, the forests retreat before grassy prairies, and Mesohippus emerges. Larger and faster than Epihippus, with longer legs and tougher teeth, it stood 24 inches at the shoulder. Its head was longer, its back less arched, its brain enlarged. Like modern horses, it had six grinders in its cheeks and just one premolar. Miohippus split off from Mesohippus some 36 million years ago. The fossils coexist for about four million years. Then Miohippus replaces Mesohippus. Again it was larger, its teeth often with an extra crest, as in all later horses. Between 24 million and 5.3 million years ago Miohippus apparently split into a variety of species. Of two major types, one returned to the forests, the other remained on the plains. Some of the forest types made it to the Old World by the Bering land bridge but then died out. The plains types gave way to Parahippus, pony-sized with an elongated skull, its lengthened middle toe bearing most of the body weight. Its first premolars were greatly reduced; the other four, like molars. The upper incisors now show a crease, like the cupped teeth of modern horses. A variety of horses fan out over the next millions of years from the basic type, Merychippus, the feet and teeth variously adapted to grazing and running on the prairies.

Modern horses of the genus Equus first appear about 3.5 million years ago. They ran on just one toe, now with a proper hoof. Weighing just under half a ton, much like today's Arabians, they reached Eurasia by the Bering land bridge some 2.5 million years ago. Variants, moving south in the Americas as the climate cooled, died out in the Ice Age. So Indians had no word for horses when Europeans introduced them. They called them elk-dog or coined some other name for them. Still, some said, "the grass remembered them."

The fossils mark the lineage of the survivors and testify to the natures of their vanished ancestors. The evidence of ancient climate change makes the causes of their loss far less mysterious than it once seemed.

Migration and adaptation

The New World replicates almost every environment known in the Old. But the species differ vastly. Likewise in Australia, South Africa, and South America. Any barrier to migration yields striking differences in flora and fauna. Arctic and Pelagic species are typically cosmopolitan. Absent barriers, adaptation is gradual:

> the naturalist in traveling, for instance, from north to south never fails to be struck by the manner in which successive groups of beings, specifically distinct, yet clearly related, replace each other. He hears from closely allied, yet distinct kinds of birds, notes nearly similar, and sees their nests similarly constructed, but not quite alike, with eggs coloured in nearly the same manner.[91]

Yet "Oceanic islands are sometimes deficient in certain classes, and their places are apparently occupied by other inhabitants; in the Galapagos Islands reptiles, and in New Zealand gigantic wingless birds, take the place of mammals."[92] Yet some species are far flung. Can plants and animals cross mountain ranges or even oceans? Darwin knew of theories of continental drift and an early union of the continents, ideas now confirmed but still ridiculed in my schooldays. But he balked at relying too heavily on speculative ideas: "to the best of my judgment," he writes, "we are not authorised in admitting such enormous geographical changes within the period of existing species."[93] He knew that volcanic islands and coral atolls rise or sink, that altered terrain might shift river courses and disperse freshwater fish,[94] that climate change can spur migrations. But could species spread to distant continents?

Experimenting with seeds, Darwin found that 64 of 87 species could germinate after 28 days in sea water – some after 137 days. Many seeds would float, especially when dried. Simulating the fate of seeds still attached to a broken branch, another naturalist found that seeds survived six weeks in a wooden box at sea, long enough to travel hundreds of miles. Birds spread seeds over great distances. So do icebergs. The ancient glaciers could strand plant and animal species on mountain tops:

> as the snow melted from the bases of the mountains, the arctic forms would seize on the cleared and thawed ground, always ascending higher and higher as the warmth increased, whilst their brethren were pursuing their northern journey. ... We can thus also understand the fact that the Alpine plants of each mountain-range are more especially related to the arctic forms living due north or nearly due north of them.[95]

Animals can swim; birds and insects fly, or drift like kites in a storm. But non-domesticated land mammals did not appear on oceanic islands beyond 300 miles from land.[96]

The most striking and important fact for us in regard to the inhabitants of islands, is their affinity to those of the nearest mainland, without being actually the same species. ... There is nothing in the conditions of life, in the geological nature of the islands, in their height or climate, or in the proportions in which the several classes are associated together, which resembles closely the conditions on the South American coast: in fact there is a considerable dissimilarity in all these respects. On the other hand, there is a considerable degree of resemblance in the volcanic nature of the soil, in climate, height, and size of the islands, between the Galapagos and Cape de Verde Archipelagos: but what an entire and absolute difference in their inhabitants! The inhabitants of the Cape de Verde Islands are related to those of Africa, like those of the Galapagos to America. I believe this grand fact can receive no sort of explanation on the ordinary view of independent creation; whereas on the view here maintained, it is obvious that the Galapagos Islands would be likely to receive colonists, whether by occasional means of transport or by formerly continuous land, from America; and the Cape de Verde Islands from Africa; and that such colonists would be liable to modifications – the principle of inheritance still betraying their original birthplace.[97]

Similarly, "the several islands of the Galapagos Archipelago are tenanted, as I have elsewhere shown, in quite a marvelous manner, by very closely related species; so that the inhabitants of each separate island, though mostly distinct, are related in an incomparably closer degree to each other than to the inhabitants of any other part of the world."[98]

The passage recalls the Galapagos finches Darwin had collected over five weeks during his voyage on the *Beagle*. These birds, now thought to be among the first animals to find the island group, some 600 miles west of Ecuador, found a varied environment free of avian competition. As they fanned out among the islands, competition and diverse opportunities promoted increasing specialization, salient in the finches' beaks, some now massive, some slender. The sixteen main islands boast three species of seed-eating ground finches with large, medium, and small beaks, another with a sharp, pointed beak, and two that feed on cactus. There are three insect-eating tree finches, a vegetarian tree finch, another that lives in mangroves, one that looks and behaves much like a warbler, and a woodpecker-like finch that probes in tree bark with twigs and cactus spines for grubs and insects. In his *Journal of Researches*, Darwin wrote:

Seeing this gradation and diversity of structure in one small, intimately related group of birds, one might really fancy that from an original paucity of birds in this archipelago, one species had been taken and modified for different ends.[99]

Darwin did not immediately work out the relationships. But the ornithologist John Gould saw that the birds were not mere variants but of distinct species, all unique to the Galapagos. Even as he pondered the classification of his finches, Darwin took in a new piece of information: He had noted the resemblance of the Lesser Rhea of Patagonia to the more common South American type, suspecting a common ancestry. Gould confirmed that the Lesser Rhea was a distinct species and named it for Darwin. "This moment more than any other in Darwin's life," Janet Browne writes, the 1837 meeting when Gould presented his findings at the Zoological Society in London and Darwin himself rose to describe the rheas' eggs, "deserves to be called a turning point." He saw his life's work before him and began reading voraciously and assembling in notebooks the evidence for evolution, his mind racing as he envisioned species transformed as their populations spread across a continent or an archipelago, the phenomenon that Darwin labeled "divergence," but now called adaptive radiation.[100]

The honeycreepers of Hawaii afford a striking example. These finchlike birds, arrived in the Islands some 3.5 million years ago, rapidly diversified into niches as woodpeckers, nectar sippers, grub probers, seed crushers, and moth eaters. Their beaks range from scimitar to nut-cracker shape. Their vivid and varied plumage and anatomic differences belie what the DNA shows: All descend from a single bird or mated pair windblown to islands with few competitors and no terrestrial predators.

Recent biologists find further confirmation of the evolutionary impact of migration in circumpolar ring species. If we fly west from the range of the American Herring Gull in North America, we find a related species, the Vega Herring Gull, across the Bering Sea, then the Birula's Gull along the Eastern Siberian Sea, the Heuglin's Gull further west toward the Laptev and Kara Seas, the Lesser Siberian Black Backed Gull toward the Barents Sea, and Herring Gulls again toward Murmansk and Norway. The contiguous species can interbreed – until we reach the Norwegian Sea and North Atlantic: The Lesser Black Backs and the Herring Gulls of Norway and Murmansk, where we come full circle, cannot interbreed. Stepwise change has gone too far.

Three questions Darwin answered, and one that he could not

Darwin addressed objections so fully in the later editions of the *Origin* that the last edition reads almost like a commentary on the first. Beyond the perennial issues about transitional forms, he faced recurrent doubts that any stepwise process could reach a remote, unforseen goal like the human eye. Similarly, with complex behavioral strategies like hive building in bees. Then there was hybrid sterility, which seemed to segregate discrete living species. Repeatedly Darwin marshaled evidence that disarmed the objections. But when Lord Kelvin argued that the laws of thermodynamics give evolution far less time than Darwin counted on, vindication awaited new discoveries in physics as yet unknown to Darwin.

Intricate organs

It's often hard to imagine, Darwin grants, how natural selection could produce complex organ systems – but the deficiency lies not in nature but in human imagination:

> When it was first said that the sun stood still and the world turned round, the common sense of mankind declared the doctrine false; but the old saying *Vox populi, vox Dei*, as every philosopher knows, cannot be trusted in science. Reason tells me, that if numerous gradations from a simple and imperfect eye to one complex and perfect can be shown to exist, each grade being useful to its possessor ... then the difficulty of believing that a perfect and complex eye could be formed by natural selection, though insuperable by our imagination, should not be considered as subversive of the theory.[101]

Darwin notes many adaptations that seem to have been gradually accrued. The swim bladder that steadies fish in the water can, he reasons, be ancestral to lungs. Indeed, some fish with chambered, ducted swim bladders can breathe in open air.[102] The flying squirrel suggests how mammalian ancestors of bats might have acquired wings, using loose skin as a parachute against a fall, or as a kite to glide on, before powered flight was possible. In the so called flying lemur a wide flank membrane extends from mouth to tail. The limbs are within it, and there's even an extensor muscle. Bats don't descend from lemurs, but we can see how a wing might have come from quite a different organ.

Webbed feet, Darwin argues, are useful to the otter-like mustela, even if it doesn't use them year round: They give access to new refuges and hunting grounds. A whale's baleen, in its early stages, suggests the lamellated beak of ducks.[103] Such cases reveal no missing link, but they do show how paddle feet, or flippers, or a sifting baleen might have evolved from parts with other functions.[104] Penguins swim with their wings. Why wings and not fins? Descent from birds is Darwin's answer. The idea of invariant species provides none.

Advocates of special creation have their work cut out for them if they want to explain why upland geese have webbed feet, although they "rarely go near the water," or why some island plants have "beautifully hooked seeds," despite the absence of mammals in whose wool or fur the hooks might lodge for transport. Darwinians can refer to ancestors that once made use of these features – plants that did rely on mammals to spread their seeds, geese that did live by the water. Grebes and coots, Darwin writes, "are eminently aquatic, although their toes are bordered only by a membrane."[105] They lack webbed feet because they did not inherit them; adaptation can't work over-night. It needs variants as well as selection pressures.

Following "the contrivances" orchids use to attract their insect pollen porters, Darwin can often trace incipient forms of more elaborate adapta-tions: "I have been astonished," he writes, "how rarely an organ can be named, towards which no transitional grade is known to lead."[106] In sea urchins, "the steps can be followed by which a fixed spine becomes articu-lated to the shell, and is thus rendered movable," suggesting a pathway "from simple granules to ordinary spines, to perfect tridactyle pedicellariae." Agassiz, a lifelong foe of evolution, had followed these steps, through "all the possible gradations," from tiny footlike organs to the hooks of ophiur-ians and the anchors of the holothuriae. Likewise, with crustacean pincers.[107]

The classic case for providential design is the human eye. Here, surely, was proof of special creation. Darwin augments the traditional tally of the eye's wonders by citing properties studied in modern optics: color vision, variable focus, a diaphragm that swiftly adjusts to prevailing light levels, a lens that corrects for spherical and chromatic aberration. To these we can add the remarkable coordination of binocular, stereoscopic vision, and the biochem-istry of rhodopsin, which translates retinal images painted by light into electrical impulses transmissible by the nerves. Could the crude workshop of natural selection build such an instrument stepwise? Surely half an eye would be useless, and what good is an eye that cannot focus?

Still, Darwin argues, a light-sensitive patch might be the origin of an eye. The gelatinous coating of small pigmented depressions found in certain starfish resolve no image but do suggest how a natural lens might have formed from a surface that first served only as a transparent covering, and then, perhaps, only to gather and concentrate scarce light. One function might lead to another as advantage defines new uses for old structures. The steps from the eyespot of the amphioxus (lancelet) to the eagle's eye may be piecemeal.[108] But gradual improvements appeal to the spirit of Darwin's age.

Reason must conquer imagination, Darwin argues, to see how complexity could emerge from simplicity. But developmental studies help, since "it is notorious that the wings of birds and bats, and the legs of horses or other quadrupeds are indistinguishable at an early embryonic period, and that they become differentiated by insensibly fine steps."[109] Similarly, with the eye: "the beautiful crystalline lens is formed in the embryo by an accumulation of epidermic cells, lying in a sack-like fold of the skin; and the vitreous body is formed from embryonic sub-cutaneous tissue."[110] The likely evolutionary steps are all but illustrated for us!

And yet, Darwin insists, the work is not perfect. How could it be? For (to give contemporary examples) we see only certain wavelengths, useful as infra-red or ultra-violet, or x-ray vision might be. Our eyesight suits our environment – more specifically, the needs of our ancestors. Its strengths and limitations fit our milieu and reflect the resources we've inherited. So evolution can explain both the strengths and the defects of our senses. We can't see as sharply as eagles or follow scents as keenly as dogs. It's vapid and vacuous to say that's because we're not made the way dogs or eagles are. Darwin's explanation: Our ancestors faced different challenges and had different inherited resources from the outset. Natural selection does not promise perfection. Evolution is an ongoing dialectic, not a finished process. Even longevity is not its goal. For some species a brief season and rapid generational turnover are advantageous.[111] Conditions vary. So natural selection imposes no unilinear scheme.

Elaborate instincts

With instincts too Darwin proposes graded steps by which complex behaviors might evolve. European cuckoos, he explains, steal a march by laying eggs in other species' nests. Their young push their rivals from the nest, monopolizing the food brought by the parent birds. But some American cuckoos lack this behavior; other varieties show it only occasionally. The intermediate case shows how variant behaviors might become the norm if reproductively advantageous. The small eggs of the exploiters mark their behavior as part of a complex. For cuckoos that use their own nests lay full-sized eggs, not furtive miniatures.[112]

Similarly, with slave-making in ants.[113] *Formica rufescens*, Darwin reports, is utterly dependent on slaves of another species, *Formica fusca*. Workers capture the slaves as pupae, to be reared in their own nests. The users don't clean the nest or even feed themselves or their larvae or pupae, even if starving. The slaves perform all menial tasks, even carrying the much larger ants in migration to a new nest. "If we had not known of any other slave-making ant," Darwin writes, "it would have been hopeless to speculate how so wonderful an instinct could have been perfected."[114] But intermediate cases suggest the steps that might have preceded behaviors so elaborate and complex in a tiny invertebrate.

Formica sanguinea also enslave *F. fusca* ants, but these masters work and fight defensively alongside their slaves. In the English variety, the slaves are kept largely in the nest; in Switzerland they were seen hunting for aphids. But in both cases most of the foraging was left to the larger ants; and in migration the sanguinea carried the slaves. The slaves tended the larvae, and only the masters fought to capture new pupae to rear as slaves. Rufescens ants don't even set the path of their own migration. Darwin, then, can chart a progression to the helpless rufescens from a lesser dependency, perhaps initiated in the occasional usefulness of alien ants grown from pupae first brought into the nest for food: "natural selection might increase and modify the instinct – always supposing each modification to be of use to the species – until an ant was formed as abjectly dependent on its slaves as is the *Formica rufescens*."[115]

In another classic case, Darwin considers the honey bee. He expatiates on the geometry of the hive's hexagonal prisms, explaining how the cells maximize the volume of honey stored, with minimal expenditure of wax and precious energy. Again gradation reveals nature's "method of work."[116] Bumble bees "use their old cocoons to hold honey, sometimes adding to them short tubes of wax, and likewise making separate and very irregular rounded cells of wax."[117] Intermediate between these crude storage cells and the hive bees' elegant double-layered, bevel-edged cells, fall the cylindrical cells of the Mexican *Melipona domestica*, "in which the young are hatched," and its large, nearly spherical, irregularly massed honey storage cells. The Mexican bees do join their storage globes with flat surfaces, saving wax by avoiding a double wall. Where three spheres come together, they anticipate the finer geometry of the honey bee's hive:

> It would be an advantage to our imaginary humble-bee [bumble bee] if a slight modification in her instincts led her to make her waxen cells near together, so as to intersect a little; for a wall in common even to two adjoining cells would save some little labour and wax. Hence it would be continually more and more advantageous to our humble-bees if they were to make their cells more and more regular, nearer together, and aggregated into a mass. ... it would be advantageous to the Melipona, if she were to make her cells closer together, and more regular in every way than at present; for then, as we have seen, the spherical surfaces would wholly disappear and be replaced by plane surfaces; and the Melipona would make a comb as perfect as that of the hive-bee. Beyond this stage of perfection in architecture, natural selection could not lead; for the comb of the hive-bee, as far as we can see, is absolutely perfect in economising on labour and wax.[118]

The less efficient design persists, perhaps because bumble bees face lighter selection pressures or enjoy compensatory adaptations. Even if Melipona does not compete directly with honey bees, Darwin clearly turns the tables on the objection that such an intricate behavior as that of hive building in the honey bee could not arise unguided, by natural selection. He can trace credible paths of transition without conceptual seven league boots.

Sterile castes and crosses

Questions about sterility may seem to pose formidable problems for evolution. How are the traits of sterile worker ants, termites, or bees inherited? Sterile insects can't pass on their traits. Yet even sterility, Darwin argues, if useful to a colony, might be inherited, provided "fertile males and females have flourished, and transmitted to their fertile offspring a tendency to produce sterile members with the same modifications."[119] Hybrid sterility is the real challenge, marking a natural barrier, as if to confirm that species are discrete. Varieties, by definition, are inter-fertile; species are not. But hybrid sterility, Darwin notes, varies in degree. Like species differences, it "graduates away so insensibly ... that for all practical purposes it is most difficult to say where perfect fertility ends and sterility begins."[120] Plants often hybridize sooner than accept their own pollen.[121] Difficult plant crosses are typically very sterile, but not always. Sometimes the hybrids are impressively fertile, whereas some readily crossed species yield "remarkably sterile" offspring.[122]

Still, hybrids gave evidence for Darwin. "The pear," he noted, "can be grafted far more readily on the quince, which is ranked as a distinct genus, than on the apple, which is a member of the same genus. Even different varieties of the pear take with different degrees of facility on the quince; so do different varieties of apricot and peach on certain varieties of the plum." Yet "no one has been able to graft together trees belonging to quite distinct families," although "closely allied species, and varieties of the same species, can usually, but not invariably, be grafted with ease."[123] Such patterns gave Darwin his clue for explaining hybrid sterility, and turning it from counter-evidence to confirmation: "the fertility of first crosses, and of the hybrids produced from them is largely governed by their systematic affinity."[124] Something internal, in "the sexual constitution" of prospective mates, must be the key.

Only with the advent of genetics did a clear explanation of hybrid sterility, hybrid fertility, and hybrid vigour come into view. Darwin's thoughts here were hesitant and conjectural. But he knew that species ranked closest by taxonomists are generally most successfully crossed. The reason was implicit in evolution: The interfertile types share a pedigree. They have not diverged enough to be incompatible. Hybrid sterility, then, turns witness for the prosecution: The Linnaean tree takes its shape because its members are akin, literally; and kindred forms cross readily, where distant types do not. Notions of species fixity offer no corresponding explanation for the varying degrees of hybrid fertility and sterility, or even for the possibility of grafting branches from one tree onto another.

Kelvin's challenge

Darwin's long delay in publishing the *Origin* and his further delay in publishing *The Descent of Man* were due in part to worries about the reception of his work. He clearly wanted to put all his evidentiary ducks in order. But part of the problem was that he did not know just how long evolution needed. A nasty fly in the ointment came from the thermodynamics of William Thompson, later Lord Kelvin, the great Glasgow physicist who formulated the Second Law of Thermodynamics and devised the temperature scale now renamed in his honor.

Nineteenth-century scientists traced energy ultimately to just two sources: gravitational and electromagnetic – typified in the mill race of an earlier age and the heat engine (e.g., steam engine) of the industrial revolution. Kelvin, a passionate critic of evolution, argued that if solar heat came from combustion (liberating energy stored in the electromagnetic bonds of chemical compounds), the sun could not have been burning for more than twenty million years. If the energy source was gravitational, as Kelvin assumed – from compaction, say, of the solar mass – the sun's lifespan still seemed too short for evolution. Summing up his calculations in 1862, Kelvin judged it "most probable that the sun has not illuminated the earth for 100,000,000 years, and almost certain that he has not done so for 500,000,000 years."[125]

The earth's age too was a problem. Noting that temperatures rise one degree Fahrenheit for each 50 feet below the surface, Kelvin calculated that the planet's original molten core had cooled to its present temperature in at most 100 million years – far too swiftly, it seemed, for evolution to do its work. Concerned, Darwin removed the time estimates from the *Origin* in its third and later editions and sidestepped such estimates in *The Descent of Man*. But nature vindicated evolution in the end. For solar heat does not come from combustion or compaction. Sir Arthur Eddington, suspecting as much in 1920, called the theory that the sun's heat comes from the pressure of its mass "an unburied corpse." He wrote, "A star is drawing on some vast reservoir of energy by means unknown to us." Then, boldly: "let us frankly recognize" that reservoir "can scarcely be other than sub-atomic energy." Fusion was still unknown, but the discrepancy between the atomic weights of hydrogen and helium allowed Eddington to calculate the energy it would release and predict that it would one day be understood and even harnessed, yielding a store of energy "well-nigh inexhaustible."[126] By present estimates, the sun's age is close to five billion years.

As for the earth, Henri Becquerel discovered radioactivity in 1896. Two years later Marie and Pierre Curie discovered polonium and radium, the first known radioactive elements. Julius Elster and Hans Geitel, German school teachers, found radiation in the air and soil in 1901, and Robert Strutt of London proposed that radioactive elements were major sources of heat within the earth. In 1903, Pierre Curie and an associate showed that radium generates enough heat to melt its weight in ice in less than an hour. That same year Darwin's son George and an Irish physicist, inventor, and geologist, John Joly, argued that this heat had slowed earth's cooling enough to refute Kelvin and confirm Joly's rival estimates, based on the gradual leaching of salts into the seas. Kelvin doggedly defended his numbers until his death and only privately confessed his error.[127] Estimates of the earth's age, based chiefly on rates of radioactive decay, hover today around 4.5 billion years.

NeoDarwinism

Mendel's work

Not everyone was as unaware of the laws of heredity as Darwin thought. Gregor Mendel, an Augustinian monk in Moravia, educated at the universities of Olmütz and Vienna, was turned down for a high school teaching job, largely because his biological knowledge far surpassed what the provincial licensing examiners knew. But in the monastery's large experimental garden, established by the abbot, who hoped humanity might benefit from what was learned there, Mendel bred some 30,000 plants, tracking specific traits. Knowing sweet peas well, he designed an elegant series of experiments that yielded stunning results.

The peas, as Mendel knew, might be yellow or green. Using carefully purebred plants, he crossed yellow with green-pea plants. The offspring all had yellow peas. Whatever made for yellow peas was "dominant," Mendel wrote. But self-pollinating this first filial or F-1 generation, as it's now called, consistently gave an F-2 generation with three yellow-pea plants for every green. The green-pea factor, evidently, was still present but latent in the F-1 plants. Mendel called it "recessive." Strikingly, the colors were not blended: There were no yellow-green peas. Mendel found similar patterns with six other traits. And the traits, he noted, were not connected: Color was inherited separately from plant height; height, independently of the smooth or wrinkled skin of each pea. Hence, the two great Mendelian laws: genetic segregation (the traits were discrete; there were no intermediates) and independent assortment (the traits were inherited separately, not influencing one another). These two features of the logic of inheritance gave Mendel a clue as to its mechanism: The governing factors (genes, as they were dubbed in 1909) for all seven traits must reside in discrete particles passed from one generation to the next.

If each of Mendel's plants received one gene for a given trait from each of its parents, the dominant genes were those whose expression needs only one gene. A recessive gene is expressed (phenotypically, we now say) only when both parents contribute a gene of that type. That would explain the ratios Mendel saw in the F-2 generation: A quarter of the plants, on average, inherit two green-pea genes. They're homozygous, as geneticists put it, for the recessive gene. Another quarter are homozygous for the dominant. And half are heterozygous, inheriting one gene of each type. They bear yellow peas, since the yellow-pea gene is dominant, but carry the gene for green peas that show up in later generations, whenever two green-pea genes coincide.

Mendel began his sweet pea work in the 1850s and completed it by 1863. Not long after, he read Darwin's *Origin* in German translation, writing notes in the margins. Franz Unger, one of his professors in Vienna, was a committed transmutationist, arguing that "new combinations" of material in plants, "always reducible to certain law-combinations," must surely allow the members of existing species "to emancipate themselves" from their former characteristics and "appear as a new species."[128] So Mendel knew Darwin's work and was quite familiar with the idea of evolution. But Darwin did not know Mendel.

Mendel published his findings in German in the1866 *Proceedings* of the Brno Natural Sciences Society. But the work remained unknown to Darwin. Darwin did own a German book on plant breeding by W. O. Focke that cited Mendel's work, but those pages in his copy of Focke remained uncut. It was neither the German nor the provincial venue of his publication, however, that left Darwin in the dark about Mendel's results. Some 134 scientific institutions received the Brno *Proceedings*, and Mendel sent out many off-prints, including a rare surviving copy to his Professor Unger, whose evolutionary views the Viennese clergy had been castigating years before Darwin published. Writing about his own work to the eminent botanist C. Nägeli, Mendel got only negativity in reply. Convinced that inheritance was gradual and blended, Nägeli – although he was in touch with Darwin – misled Mendel about the work of others and sat on his discoveries.[129] Mendel held by his results, and held fast to his faith. But his election as abbot drew him away from intensive plant experiments, and he turned to meteorology, never knowing that his work would initiate a revolution.

Even as Mendel was trying to call attention to his paper, Darwin was combing the world for evidence pertinent to evolution. But his many allies were seeking causes of change, not stability. Classical, non-evolutionist biologists expected organisms to breed true. Deviations and individual differences seemed to offer no consistent pattern to marshal under scientific laws. But Darwinians were fixated on continuous variations, not discrete traits like yellow peas or green, wrinkled or smooth. It didn't help that Mendel reported his results quantitatively, not in the discursive style then widely fashionable. Investigators who did work quantitatively focused on traits they could measure, not variants to be counted. Still, as biology grew more analytic and debates flared about heredity, new investigators emerged, prepared to speak Mendel's language.

The new genetics

Mendel's paper appeared the same year as the fourth edition of the *Origin*. Even ten years later Darwin had no inkling of genetics. He knew that Weismann "has lately insisted" on the isolation of the germ line. But he never recognized the impact of Weismann's demonstration that acquired traits are not inherited.[130] The build up of muscle mass or memory, the loss of a limb or gain of a suntan are not heritable. No matter how many generations of ancestors are shaved, circumcised, or tattooed, the effects are not transmitted. As David Joravsky notes, "Darwin himself published a report that the Muslims of Celebes are born with shortened foreskins."[131] In fact, however, inherited traits reflect one's forebears' genetic makeup, not what they did or suffered. In a famous experiment, Weismann docked the tails of 22 generations of mice without effect on their offspring.

Heritable change, as we now know, does originate in changes to the germ line, genetic mutations, as we call them. They are not typically responses to need. Indeed, their effects are rarely adaptive. Species will change when natural selection culls the less adaptive variants, or when those carrying genes for beneficial traits out-reproduce the rest. But Darwin counted on adaptive variation to speed and steer the course of evolution. Weismann's findings left him bemused. He appealed vaguely to the complexity of inheritance but did not forswear Lamarck. "Gemmules," he conjectured, unseen particles gathered from all parts of the parental body, might underlie inheritance. Aren't inherited traits found throughout the offspring's body?[132] In his book *Variations of Animals and Plants under Domestication*, Darwin included a full chapter on "the provisional hypothesis of pangenesis," writing in summary:

> I venture to advance the hypothesis of Pangenesis, which implies that every separate part of the whole organization reproduces itself. So that ovules, spermatozoa, and pollen grains the fertilized egg or seed, as well as buds include and consist of a multitude of germs thrown off from each separate part or unit.[133]

Pangenesis, an ancient, intuitively appealing idea, sat well with Darwin's gradualism. But, as Fleeming Jenkin, business partner of Kelvin, explained in reviewing the *Origin*, blended traits would tend to settle at an average, swamping any evolutionary trend and leaving no variants to spearhead change.[134] Darwin's cousin Francis Galton defended his approach; but in three years of experimental work, encouraged by Darwin, Galton's gray rabbits bore gray offspring, even when transfused with blood from white ones. Pangenesis was a non-starter. Both men regrouped. Galton allowed that traits could be preserved if inherited discretely. Gemmules were particles, after all. But some traits, like stature, surely must be subject to blending inheritance. Darwin, for his part, quietly dropped strictly blended inheritance in his fifth edition. To ensure the impact on speciation of tiny, even imperceptible changes, he pictured like offspring flocking together.[135] Mendel's "potentially formative elements" remained unknown.

In 1900 Carl Correns in Germany, Erich Tschermak in Austria, and Hugo de Vries in the Netherlands, stirred by the rising debates over inheritance, simultaneously unearthed Mendel's paper, confirming their own plant hybridization experiments. William Bateson, a British biologist, immediately grasped the import of Mendel's work and coined the terms 'heterozygous,' 'homozygous,' and 'allelomorphs' (later shortened to 'alleles') – for the alternative genes governing a trait. In 1905, in an unsuccessful application for an academic chair, Bateson named the emerging Mendelian science genetics. The following year he and R. C. Punnett found that flower color and pollen length, seemingly unrelated traits, *do not* assort independently in sweet peas. This flagrant breach of Mendel's Law of Independent Assortment was later explained by the fact that these genes, unlike the seven Mendel studied, lie on the same chromosome. In 1908 Bateson was named to a new chair, in genetics.

Chromosomes, as we now know, are the particles behind Mendel's laws. They settle the bitter war between the geneticists, who thought heredity must move by discrete steps, and Darwinians, who expected evolution to be continuous. Tiny steps allow for Darwin's gradualism – although a single mutation, as de Vries suspected when he coined the term, may sunder a population reproductively and lead to speciation. Multiple genes can influence a single trait – stature, say – smoothing population variance. And, as Udney Yule showed, not every gene is dominant or recessive. Some are codominant – partially expressed in heterozygotes. This too makes variation more continuous.

Chromosomes were described by Walther Flemming in 1882. Weismann suggested two years later that nuclear matter must be halved in the division of the germ cells that yields the gametes which transmit inherited traits. In 1902 W. S. Sutton detected the segregation of the chromosomes in cell division. With barely contained excitement, he wrote "to call attention to the probability that the association of paternal and maternal chromosomes in pairs and their subsequent separation during the reducing division [meiosis] ... may constitute the physical basis of the Mendelian law of heredity."[136] Thomas Hunt Morgan, studying mutant fruitflies at Columbia University, confirmed Sutton's hypothesis when he connected the gene governing a white rather than red eye in his flies with the X chromosome.

One anomaly that remained to be explained: Traits regularly transmitted together are sometimes inherited separately. F. A. Janssen boldly surmised the truth: In meiosis, chromosomes may break and exchange segments. In 1915 Hunt Morgan and his students, following up on an idea of Alfred Sturtevant, an undergraduate at the time, actually "mapped" genes of the fruitfly, *Drosophila melanogaster*, by assuming that the closer two genes lie on a chromosome the more rarely will they separate. Crossing over, as Hunt Morgan called the exchanges, proves crucial to evolution. It allows sexual reproduction to produce new gene combinations without erasing existing libraries of genes.

Mutations produce the variance critical to evolution. Is mutation sufficient? H. J. Muller and others showed in the first half of the twentieth century, that radiation, heat, and chemical agents promote mutations. But only rarely does a useful variant crop up. Hence the notion that nature simply suppresses deviant forms: Freshets may jump the stream banks. But how can they carve a streambed of their own? Still, as the outlines of inheritance grew crisper, De Vries hoped that mutation might suffice to explain evolution. That hope was dashed by work done independently in 1908 by the German physician Wilhelm Weinberg and the British mathematician G. H. Hardy. Building on the insights of Punnett, Yule, and R. A. Fisher, Hardy and Weinberg demonstrated that without new mutations or selection, the relative frequency of alleles in a population remains constant. Traits are not lost, as they might be in blended inheritance. But neither do they spread. New mutations may alter the relative frequencies of alleles. But they establish no trend: Genetics alone cannot explain evolution.[137] What's needed, as Darwin saw, is natural selection.

Relying in part on breeding experiments, R. A. Fisher, J. B. S. Haldane, and Sewall Wright modeled the spread of genes in a population as a function of the genes' adaptiveness and mode of expression (dominant, co-dominant, or recessive). Starting with a single mutation as rare as one in a hundred thousand, and assuming, say, the intermediate case of co-dominance, one could calculate that a gene of very slight selective advantage, only 0.1% over the general population, would be fixed at 90% frequency in 11,500 generations. If the advantage were, say, 10%, the new gene would become fixed at 99% in 120 generations.[138]

Where a generation takes 20 years or more, as in human populations, evolution would be slow. But where generations pass in a matter of days or hours, as with fruitflies or bread molds, evolutionary changes move swiftly. So evolution does not need limitless time; it can proceed by tiny mutational steps in a realistic span of generations. Nor does it need more variation than mutation can naturally produce. For even with very low mutation rates differential fertility will profoundly change a population. In a reasonably large population, moreover, co-adaptive gene complexes will emerge. The rarity of mutations and the even greater rarity of beneficial mutations does not stymie evolution.

Where Darwinists and mutationists once battled for the explanatory turf, Darwinism and genetics have come together. In today's neo-Darwinian synthesis, genetics and evolution form an integrated whole, welded together by the conceptual and experimental work of Theodosius Dobzhansky. Mendel and his successors now displace Lamarck. Species do have ancestors unlike themselves. They are neither separate creations nor eternal types. But genetic variants arise with no view to advantage. Natural selection culls the population, for failure or success.

Adaptation observed

Anti-Darwinists often say that evolutionary change has never been observed. But that's not exactly true. Such changes are well known in rapidly evolving species. The oft-repeated claim that there is no laboratory evidence of evolution must be qualified by the protean changes of bacteria. What about multi-cellular organisms? Our clearest confirmation comes not from fossils but from taxonomy: The DNA confirms that the Linnaean chart is a family tree. Whales and dolphins can be traced to their hippo-like ancestors, camels and alpacas are linked not just by external resemblance but by DNA, as if in a paternity suit. Hundreds of large-scale studies confirm the picture, allowing us not only to chart the lines of descent but to fill in the missing Y-axis that Darwin lacked the data to supply, that is, the time dimension.[139]

Kettlewell's moths

Industrial melanism affords striking evidence of adaptive change. Pigeons, squirrels, sparrows, and other urban animals, at least a hundred species in Britain alone, darkened as industrial pollution blackened the landscape. The trend was first reported in the peppered moth *Biston betularia*. The moths were commonly a pale, speckled gray. But a black specimen was observed near Manchester in 1848, probably a rare mutant. As the industrial revolution took hold, the black form grew increasingly common; pale moths became rare. By 1900 more than 90% of the peppered moths in English industrial regions were black – 98% in some areas.

J. W. Tutt proposed in 1896 that birds were finding the pale moths more readily, the black moths camouflaged in the darkened environment. Speckled moths, he reasoned, had once blended in with the lichen-covered tree bark. Where soot had covered the trees and killed the lichens, the black carbonaria type was advantaged. A lepidopterist proposed that the moths were simply ingesting matter that darkened their bodies. But breeding experiments showed that the coloration was genetic, and in 1924, J. B. S. Haldane calculated the selection coefficients that would yield the observed shifts in color frequencies.

H. B. D. Kettlewell, a physician turned ecologist, took up Tutt's idea in the 1950s.[140] He correlated the color shifts with habitats downwind of industrial centers, confirmed that birds prey upon the moths, and saw that birds have trouble spotting melanic moths on darkened tree trunks. Experimenting with birds in an aviary and then with a release of specially marked moths, he found black moths roughly twice as safe from predation as light ones in the blackened woods outside Birmingham. The trend was reversed in Dorset, where lichens and birches, far from industrial effluent, provided lighter resting places. Niko Tinbergen filmed birds preferentially preying on the more visible moths in both types of habitat.

Kettlewell worried that in his eagerness for statistical significance he had introduced too many moths and perhaps skewed his results. He also had doubts about his assumption that the moths tend to rest on tree trunks and not higher up and less exposed, in the foliage. Others wondered if mixing wild caught and lab-bred moths might have affected Kettlewell's figures. A bigger problem, perhaps, was his release of the moths in daylight hours, when this nocturnal species would likely alight on almost any surface and "clamp down" until nightfall. The concerns were fairly typical of field experiments, matters to be settled by later work.[141]

Quite another sort of critique arose as Kettlewell's findings and vivid photographs of the moths against dark and light backgrounds became favorite textbook illustrations. Now came charges that the pictures were staged, the findings oversimplified, even misrepresented. Like most things human, the work was never perfect. But the speculative and gossipy charges and even the flaws did not invalidate the findings, borne out in later studies.[142] Stunning confirmation came unexpectedly: As pollution controls took hold, the proportions of black moths fell from 90% back to 10% by the end of the twentieth century.

Biston betularia remains, as Sewall Wright wrote, "the clearest case in which a conspicuous evolutionary process has been actually observed."[143] The swift changes make it hard to deny the impact of genetic variation and environmental selection. But anti-Darwinists remain unconvinced: "The change observed in Kettlewell's moth produces a different phase, not a new species. It is not evolution."[144] This response, Philip Kitcher argues, is "absurdly naive." All evolution is micro-evolution.[145] Besides, the moths don't stand alone. As Michael Rose writes, "more than a hundred Lepidopteran species have undergone this change in melanism." Beyond that, there's evidence of ongoing adaptive radiation in the wild, among Hawaiian fruitflies.

Drosophila evolving

Hampton Carson made Hawaii his natural laboratory for studying Drosophila. The 6,500 square miles of Island terrain hosts some 800 native species of fruitflies, ranging from less than a sixteenth of an inch to over three quarters of an inch in body length and differing widely in anatomy, habit and habitat. DNA studies indicate that all of these species, across two genera, Drosophila itself and the allied genus of Scaptomyza, descend from a single gravid fly blown to Hawaii millions of years ago. The progeny diverged in habitats varying in humidity, temperature, food supply, nesting areas, and the like.

Focusing on some 100 species called "picture winged" (for their characteristic light and dark wing markings), geneticists find distinctive banding patterns in the so-called polytene chromosomes. Readily seen under the microscope in larval salivary cells, the patterns are reversed in some flies, evidently by chromosomal inversion. Tracing the variant patterns, Carson and his associates followed the spread of picture wing Drosophila in the Hawaiian chain. New species were found at each step along the way. The Big Island, for example, has 26 picture wing species, most traceable to 15 founder events in which one or a few flies from Maui and its nearby satellites made it across the Alenuhana channel to the Big Island, where their descendants established one or several new species. Other Big Island species originated from three founder events originating in Oahu, further off. One group is actually traceable to ancestors from Kauai, the oldest surviving island in Hawaii, and the furthest from the Big Island. All 26 Big Island species formed within the past half million years. They are found nowhere else.[146]

One species, *Drosophila sylvestris*, found in cool, wet forests above 2,500 feet on the Big Island, lays its eggs in decaying tree bark. The males have special hairs on their forelegs, used to brush females in courtship. Males on the northern (Hilo) side of the island have far more of these hairs than flies from the southwestern (Kona) side. Anatomical and behavioral differences like these, Carson reasoned, could divide the populations into different species. Here evolutionary change seemed to be caught in the act.

The DNA evidence

Now that scientists have sequenced the human genome and that of many other species we have a wealth of new evidence corroborating the fact of evolution generally and the human pedigree specifically. Scientists have matched the human gene sequence against that of chimpanzees and other great apes and even identified the spot at which two chromosomes merged, yielding our characteristic 23 pairs, where chimps have 24.[147] Transposed bits of DNA and multiple copies of existing genes tell a similar story. Often non-functional as a result of mutation or transposition, such sequences are adaptively neutral once their function is lost. Neither spreading nor disappearing as a result of selection pressure, such so-called pseudogenes serve the same evidentiary function for today's evolutionary geneticists that vestigial organs served for Darwin. They repeatedly reveal our close kinship to chimpanzees, and more distant relationships with other primates. A good example is the GULO pseudogene, a relic of the GULO gene that, say, dogs and cats need in producing vitamin C. A varied diet has rendered that gene unnecessary in humans and chimps, since we can get vitamin C directly from fruits and vegetables. Absent selection pressure to sweep away disabling mutations, the DNA at this site has mutated sufficiently to render the gene non-functional in both humans and chimps. But the 98% identity in the sequence that remains is a clear record of common ancestry.[148] Numerous other parallels confirm the pattern.[149] As Daniel Fairbanks writes:

> genome-wide comparison of the human and chimpanzee genomes "spectacularly confirms" what previous individual studies have shown: the genes, chromosomes, transposable elements, and pseudogenes of humans and chimpanzees are strikingly similar. Although the molecular differences constitute only a fraction of the two genomes, they are not trivial. They represent some of the most powerful evidence of common ancestry because they are fully consistent with known mechanisms of chromosome rearrangement, generation of recent transposable elements and pseudogenes, and the effects of natural selection we expect to observe in certain genes and their regulatory regions. The comparison is massive, including thousands of genes and pseudogenes, millions of transposable elements, and billions of base pairs in DNA.[150]

4

Three lines of critique

We've already encountered some of the early ripostes to Darwinism, issues about hybrids, probability, and entropy. But three abiding lines of attack are worth considering here. I don't think the critics succeed in pulling down Darwin's citadel. But they help reveal evolution's strengths and limits.

The first of the three was voiced by Darwin's teacher Adam Sedgwick: Evolution was atheistical, cold, materialistic. It ignored "all rational conception of a final cause." Those were motives of the critique. But motives don't render a theory false. Sedgwick's argument was that evolution rests on a tissue of circumstantial evidence. It fails to meet the standards of inductive reasoning. By the late nineteenth century that charge had become boilerplate. It was pursued in the twentieth by the creation science movement and elaborated by Alvin Plantinga.

The second charge is Karl Popper's: evolution is a near tautology. It ascribes the survival of adaptive forms to their fitness. But Darwinian fitness just means survival, as measured in ratios of viable offspring. Types that survive are, by definition, well adapted; but adaptive traits are those that promote survival. So Darwinism seems to explain nothing and make no real predictions. Its story is not falsifiable: No conceivable evidence could count against it – a sure sign of vacuity.

Third comes Intelligent Design. The core objection: Living structures and processes are irreducibly complex. They cannot evolve piecemeal, since there's no utility, thus no adaptive edge, in their isolated components. Darwinism is trapped in its own mechanistic dogma.

Darwinian induction

Sedgwick was a geologist, known for his work in Devon and Wales that led to the naming of the Cambrian and Devonian epochs. Darwin's gift of an advance copy of the *Origin*, Sedgwick wrote, brought him "more pain than pleasure." It slighted the idea of purpose, "the crown and glory of organic science" – linking "material to moral." Reviewing the book anonymously, Sedgwick mingled irony in the customary concessions of worth: It was "admirably worked up," contained "a great body of important truth," and was "eminently amusing." But it failed for want of evidence – no direct observation of species change. Breeders' experience was irrelevant. Hobbyists and husbandmen breed varieties, not species. Specialists' disputes over species distinctions expose not blurred boundaries but lack of finesse. The rare progeny of interspecies crosses soon revert to the original forms. For "The Author of Nature will not permit His work to be spoiled by the wanton curiosity of Man." In nature, "wild animals of different species do not desire to cross and unite."[1]

Darwin's appeals to morphology and embryology, the testimony of taxonomy and the fossils seem not to count: New strata do show new forms, Sedgwick acknowledges. But each type remains perfect in its kind – "the noblest cephalopods and brachiopods that ever existed; and they preserve their typical forms till they disappear." Where are "the connecting organic links that ought to bind together the older fauna" with the new? Evolution, in the end, is pure conjecture: "You cannot make a good rope out of air bubbles." Where is the *vera causa* to explain extinction or adaptation? Natural selection is no more a cause than the passage of time.

Confessing a "deep aversion" for Darwin's "unflinching materialism," Sedgwick mingles his motives with his argument: Darwin's repudiation of final causes betrays "a demoralized understanding." Were the new approach to take hold, Sedgwick pleads in his personal letter, it would brutalize humanity. Exponents of evolution, then, are also its victims. Robbed of God and all thought of immortality, they've lost their moral compass and spiritual sextant. So much for the costs of evolution. But Sedgwick's scientific charge is epistemic: Darwin "has deserted the inductive track, the only track that leads to physical truth."

Darwin had not excluded final causes, in fact. But he had localized them. Organs, life processes, and behaviors still fulfill purposes. The strivings of living beings must now serve the interests of their populations. Biology will not speak for salvation history or its secular counterpart, inevitable progress. Purposes will not center on the human case, and most arise without forethought by their beneficiaries. If there is a single Darwinian good in which all creatures partake, it will be the flourishing of living beings "after their kind."

It's true that Darwin sought naturalistic explanations for phenomena long swept under the lush carpet of religious awe. But he's hardly alone in this. We don't damn physicians for tracing illnesses to micro-organisms, pollutants, or congenital defects, rather than evil spirits. Indeed, one strength of monotheism is its power to avoid ascribing salient events to capricious interventions. Religion, here, is allied with science against all bogeys – and all attempts to bribe, hoodwink, coerce, or manipulate the divine. As Wittgenstein says, "Religious faith and superstition are quite different. One of them results from *fear* and is a sort of false science. The other is a trusting."[2]

To deny natural causes their natural effects, Maimonides argues – as if forgetting that food sustains or medicines heal – is to treat such causes as created in vain.[3]

What about Darwin's reasoning? William Jennings Bryan echoes Sedgwick in calling evolution pure speculation. The accusation persists when evolution is called theory and not fact. That last charge rests on an equivocation: 'Theory' contrasts with 'fact' when it means conjecture, not when it tags a hypothesis well founded in evidence – like the theory of gravity. Theory is the fruit of inquiry. Facts are the seeds. They need to be interpreted – grown and cultivated, as it were – before we can see a definite meaning in them. Theories are corrigible. That's the beauty of science. But corrigibility does not mean subjectivity. Quite the contrary. What corrects, enlarges, or redirects a theory, tightening its grip on reality, are not our private or shared preferences but our fuller understanding of the world.

Plantinga courts the vulgar equivocation, chiding evolutionists like Ayala, Dawkins, and Gould for intolerance in their heated responses to the charge that evolution is mere theory. Given theism, he writes, special creation is "somewhat more probable" than common descent through natural selection,[4] and asks "whether evolution should be taught as the sober truth of the matter ... in the way arithmetic and chemistry and geography are taught" and not, "for example, the best current scientific hypothesis."[5] He caps that question with a gesture toward Creation Science: "the claim that the universe is young – is very hard to square with a variety of types of scientific evidence. ... Nonetheless, a sensible person might be convinced, after careful and prayerful study of the Scriptures, that what the Lord teaches there implies that this evidence is misleading and that as a matter of fact the earth really *is* very young. So far as I can see, there is nothing to rule this out as automatically pathological or irrational or irresponsible or stupid."[6] Plantinga here assigns scripture an epistemic role that wildly cants his brief for open minded appraisals of all the evidence. Despite Plantinga's hard-earned epistemological credentials, Sedgwick comes off the fairer critic, for laying his moral and spiritual cards on the table and not throwing his Bible onto the scales of evidence.

Sedgwick felt wounded by the *Origin*, but his critique is not mere rant. It hankers after Francis Bacon and his demand that science move beyond sheer speculation. Still Sedgwick's critique was wrongheaded. Darwin's reasoning was far different from induction in any vulgar sense: Evolution is no rule abstracted from multiple observations of species change. Its credibility rests on its power to explain. Its heuristic success transformed biology and accounts of inquiry as well. But Darwin's aim was not to change epistemology. His methods were not newfangled. He had reasoned much as we all do in relating seemingly disparate phenomena.

Rising to Darwin's defense, Thomas Henry Huxley ridiculed objectors "who have never determined a scientific fact in their lives by induction from experiment or observation" yet "prate learnedly about Mr Darwin's method, which is not inductive enough, not Baconian enough, forsooth, for them." Darwin's reasoning was "in exact accordance with the rule laid down by Mr Mill; he has endeavored to determine the great facts inductively, by observation and experiment; he has then reasoned from the data thus furnished; and lastly, he has tested the validity of his ratiocination by comparing his deductions with the observed facts of Nature."[7]

As his ironic Elizabethan interjection intimates, Huxley finds Sedgwick's epistemic strictures hopelessly outdated. John Stuart Mill's detailed analysis of scientific method plainly licensed Darwin's type of inferences. They were models of scientific reasoning. Hence Huxley's impatience. Yet Sedgwick was no fossil. He was not just a professor of Darwin's. He had taken him along on his pioneering geological survey of Wales in 1831 and trusted his novice assistant's independent observations. Indeed, Sedgwick had taught Darwin the rudiments of the method he would use in framing his theory. Near the start of their journey, Darwin, already an accomplished amateur beetle collector but hardly a master scientist, had tried to impress Sedgwick by telling about a tropical shell unearthed in the gravel pits near the family home in Shrewsbury. Sedgwick only laughed: One can't upend all we know with one pinprick of data. Facts must fit together if new hypotheses are to weather the counter-evidence. That seashell must have been someone's discard. No tropical sea had overlain that gravel pit. "Nothing before had ever made me thoroughly realise," Darwin wrote, "though I had read various scientific books, that science consists in grouping facts so that general laws or conclusions may be drawn from them."[8]

Huxley cites Mill's account of induction in *A System of Logic* (1843), to render canonical the inferences of the *Origin*. But the pattern followed in Darwin's reasoning is best described not there but in the *History of the Inductive Sciences* (1837) by William Whewell, a brilliant polymath known to Darwin since his student days at Cambridge.[9] Whewell coined the term consilience to characterize the convergence of evidence that conspires to sustain sound theories: A good hypothesis is no mere generalization but an explanation that yields new knowledge by piecing together facts from different quarters. A theory grows in cogency when it explains ever more of what we know, bringing the welter of experience not just to order but to understanding. Sedgwick knew this. It grounded his comments about Darwin's tropical shell. What blinded him to the strengths of evolution was what he took to be the tenor of Darwin's findings.

Sedgwick had long chafed at Lyell's uniformitarianism (another coinage of Whewell's), not from any love of catastrophism[10] but because Lyell had denied advancing trends among the fossils. An ally of Sedgwick's had even anticipated his put down, calling Lyell's work "amusing"! Both Lyell and Sedgwick fought shy of transmutationism – although Lyell was, in time, reluctantly won over. Sedgwick saw the fossil trends but balked at Darwin's "materialism"; the Designer's hand was plain in each new species. Darwin honored Lyell's method. But uniformitarianism for him meant gradual change, constancy of principles, not unchanging types. And Sedgwick's guiding hand gave way to the "invisible hand" of Adam Smith – that is, natural selection.[11] Increasing complexity bespoke no inner drive or external push for betterment. It was a byproduct of "the struggle for survival."

By qualifying Sedgwick and Lyell's views, Darwin overcame their differences and inconsistencies. His synthesis of the evidence[12] was the essence of good science on Whewell's account. Few theories have done that so well. No one today can advance a step biologically without Darwinian assumptions, whether in the cancer clinic, the epidemiological office, genomics or pharmaceuticals lab, dissecting room, tundra, forest, or desert. Does this ubiquity make evolution not a fact at all but a hope? That was Karl Popper's charge.

Is Darwinism vacuous?

Popper himself was an evolutionist, and the model of scientific progress for which he is best known is evolutionary. Uncomfortable about seeming to malign Darwinism, he searched for the right words and determined to call evolution not a theory but a metaphysical research program. Darwinians were not amused. No label but sound science would do. As they feared, the foe took up Popper's complaint.[13] Popper, always a maverick, trimmed his sails but did not readily recant. The structural weakness in Darwinism seemed plain to him. His personal trajectory made it a sort of moral imperative for him to state his case. Born in Vienna in 1902, he was impressed early on by the logical positivists of the Vienna Circle. Although not a member of the *Wienerkreis* himself, he was much taken by the project of these logicians and philosophers, marking off science from non-science. For them that meant sense from nonsense. Meaning, they argued, depends on verifiability. Empirical propositions were verifiable by the senses; those reducible to tautology lay in the sphere of logic and mathematics. Beyond formal truths and empiric facts loomed metaphysics – mere nonsense. Inquiring broadly into the character of being, metaphysics is filled with claims that look unverifiable – not propositions at all, then, but pseudo-statements, counterfeits of meaning.

The positivists' harsh criteria stripped all ethical and aesthetic claims of meaning. All affirmations *and denials* about God were nonsense, answering no question at all but addressing only pseudo-questions. Many claims about the past and future seemed to fail in meaning as well. So did all claims about what might have been. The verification criterion of meaning (VCM) was severe. So strict, in fact, that it failed by its own test: It did not look like a formal statement. For it seemed too controversial to pass as a definition. But if intended empirically it hardly captured what people often mean by meaning. It looks like a norm, in fact, about how to treat the idea of meaning. If so, its application (or imposition) involves a value judgment. But value judgments were supposed to be unverifiable.

To Popper the vcm looked no better than the metaphysics it proposed to displace, preening itself on the same pretensions it intended to discredit. Popper was not as chary as the Vienna purists of every discourse that reaches beyond the empirical. But he had been sensitized by the eely evasions of early interlocutors who were enchanted by the then fresh myths of Marx and Freud. He was frustrated by how hard it was to pin them down in argument. They seemed to turn every countercase into new support for their pet theory. That led Popper to turn from verificationism to falsifiability as a standard, not of meaning but of science: If a theory held regardless of all possible evidence, then whatever its intent it was not science. A proposition true in all possible worlds makes formal, not material claims. Scientific hypotheses take risks. They field predictions testable against experience. No claim about the world, Popper thought, is ever verified conclusively. But evidence can confirm (or strengthen) a hypothesis – or, he held, decisively refute one. So falsifiability is the acid test: An irrefutable proposition is not scientific.

Fascinated by evolution from his youth, Popper described scientific history in evolutionary terms: Discredited hypotheses are the extinct species. Evolution was not one of those. But it was unfalsifiable. So it was not science but just "a possible framework for testable scientific theories." In a world of some constancy, organisms adapted to their surroundings survive; "those which clash with the conditions," could be expected to be "eliminated." In such a world, "Darwinism becomes not merely applicable, but almost logically necessary."[14] It was not tautologous outright: It did not hold in all possible worlds. But biologists do apply it to any world where organisms bear heritable variations that enhance or compromise their reproduction. So Darwinism was not a sheerly formal claim. But in our world, Popper argued, Darwinism only seems to make falsifiable predictions. Its explanations don't really explain anything: They account for the survival of any living species by calling it adapted, and for all extinctions by calling the vanished types misfits. But that's just the way biologists use language. The whole evolutionary story turns on a circularity: "assume that we find life on Mars consisting of exactly three species of bacteria with a genetic outfit similar to that of three terrestrial species. Is Darwinism refuted? By no means. We shall say that these three species were the only forms among the many mutants which were sufficiently well adapted to survive."[15]

Popper admires Darwinism for offering an alternative to theistic accounts, which were "worse than an open admission of failure," since they "created the impression that an ultimate explanation had been reached." But when "Darwinism creates the same impression, it is not so very much better."[16] Popper's motives peep out here: He wants an open universe, where any claim can be overthrown. It's by edging toward universality that Darwinism

smacks of metaphysics. What sets off Popper's allergies is the whiff of dogmatism he scents in all claims to ultimacy. Theism, I would argue, is the
proper place for claims of that kind; it's because ultimates are its province
that theism needs to be so chaste and careful in its pronouncements – and so
open minded when it sets about to promulgate them. But is evolution vacuous?
Does it say simply that the fit survive because they're fit?

Darwinism is pretty clearly not trivial. Otherwise, why all the fuss? It does
make factual claims, evident when it talks about what there is: Existential
claims don't just spell out the meanings of words. Darwin, as Popper knows,
claims 1) that living beings vary, 2) that some variations are heritable, 3) that
resources (food, space, mates) are limited, 4) that life forms, therefore, face a
struggle to survive, and 5) that some traits are more helpful than others in
that struggle. True, it's tautologous to say that the fittest are the types that
best reproduce, if we measure fitness by reproductive success. But it's not
tautologous to say that some heritable traits confer reproductive advantage
or disadvantage – let alone to try and name them.

In calling Darwinism a metaphysical research program Popper meant to
honor biology while denying a key premise the status of fact. But adaptation
is a factual claim, meant to explain life's variety by way of natural selection. It's
because environments can make a trait adaptive or maladaptive that Darwinism is not circular. Adaptations are inherently relational, always tied to a
milieu. So claims about fitness are not empty. They always refer, obliquely, to
the facts about environmental challenges and the means by which they're met.

Darwinians do skilfully cover the bases: Useful traits are adaptations;
useless ones, markers of descent, preserved by their very irrelevance: What
was once useful may now survive just because it's tolerable.[17] Reasoning that
way, Darwin can accommodate divergent streams of evidence. But broad
coverage does not invalidate a theory. Abstract talk about adaptation may
sound circular. As Ernst Mayr writes, mimicking Popper's critique: "Who
survives? The fittest. Who are the fittest? Those that survive." But, "As soon
as one deals with specific cases, one can make predictions that can be falsified
in principle."[18] Vacuity vanishes.

One reason for the iridescent appearance and disappearance of circularity
is the alternating presumption or bracketing of Darwinian premises. Any
theory will look tautologous if its findings are made givens.[19] But Darwin's
ideas of fitness were matters of discovery. They were not always obvious.
Fleeming Jenkin actually labeled improved offspring *disadvantageous*, since
they compete with their parents![20] Much depends on where one locates biological interest and advantage – in parents, or offspring, or the lineage. But
to call a trait an adaptation is not to read off a definition but to tell a story
about enduring (or lost) benefits. Such stories are hardly truisms. The scope
of adaptation remains controversial in biology today: Some biologists seek a
use for every trait. Others stress genetic drift or founder effect. None of this
would be contested if a dictionary could settle the disputes. It's untrue that

Darwinism can accommodate just any data. If biologists did find life, but only a few species, on Mars (or in any exotic habitat), they would expect to see a relatively uniform environment. Darwinism would be discomfitted insofar as that prediction failed. It predicts biological diversity in a diverse environment. Manifold econiches open diverse opportunities; populations tend to push the resource envelope. But differences in reproductive success are not caused by tautologies.

Darwin himself did not seek safety in irrefragability. He does like to turn the tables on countercases, as we've seen. But his stepwise model of the emergence of complex behaviors like nest poaching by cuckoos, or slave making by ants, or the honey bee's hexagonal prisms, is hardly special pleading. Far from trying to stretch his story around the facts, Darwin characteristically enriches the evidential base when answering an objection. He's equally ready to name conditions that would invalidate his work: "If it could be proved that any part of the structure of any one species had been formed for the exclusive good of another species it would annihilate my theory," he writes. Again, if organic structures were shown to be created solely for their beauty or variety, that "would be absolutely fatal to my theory."[21] Claims about beauty, variety or exclusive dedication to other species would be hard to prove. So the admission may seem hollow. But it does highlight the contrast between Darwin's claims and much of the "transcendental biology" of his day. Natural selection demands that teleology remain local at its roots.

A critical admission stems from Darwin's insistence on gradualism: "My theory would absolutely break down," he says, "if it could be demonstrated that any complex organ existed, which could not possibly have been formed by numerous, successive, slight modifications."[22] Evolution, Darwin insists, does not move by leaps and bounds. He freely echoes Linnaeus: *natura non facit saltum*.[23] Saltation here would mean that "species have suddenly given birth, through quite unexplained means, to new and totally different forms." Such an account would hold "but little advantage" over "the old belief in the creation of species from the dust of the earth."[24]

Can evolution proceed by tiny steps? That's the question raised by exponents of Intelligent Design under the rubric of irreducible complexity. "By *irreducibly complex*," Michael Behe writes, "I mean a single system composed of several well-matched, interacting parts that contribute to the basic function, wherein the removal of any one of the parts causes the system to effectively cease functioning." Such systems, Behe argues, "cannot be produced directly ... by slight, successive modifications of a precursor system, because any precursor to an irreducibly complex system that is missing a part is by definition nonfunctional."[25]

Intelligent Design

Many biologists see this issue of gradualism as Darwin's Achilles' heel. C. H. Waddington, a committed evolutionist, called it the problem of "unbridgeable gaps." He hoped to bolster Darwinism to meet the challenge. But ID advocates aim not to shore up evolution but to find a place for God's work by testing the limits of natural selection. The brilliant structures and intricate processes of life, they argue, clearly bespeak a wise and purposive designer. They could not have emerged by natural means. ID advocates are not biblical inerrantists. They don't search for the hull of Noah's ark or hold creation to a strict six-day deadline. Chary of the sectarianism of creation science and wary of the extremes of the young earth, flood geology movement, they frame a minimalist position, welcoming allies of varied persuasions but reticent in speaking about God, lest ID be labeled a religious stance and barred from public classrooms. They prefer to state their critique and leave the creator's name and nature to their hearers.

Behe, a Catholic biochemist at Lehigh University, cites the cilium, the organelle that propels a sperm. Several hundred cilia beat rhythmically in each cell of the respiratory lining, clearing fluid from the air ducts. Each cilium is a bundle of fibers sheathed in an extension of the cell membrane. Viewed in cross section under the electron microscope, each fiber reveals a pair of microtubules, made up in turn of thirteen strands of a protein, tubulin. The pair is surrounded by nine more microtubules, each composed of fused thirteen-strand and ten-strand members. The charges on the protein chains line them up as fibers. Lateral connections align the central pair and link them to the nine peripheral tubules; and those, to each other. A knobby bulb caps the strand. "Motor proteins" called dynein project laterally from each peripheral microtubule. Experimental work with proteases, enzymes that snip proteins at key points, shows that the cilia beat when the parallel microtubules slide past each other as the dynein laterals move up and down their length. Connectors of a protein called nexin prevent overshooting, lest the mechanism unravel.

All the parts are needed, Behe argues. None has any use alone. So what would select for any, absent the organelle? How could the components arise piecemeal? "Just as a mousetrap does not work unless all of its constituent parts are present, ciliary motion simply does not exist in the absence of microtubules, connectors, and motors."[26] How, Behe asks, could anything as complex as a cilium emerge without foresight? Yet, as Dawkins insists, Darwin can't have it any other way: If complex organs (and behaviors) don't evolve gradually "we're back to miracle" and "evolution ceases to have any explanatory power at all."[27]

The flagellum, a whiplike filament anchored in the cell membrane of certain bacteria, actually rotates, turned by a ringlike "motor" at its base. Rather than count on ATP, the usual intracellular energy source, "a flow of acid through the bacterial membrane" powers the flagellum – another irreducibly complex organelle, Behe argues, seeing no way for natural selection to assemble its components: Thousands of papers have been published on the structure, yet "no scientist has *ever* published a model to account for the gradual evolution of this extraordinary molecular machine."[28]

Behe's appeal is not to complexity alone but to organicity: Components are useless outside the complex; organic systems bespeak a prior plan. Darwin faced similar objections when Sedgwick cited "the mutual adaptation of parts" and drew the familiar inference: "all around me a design and purpose."[29] St George Mivart wrote similarly in Darwin's time: "'Natural Selection' is incompetent to account for the incipient stages of useful structures."[30] The critics echo versions of the design argument running all the way back to Plato. Sailing a fleet or deploying an army, the Stoics said, demands direction; how much more so the budding of a vine – or the harmony of the cosmos: Either nothing is ruled by intelligence, or all things are. How can the little wisdom of a part exist without wise governance of the whole?[31] Organs would be useless, Galen argues, without coordination; animals would be helpless without behaviors to match: What use are wings unless birds can learn and teach their young to fly?

Even a clock or an orrery modeling the motions of the planets needs a designer, the Stoics said – a fortiori the vast clockwork of the heavens! How could these arise, as the Epicureans pretended, by random atomic collisions?[32] As in modern visions of monkeys at the keyboard, the Stoics invited their hearers to picture golden alphabets rattled and spilled from some great vessel. None would yield a line of verse, let alone an epic – not just because words would be rare and sentences rarer. A work of art – epic, tale, or play – is a coherent whole. Its parts connect in ways that mindless letters can't devise. Organisms, far more complex, point to a higher integration – ultimately, to the intelligent interaction of all things that Stoics called *sympatheia*. System matters here. ID, in the same spirit, takes seriously Aristotle's thought that parts in an organism are organs precisely by their active integration in the whole.[33] Aristotle finds proof that nature is not ruled by chance – first in causal regularities; but more pointedly, in the fitness of living beings. Nature imparts constancy – but also purposiveness: Incisors erupt in the front of the mouth, molars at the back.[34] Etienne Gilson sums up the thought: In living beings parts depend on wholes just as much as wholes depend on their parts.[35]

We've seen how Darwin answered the claim that wing stubs or eye parts would have no adaptive value before there was actual flight, or sight, proposing that there might have been "numerous gradations from a simple and imperfect eye to one complex and perfect," each useful in its own right. The "so-called flying lemur" showed how bats might have gained their wings. Existing organs take on new uses: Wings serve as fins and forelegs to the penguin, as sails to the ostrich, as flappers to the logger-head duck.[36] Selection pressures vary. So one can't presume that an organ's precursor had no useful function.

Darwin's answer didn't silence the critics. The debate continues. In 1994 Dan-Erik Nilsson and Susanne Pelger modeled the evolution of a serviceable eye from a light sensitive patch:[37] Steady selection pressures favoring fine tuned spatial data would make invagination inevitable in time, creating a hollow, its aperture constricting as if to form a pinhole camera. Changes in the matter inside would yield a focal length 2.55 times the chamber's radius, "ideal" for "a graded-index lens with a refractive index of 1.52" – "close to the upper limit for biological material."[38] In 1829 steps, successive 1% improvements would expand the initial patch some 80 millionfold, to a simple focusing eye like that of an aquatic animal. That would take 363,992 generations, or as many years, in small aquatic animals that spawn annually.

It was not explained how each generation could steadily improve by a full percent. Nor does the model account for binocular vision, or the origin of rhodopsin, the retinal pigment that shifts chemically when struck by light, producing an electrical impulse. Nor does it cover the nerves and the brain advances needed to make vision usable. The evolution of the iris, which enhances blood flow to the eye and adjusts to varied light conditions, was omitted, as were the muscles that focus the lens on near or distant objects.

It was the coordination of parts with behaviors that convinced Galen that organic design was providential. ID proponents still ask how else such dovetailing could occur. Their adversaries seem to them to lay all organic complexity to chance. I think the eye, like any useful organ, did evolve. Perhaps the best evidence is the analogy of squid and mammalian eyes. An insect's compound eyes use quite different principles, but the squid's eye is remarkably like ours. Since most molluscs lack eyes, it's natural to infer a striking case of evolutionary convergence – although we can't pretend today to know each step along the way. But chance, in the polemicist's sense, seems too crude a name for the process.

Nilsson and Pelger's model was scored by David Berlinski, an ID exponent: They did not explain the origin of their light-sensitive cells, let alone the requisite blood vessels, nerves, and skeletal support structures. Berlinski criticizes their lumping together morphological and biochemical changes in a single incremental result, gauged in enhanced visual acuity. He finds the 1829 steps highly arbitrary. Dawkins and others credited computer simulations in developing the model. But Nilsson forthrightly confessed that his essays at such simulations failed.[39]

Appeals to the eye, long a fixture in arguments for design, are updated by Behe, with systems theory, biochemistry, and cytology. Far from the simplicity that some early naturalists expected to find within the cell we discover immense complexity. Hence Behe's title, *Darwin's Black Box*: When the box is opened by electron microscopy and molecular analysis, we find systems within systems. Such subassemblies, ID advocates argue, presuppose a living organism. Like the Stoics, they vault from here to a higher wisdom. For the Stoics, that wisdom resided in *pneuma*, the divine spirit, pervasive, artistic, pulsing with energy all through the world, like the soul of a living being. Such visions helped transform ancient animism into vitalism. But Behe, unlike yesterday's vitalists, is unfazed by the thought that animals are machines.

He illustrates the flagellum with schematics in the style of industrial designs.[40] But he finds mystery in mechanism, and irreducible complexity even in the smallest organic subsystems.

Lovingly detailing the cascade of stages in the clotting of blood, Behe calls living systems Rube Goldberg machines: Intricate feedback loops regulate life processes and demand coordination of the "separate pieces each acting in turn, one after the other, to accomplish its function." If "removal of any one of the parts causes the system to cease functioning,"[41] and no part has value apart from the whole, how could the cogs and levers active at each stage possibly have evolved? Rhetorical questions of this sort mark Behe's argument as a classic *reductio ad ignorantiam*, all but echoing the language Hume assigns to Cleanthes, the natural theologian in his *Dialogues Concerning Natural Religion*:

> Look round the world: Contemplate the whole and every part of it. You will find it to be nothing but one great machine, subdivided into an infinite number of lesser machines, which again admit of subdivisions, to a degree beyond what human sense and faculties can trace and explain ... [42]

Behe's claim is not just that explanation would be difficult. There's a Catch-22: You can't get A without B, C, and D ... all the way to N. But the whole series depends in turn on A. Indeed, Behe's model is not as linear as a Rube Goldberg invention: The parts all depend on one another. None would work without the rest – at least, no one seems able to say how.

That fact throws "an enormous monkey wrench" into Darwin's gradual-ism.[43] Behe reports searching fruitlessly for scientific papers that even try to answer his questions. The trouble is that at any moment just such studies might appear. Even in the few years since Behe threw down his gauntlet, many have appeared. Some, in fact, were published before his 1996 book. Neil Blackstone mentions a few: Clotting, researchers argued in 1992, may have begun as a defense against bacterial toxins.[44] Archaebacteria seem to have a prototype for the protein-degrading enzymes found in more advanced species.[45] Blackstone infers: "the antigen-presenting role of these molecules in the mammalian immune system clearly derives from such primitive func-tions."[46] T-cells, he adds, "cannot replicate without performing their immune system functions"; so they may perform functions not only in immune response but also in regulating tissue growth.[47] They may have been active at one job when adapted to another.

A telling model is found in hormones. A hormone does its work of com-mand and control through the responses of a receptor that it fits like a key in a lock. Neither component works without the other. So a mutation promoting production of a hormone would be useless without corresponding changes to promote its complement. Otherwise having a hormone would be like having a telephone that no one could answer. It's not just another phone that's needed. There have to be phone lines or cell towers, and processing systems. But recent findings suggest that pre-existing structures might have been reconfigured as receptors. Joseph Thornton and his colleagues studied hormone receptors in 59 species, including primitive, jawless fish and skates. Calculating the point of divergence of these types on evolutionary assumptions, the investigators synthesized a generic receptor that could bind with two distinct hormones. A new hormone could have arisen through a mutation and found a receptor already at work in tandem with the original hormone.[48] So the new adaptation was not drawing to an inside straight.

Similarly with the loblolly pine. As Niall Shanks and Karl Joplin explain, tree trunks get their rigidity from lignins, complex polymers of two alcohol monomers. One of these, appropriately named conifer alcohol, typically makes up 90% of the lignin. A specific enzyme forms it from a corresponding aldehyde. But a mutation can reduce that enzyme's effectiveness by 99%. Still, the mutant trees grow normally, using an alternative alcohol derived by a different biochemical pathway. Redundancy takes the sting out of the ID argument: A complex system need not be fragile and inflexible just because it's intricate.[49] Massimo Pigliucci explains,

> Redundancy is a common feature of living organisms where different genes are involved in the same or in partially overlapping functions. While this may seem a waste, mathematical models show that evolution by natural selection has to imply molecular redundancy, because when a new function is necessary it cannot be carried out by a gene that is already doing something else, without compromising the original function. On the other hand, if the gene gets duplicated (by mutation), one copy is freed from immediate constraints and can slowly diverge in structure from the original, eventually taking over new functions. This process leads to the formation of gene "families" … e.g., those governing the globins, which vary from proteins allowing muscle contraction to those involved in the exchange of oxygen and carbon dioxide in the blood … mutations can knock down individual components of biochemical pathways without compromising the overall function – contrary to the expectations of irreducible complexity.[50]

Redundancy affords alternative pathways that carry on the work of disabled genes: "there are at least 400 proteins associated with the proper control of the cell cycle alone." Some of these may pick up the slack where others fail.[51] Tank commanders think the same way. They carry spare parts and use field ingenuity to adapt parts for uses never originally intended. Sexual reproduction favors the coopting of useful alleles, bringing together potentially complementary genes. So we can hardly assume that the natural masterpieces we know did not emerge by small steps from cruder antecedents.

Redundancy is not the whole answer, then, but it does defuse the charge that living systems cannot function, let alone arise, except as completed wholes. Today's backup system might well have been the default in ages past. One can still ask how the ancestral system itself arose. But breaking down a system into subassemblies or processes with a prior function at an earlier evolutionary stage turns the big poser about the piecemeal emergence of elaborate systems or sequences into a series of smaller questions far more amenable to biological investigation. The claim that the complex that impresses us now would be useless absent just one part loses its bite. As Kenneth Miller writes, "nature is filled with examples of 'precursors' to the flagellum that are indeed 'missing a part,' and yet fully functional. Functional enough, in some cases to pose a threat to human life."[52] For example, the TTSS (Type III secretion system) used by highly virulent bacteria to inject their toxins into a host's cytoplasm is composed of proteins "directly homologous to the proteins in the basal portion of the bacterial flagellum."

> [T]he opportunism of evolutionary processes would mix and match proteins to produce new and novel functions. ... The existence of TTSS in a wide variety of bacteria demonstrates that a small portion of the 'irreducibly complex' flagellum can indeed carry out an important biological function.[53]

The electron transport chain, Blackstone writes, is a "membrane-bound series of redox carriers" that transfers energy from catalyst to catalyst – "flavoproteins, quinones, and cytochromes" – within the cell. Passing electrons "from one carrier to the next and extruding protons," it yields ATP. The "marvelous precision," of the system, "arguably the most widespread, complex, and critical biochemical mechanism known," might have made it the poster child of Intelligent Design. But Behe gave it short shrift, sidestepping "the abundant literature concerning its evolution" – since the steps needed to build this triumph of evolution, as Blackstone calls it, were not obscure.[54]

Just as Darwin reasoned that "pre-existing structures and capacities are utilised for new purposes"[55] in gross anatomy and animal behavior, his successors propose biochemical or cytological precursors with functions quite different from those of the new hormone, enzyme, or organelle. That gives evolution plenty of stepping stones. But one need not fill in every gap to gain confidence that future research will do so. Behe plays up the knowledge gaps. The processes are, indeed, amazingly complex. Still, a *reductio ad ignorantiam* is inherently inconclusive. It issues a challenge but does not prove that what it asks for is impossible, or that relevant evidence won't be found, perhaps with new conceptual tools as elegant and novel to us as the Jacob–Monod model was in explaining the genetic regulation of physiology and development. After all, when McCarty first proposed DNA as the blueprint of heredity, most biologists thought its chemistry far too simple. No substance less baroque than a protein seemed equal to the task. But, as Cronin says, it's hard, perhaps impossible, to reconstruct the steps it took to bake a cake, given only the cake. Yet that does not make baking impossible.[56]

A sanctuary of ignorance?

Spinoza was the first philosopher to call out *reductio ad ignorantiam* as a fallacy. John Locke usually gets the credit. His 1690 *Essay Concerning Human Understanding* labels it a tactic for shifting the burden of proof, "to drive others and force them to submit," by requiring them to accept one's argument or find a better.[57] The argument, Leibniz responded, "is sound in cases where there is a presumption, such that it is reasonable to hold to one opinion until its contrary is proved."[58] The natural question is how to identify the default position. After all, Darwin too frequently challenges his critics with *their* weakness in explaining, say, the shape of the taxonomic tree, or the persistence of "rudimentary" organs. Who has the burden of proof? Sometimes convention preempts the decision: The accused is innocent until proven guilty. But that presumption reflects our desire to spare the innocent. It won't settle the facts. And in Darwinian debates there is no agreement about the onus of argument.

John Woods and Douglas Walton, twentieth-century logicians, write: "it is not easy to see how there is anything fallacious in what Locke described" – as long as there's some good argument to backstop the demand for a better.[59] Unrefuted does not mean true. But neither do demands for counterarguments make a thesis false. It's easy to tilt the table by shoving a skeptical wedge under one leg of an argument. Theism is often greeted in that way. But the same can be done with atheism – despite the familiar alliance of skepticism with denial.

Most systems of logic, Woods and Walton remark, are not sensitive enough to the pragmatics of discourse to afford good rules about burdens of proof.[60] Any pat scheme would leave questions about how fair and topic neutral it was. Providing enough context to frame a workable convention would open up the space for bias. Logic can't settle every debate. It does mark the Intelligent Design challenge as dialectical, not demonstrative: ID doesn't refute Darwinism. It just points to questions still unanswered and uses any sketchy answers to prop the door open to preferred, theistic alternatives. Evolutionists promise the challenges will be met. ID advocates are dubious. I think their approach ill advised for theists, both tactically and strategically. Spinoza helps show why.

Published soon after his death in 1677, Spinoza's *Ethics* was finished by 1675. The Appendix to Part I, completed by 1665, pinions the *reductio ad ignorantiam* and coins the name. Spinoza's target, like Locke's, was over-reliance on divine agency.[61] The presumption that God acts arbitrarily and orders all things with a view to human weal or woe, Spinoza insists, turns outcomes into causes, transforms the great features and forces of nature into mere instruments, and robs God of perfection, by speaking as if God had wants or needs:

> Not to be overlooked is how partisans of this doctrine, eager to show their genius for assigning purposes, have deployed a new mode of argument to support their view, a *reductio* not *ad impossibile*, actually, but *ad ignorantiam* – showing only that they had no other way of arguing this doctrine of theirs.[62]

Spinoza focuses on partisans of personal providence: A man is killed when a stone falls from the roof. There are always those who ask why the wind blew it down at just that moment – and why the poor man walked by just then. "They won't stop asking for the causes of these causes, until you take refuge in God's will, the sanctuary of ignorance."[63] We humans, Spinoza reasons, always act for an end. Ignorant of the relevant causes, or ignoring them on the supposition that all events (or the ones we deem portentous) must have motives too, we seek intentions behind every occurrence, serving or disdaining our wants and needs.

Spinoza had earlier branded appeals to God's will the sanctuary of ignorance. Writing in 1661 to Henry Oldenburg, the man who brought together the circle of savants (Locke included) that would become the British Royal Society, Spinoza had vehemently contrasted the search for causes with empty appeals to "inexplicable forms and occult qualities."[64] The *Ethics* keeps the contrast alive, between the scientist's commitment to natural explanations and the vague obeisances to the divine offered as alternatives:

> Seeing the structure of the human body they're dumbfounded. Ignorant of the causes of such fine work, they conclude that it is fashioned not by mechanical but by divine, supernatural art, and so made that one part does not harm the next.[65]

Spinoza too sees all things as God's work. But he does not picture God tinkering with the world, every act a magical intrusion. Like Aristotle, he finds it uninformative to leapfrog over proximate causes in a rush to name the ultimate cause, which will always be the same. He has little patience for anthropocentric cosmologies:

> Finding quite a few things, within and outside themselves, that are useful in prosecuting their interests – eyes for seeing, teeth for chewing, plants and animals for food, the sun to light the way, the sea for breeding fish – they come to regard all natural things as mere means to their own advantage. They know they found these things and did not make them. So they assume the cause was someone else who provided all these means for their use.[66]

Spinoza echoes Maimonides' admonition against arrogantly imagining, say, that the stars exist simply for our sake.[67] He flares up at obscurantists who block the search for natural causes and usurp authority by projecting human appetites and passions onto the divine. They turn humble recognition of our ignorance into neglect of the very inquiries that would mend it:

> it's laughable to see Philosophers take refuge in God's will whenever they're ignorant of the causes of things … I think this mistake alone is the root of all superstition, and doubtless much knavery as well.[68]

The knavery: exploitation of ignorance and usurpation of God's good name.

Spinoza confronts irreducible complexity in an ancient conundrum about the first tools: How could tongs be made without a hammer to pound the iron flat; or a hammer, without tongs to hold it to the fire?[69] Such puzzles dissolve, he answers, when we conceive our forebears starting with the simplest devices – perhaps their bare hands – and gradually making other tools, until they could tackle the most intricate tasks. Today we need computers to make cars and can't build cars without computers. But that doesn't prove that cars and computers were never built. Evolution here is not a quandary but part of an explanation. The old conundrum was embedded in the way the problem was posed. Is that true in biology too?

Anthropomorphism can make the deity a refuge of ignorance – a God of the gaps, summoned when we're at wit's end, otherwise dispensable. That's what Aubrey Moore warned of: appealing to God in the clinches but leaving nature disconnected day-to-day. Plantinga, who was present at the foundation of the ID effort, spurns appealing to a God of the gaps. God, he insists, is active constantly, sustaining the world and those he loves. Yet Plantinga does invoke a God of the gaps when he urges that if science "after considerable study," just can't see how some event "could possibly have happened by way of the ordinary workings of matter," then, for theists at least, "the natural thing to think is that God did something different and special here."[70]

Natural, perhaps, but not rational. It means shifting our gaze from the event that caught our eye or captured our heart, to some surrogate for natural causes, rather than search for the deeper causality that made possible this event so arresting to us. Plantinga gives science the first shot at explanation. But he keeps God in the wings, egging on faith against reason. That puts piety on a false footing and denigrates creation – as if all nature were not miraculous. The trouble with a God of the gaps is plainest in pragmatic terms: Such gods will shrink as causal understanding grows. That's bad tactics for believers. It puts theism on the defensive. God cowers in the corners, where light has not yet banished every lurking hobgoblin. God retreats as knowledge advances, his dominion ever smaller. Bad strategy as well, then, since theists *should* see God everywhere, as Plantinga intends, not just where fear and ignorance (or their half-sisters, hope and complacency) take hold.

Spinoza's alternative is recognition that when things pursue their natures they're not contravening but enacting God's decree. God acts in and through nature, not despite it, not just in unsolved mysteries or stunning acts of favor but in all things. That makes understanding, including scientific understanding, not the enemy but the ally of religion. The two are not set against each other as light against darkness (each calling the other by the uglier name). Science does not advance by discrediting religion; religion need not appeal to ignorance. It need only remember that "God's will is clearest to us when we conceive things clearly and distinctly."[71]

Beyond a God of the gaps

The rhetoric of the *ad ignorantiam* is ancient, precedented even in God's challenge to Job from the stormwind, asking, if Job knew how mountain goats give birth, how ravens are fed, where the hail arises.[72] The power in such questions lies not in their having no answer but in the sense of awe they invite. Balbus, cast in Stoic garb by Cicero, finds humanity jaded. We take everyday marvels too much for granted. The sky would seem a miracle if we had never seen it:

> From daily habit and familiarity our eyes and minds have grown used to the sight, and we no longer marvel at it or seek an explanation for it, since we see it constantly – as if it were the novelty and not the greatness of a thing that should rouse us to seek its cause.[73]

The sky is not a clock or orrery that needs a tinkering craftsman. It's a natural marvel that invites a search for causes. Knowing how refraction makes the sky blue or how fusion makes the sun shine can't shrink the sense of awe it inspires. Curiosity about natural causes need not preclude but invites the sense of joy that can open up into religious experience. Science here goes hand in hand with spirituality. The sense of the sublime that familiarity may dull but art may reawaken is a natural prelude, partner, and outcome of scientific inquiry, and religious awe. That's evident in Blackstone's celebratory language about electron transfer and the discoveries that unveil its workings. The sense of mystery that matters religiously does not sink comfortably into ignorance or cower in the dark. It's a livelier, healthier response, elated by a sense of the power behind nature's manifest powers, profusion and prodigality – part of the sense of wonder that Aristotle saw at the spring of every inquiry. It's no mere failure of nerve or understanding. So, as A. J. Heschel teaches, it's not threatened by discovery.[74] Gilson explains:

> We do not come upon it only at the climax of thinking or in observing strange, extraordinary facts but in the startling fact that there are facts at all: being, the universe, the unfolding of time. We may face it at every turn, in a grain of sand, in an atom, as well as in the stellar space.[75]

These thoughts do touch on metaphysics, just where it edges beyond science, thinking more broadly, perhaps more deeply, fishing for what Aristotle called *archai*, ultimates.

The distinction between ignorance and the sense wonder that may ignite religious awe helps clarify Behe's ease with mechanism. Theists see hallmarks of wisdom in nature. Knowledge is no detriment. But Behe, adopting the role of a lonely champion who faces truculent philistines, uses the language he expects to find most telling. Ignorance looks like a nice smooth stone for his slingshot. Gaps in scientific knowledge look like chinks in Darwin's armor.

Gilson finds higher ground and a broader vision, seeing more beauty in the works of nature than in those of art. As Aristotle admonishes his some-times squeamish tyros in dissection, if we appreciate art works for their vir-tuosity in representing nature, all the more should we marvel at the originals, with their consummate "absence of haphazard and the conduciveness of everything to an end." Isn't that end, in any living creature, "a form of the beautiful"?[76] Beauty here aligns with function, and nature educates our aes-thetic sense by linking form with function. Darwin echoes that response, seeing "beautiful and curious adaptations everywhere in the organic world."[77] Such thoughts, Gilson argues, push the search for truth beyond a quest for utility.[78] But even utility bespeaks a larger good than mechanism knows – and there's beauty in mechanism too, as Behe and many another naturalist would agree.

Rejecting the reductionism of his own day, Aristotle argued that a student of nature must consider not just the least parts and matter of an organism but also the idea or plan that knits it together.[79] But if Aristotle taught us anything biologically it was that these two, form and matter, are inseparable. What shapes their union in every organism is a local good, the good of that creature and its kind. It's this thought that enables Aristotle to see order and beauty in the world and even generalize: "nature does nothing in vain."[80] Darwin carries that thought further, by discovering how living species pursue and enlarge their purposes, beyond the stable natures of their kinds. When scientists learned the role of DNA and set about decoding its language, they touched the nexus between matter and idea, where genetic messages translate into the structures and processes of life. No philistine could credibly deny that the purport of these messages was a local good, beautiful in its own distinctive way.

Einstein often reflected on facets of his work that many another inquirer lacks the courage or the words to acknowledge. Describing the emotions that spurred his quest, and reaffirming the trust that underlay it, he wrote: "I have found no better expression than religious for confidence in the rational nature of reality, insofar as it is accessible to human reason. Whenever this feeling is absent, science degenerates into uninspired empiricism."[81] Science should be inspired, not starkly empirical, blankly totting up data. Its impetus is faith in nature's rationality. Its successes confirm that faith, awed but not afraid: "In every true searcher of Nature there is a kind of religious reverence. For he finds it impossible to imagine that he is the first to have thought out the exceedingly delicate threads that connect his perceptions."[82] Einstein alludes cautiously to a higher wisdom, his humility well worth emulation. The thought that nature really is as we find it to be, that its patterns and regularities are not just our inventions or impositions, joins hands with the idea of exquisite design – not mimicking but outcoursing the human sense of the rational.

> You will hardly find one among the profounder sort of scientific minds without a religious feeling of his own. ... The scientist is possessed by a sense of universal causation. ... His religious feeling takes the form of a rapturous amazement at the harmony of natural law, which reveals an intelligence of such superiority that, compared with it, all the systematic thinking and acting of human beings is an utterly insignificant reflection. ... It is beyond question closely akin to that which has possessed the religious geniuses of all ages.[83]

Scientists, like prophets, make sense of the world – or rather, find a sense they did not make. The prophetic voices that urge us to look to the heavens and consider their Creator (Isaiah 40:26, Psalms 8:4, 19:2) soar up from the plain of gray neutrality that many reductionists expect to inhabit. So, when Isaiah says *Lift up your eyes and look about* (60:4), Heschel hears an invocation to rise above mere *sensing*, to "the silent allusion of things to a meaning greater than themselves. It is that which all things ultimately stand for." Sublimity is "not a thing, a quality, but rather a happening, an act of God, a marvel" – an opening, "a way in which things react to the presence of God."[84]

Glaucon, in the *Republic* (VII 529), suggests that the Guardians should study astronomy. It sets the mind on "higher things." Socrates laughs: As if "anyone with his head cocked back should learn something by staring at decorations on the ceiling." If it's just a matter of *looking* at the sky, one might better say the soul is looking *down*. But grasping the mathematical loveliness of the heavenly motions does draw the soul toward the Transcendent. "A scientific theory, once it is announced," Heschel writes, "does not have to be repeated twice a day." But "insights of wonder must be constantly kept alive. Since there is a need for daily wonder, there is a need for daily worship"[85] – hence the Hebrew liturgy's proclamation of God's unique and loving sovereignty, morning and evening. Linking ritual to wonder, Heschel highlights not just the contrast of discovery with archived science but also the risk of ritual's hardening into rote. The discoverer's joy can be trapped in hidebound volumes, but it can also be rubbed away by the friction of polemic, leaving only anger, anxiety, and dogmatism.

Heschel sees three ways of relating to nature: "we may exploit it, we may enjoy it, we may accept it in awe."[86] Science and technology pursue the first two. Awe goes further. As Wittgenstein wrote, "Man has to awaken to wonder – and so perhaps do peoples. Science is a way of sending him to sleep again."[87] Science is not to blame here but the scientism that hides behind the good name of science. Technology need not be exploitative, and science need not be soporific. But both can be used and taught that way. So can religion. Wonder is an art, not just a state of mind, an awakening for both science and religion. Awe, of course, is no substitute for understanding. That's the lapse Spinoza condemned. As Heschel warns,

> The sense of wonder and transcendence must not become "a cushion for the lazy intellect." It must not become a substitute for analysis where analysis is possible; it must not stifle doubt where doubt is legitimate. It must, however, remain a constant awareness if man is to remain true to the dignity of God's creation, because such awareness is the spring of all creative thinking.[88]

Awe is hardly foreign to science, or technology. But reverence for the ultimate source of the marvels we encounter, in nature or in human creativity, is the province of religion. To displace that reverence, project it onto the works of our own hands or the figments of our fears and wishes, is the heart of idolatry, returning the extraordinary to the ordinary, for presumptive ease of handling. Better no religion than that. Here monotheism and atheism can agree. But monotheism takes wing in the recognition that awe is not the same as terror, and gratitude not the same as greed; religion is not fire insurance and is never the same as self-satisfaction.

What prompts some to seek shelter in Intelligent Design is the scientistic insistence that only naturalistic explanations score. The polemicists who use Darwin as a stick to beat religion readily assume that natural causality is the enemy of theism. Their rivals can fall into the same trap: The *reductio ad ignorantiam* echoes the notion that natural causes diminish God's role. Buying into the assumption that miracles are contraventions of nature instead of its marvels, the exponents of ID set up their own defeat when they demand supernatural explanations where they find science lacking – as if any natural process could be wrenched from its natural setting and still yield its natural effects.

But ID advocates rightly bridle at the notion that when we're out of mechanism we're out of truth. On the contrary, it's as misguided to substitute proximate for ultimate causes as it is to proffer ultimates when more immediate explanations are sought. If we want to know the ultimate source of value – of beauty, truth, goodness, even existence – mechanism has nothing to contribute. Fobbing off seekers with tales of subtle infracellular reactions is no response. Writers like Dennett and Dawkins reject the very idea of an

ultimate source of value. Mechanisms are the only explanations they countenance. But, like any claim about ultimates, this exclusion too belongs to
metaphysics. It's not a discovery of Darwin's but just another attempt to
squeeze evolution for implications far beyond its reach.

It was seeing Darwinism dragooned into the service of denial that provoked the attorney Phillip Johnson to help found the ID movement, aiming
to confront dogmatic naturalists who rule out any role for God and try to
block even discussion of ultimate questions. Johnson reads in Dawkins that
all scientific evolutionists "despise" creationists, as "dishonest propagandists,
persons who probably only pretend to disbelieve what they must know in
their hearts to be the truth of naturalistic evolution."[89] Barbs of that sort
hardly clear the air. Richard Lewontin, a Marxist geneticist from Harvard,
long inveighed against reductionism in biology. Having often faced the ire of
his fellow scientists, he adopts the accusatory *we*:

> We take the side of science *in spite* of the patent absurdity of some of its
> constructs, *in spite* of its failure to fulfill many of its extravagant promises
> of health and life, *in spite* of the tolerance of the scientific community
> for unsubstantiated just-so stories, because we have a prior commitment,
> a commitment to materialism.[90]

Lewontin's confessional resonates with ID writers.[91] The adversaries of
theism begin innocently enough, as epistemological naturalists. They rightly
define the scientist's job as finding natural explanations for natural phenomena. But they and their camp followers often move on to claim a
broader mandate. Slipping from methodological to metaphysical naturalism,
they ridicule any sort of explanation beyond what they approve and practice,
debarring not just from science but from conversation any reference to realities beyond what their favored methods countenance. That kind of pre-
emption, ruling theistic claims out of court, is what got Johnson's dander up
and prompted the ID confraternity to join ranks in seeking to shift the
burden of proof and calling out the gaps in evolutionary theory. Yet, as Ruse
writes, "No sound argument has been mounted showing that Darwinism
implies atheism. The atheism is smuggled in."[92]

Seeing reductionists lean back in their adirondack chairs, blowing smoke
rings at the very idea of design, Behe, for one, took a swift kick at the two
chair legs still on the floor. Organisms, he argued, are not just complicated.
They're irreducibly complex; their parts, interdependent. Their subsystems
could not have arisen without prior purpose and intent. I think Behe over-
states his case. Design, as I see it, is an emergent property in living species. If
life is not a throw of the dice, neither is it a preset script. That would belie
the open future. But the imagery of chance, cherished by mechanists from
Democritus to Monod, is no more apt in describing evolution than Paley's
watchmaker image is in speaking of the living God.

God is not Rube Goldberg, starting with a need and then building some contraption to win through to the end in view. Eternity does not march from niche to niche, as evolution does, or work back from ends to means, as human projects do. In God the Alpha is the Omega. How eternity manifests itself in a world of temporal sequences and purposive projects is a question that science makes us more able to chart than we are to map the thoughts of a timeless Creator. Time, Plato said, is the moving image of eternity. But time is where we live. We learn its games, sometimes in the sciences, sometimes in the arts, or in our lives with one another. For it wasn't only Einstein who caught a glimpse into God's mind. So did Darwin, and Mendel, and every inquirer who sees sense in nature, every artist who responds to beauty, and every person who sees the light in a child's eyes. We catch a glimpse of God's idea not within his mind but actively expressed in the world we know.

God gives living beings an impetus toward their own good and that of their kind. Godgiven strengths aid in the seeking of those goods. The act of creation sets each organism in an environment where its good can be sought – not scripted, not guaranteed, since the surround is thick with the projects of other beings, each reaching for its own good in its own way.

Glossing the verse *Will He who plants the ear not hear; will He who forms the eye not see?* (Psalms 94:9), Maimonides observes that the imagery does not imply, as if by parity of reasoning, that "the Creator of the mouth must eat, the Creator of the lung must shout" (*Guide* III 19). Divine knowing is of a different order from human understanding. But one can't fashion a needle without any idea of sewing: The absolute Inventor must know his creatures not by study and experience, as we might learn about a mechanism by taking it apart, but timelessly – working not as an artisan but as an immanent and eminent cause – eminent in the sense of adequacy to the effect out of the richness of a fuller reality. The creations, in this case, are living species, brought to birth through the midwifery of all that *does* lie on their plane. Created nature affords the matter and milieu and engine of ongoing creation.

5

"That has its seeds within it"

Genesis tells us that God created heaven and earth, but not how. For that we need science. Science tells us how things work, but not why. For that, if such questions deserve an answer, people turn to religion. Religions seek meanings, as it's sometimes put. That seems a fair division of labor. But religion cares about facts too, and science is incomplete if it ignores values.

Many Bible readers press scripture for a cosmology. Others assume that science preempts whatever scripture may relate. Religions, they assume, like mushrooms, thrive best in the dark. Focusing on the colorful words, quaint rituals, and sometimes violent doings of extremists, they cast all piety as regressive and repressive. Darwin becomes a culture hero for topping off the labors of Democritus and Epicurus by reducing teleology to mechanism, freeing humanity from baneful fantasies, making atheism not just respectable but obligatory. Modernity means replacing myths of value and purpose with hard facts about necessity and chance. Human nature, choice and freedom, reason, insight, awe, and love are just the products of vast, uncaring subatomic and molecular roulette.

More than a little autobiography may hide between the lines of such valedictories. Choler bespeaks a sense of loss: All deities must be swept away once feet of clay are glimpsed on childhood's household gods. Even right and wrong may be tossed into the same bin as God's six-day work week. These too, Nietzsche said, are ghosts of God. If scripture can't be silenced it can at least be gagged, squeezed into the crudest possible reading. Some people, of course, love the dark and don't want to know how God creates, fearing, like children at a magic show, that miracles will vanish once the mystery is known. Yet there's broad and fertile ground between the literalism that finds no truth in poetry and the rival literalism aghast at the thought of poetry in prophecy, eager to offer up science on the altar of a God who never asked for that sacrifice.

Still, Darwin did not purge value from nature or reduce biology to chance. Nor does Darwinism dissolve human dignity and freedom. Living beings do have worth, nearest to hand in the human case, where values are chosen and projects devised with conscious intent. If evolution announces anything, it proclaims precedents for the pursuit of value. Just as the worth of being and the dignity of persons opened the way to the discovery of monotheism, so do the emergence of purpose and subjecthood make evolution itself a powerful argument for creation. Reductionists may slight such values. But who then is turning a blind eye to the evidence?

Seeds

Biblically, God caused plants and trees to spring up from the earth, not from thin air. The plants bore seeds, and fruit, also holding seeds to propagate their kind (Genesis 1:11–12). New plants were not continually created afresh. God works through nature. Science shows us how. Does God enlist the DNA as well – what my mother, in a poem of hers, once called God's love letters to humanity? Smoothing over the Hebrew, translators offer something like this: *God blessed the seventh day and made it holy. For then He ceased from all the work He had done* (Genesis 2:3). But the Hebrew trails an infinitive: *all the work God had created to make* (la-'asot). Ibn Janah and Nahmanides link that last with *ceased* – thus, "ceased making": God's work finished, He stopped. That parses. But it does suggest that God went into retirement once the world was done. Ibn Ezra and Kimhi, as we've seen, find a hint that creatures must finish God's work. As Ernan McMullin writes: "instead of inserting new kinds of plants and animals ready-made, as it were, into a pre-existing world, God must be thought of as creating in that very first moment the potencies for all the kinds of living things that would come later, including the human body itself."[1]

Glossing *the day the Lord God made earth and heaven* (Genesis 2:4), the Rabbis suggest that all was ready on the first day.[2] Augustine develops the theme, which we've already met in the Midrash and Maimonides: "Latent in the seed was all that would in time become a tree." God made "not just the heavens, with sun, moon, and stars ... but also the beings that water and earth contained, in their potency and in their causes, before they issued over time."[3] God imparts capacities to develop – including, we now know, the potentials of species to adapt. Thus Darwin speaks of "the laws impressed on matter by the Creator,"[4] and suggests: "some few organic beings were originally created, which were endowed with a high power of generation, and with the capacity for some slight heritable variability"[5] – keys to evolution.

The Midrash imagines nature empowered to bring forth new things, as figs ripen on a tree (Genesis Rabbah 12.4). The earth was not pregnant with plants. But it held what they needed to spring up and flourish. The Malbim elaborates: "Creation advances from stage to stage: mineral, vegetable, animal, human. All that went before prepared for what came after. As in climbing a ladder, creation, we know, does not skip steps. It moves one rung at a time ... the earlier rungs subsumed in the later."[6] That last describes emergence well: Living beings have a chemical nature, but they aren't mere chemicals; nor are humans adequately described simply as animals – although biology still applies.

Echoing Augustine's thought, McMullin sees evolution as clear evidence that "the universe has in itself the capacity to become what God destined it to be."[7] Plantinga calls such views "semi-deistic."[8] But Iverach would disagree. It was confinement of God's act to rare and portentous occasions that Aubrey Moore in 1890 called a "moribund deism." Charles Kingsley wrote, in Darwin's time: "it is just as noble a conception of deity to believe that he created primal forms capable of self development" as it is "to believe that he required a fresh act of intervention to supply the lacunas which He himself had made."[9] Emergence, after all, is a central theme in Genesis. Freedom, as Kant wrote, is "the inner principle of the world."[10]

For Augustine and the Rabbis, nature was created and is sustained by grace. "What more could be needed?" McMullin asks. "Defining God's relationship with the natural order in terms of creation, conservation, and *concursus*, has been standard, after all, among Christian theologians since the Middle Ages."[11] If God remains creative in the world, using natural means, then discovering how does not derogate from God's work. Those who force a choice between natural and religious explanations, whether hoping to protect or to dismiss divinity, have missed a core impulse of piety, seeing and seeking God's handiwork in the most mundane and immediate of things. Theists don't need to relegate God to intercosmic spaces. They see God's work everywhere.

God, in the rabbinic idiom, is not in the world but is the world's Place, the ground of being, the Rock (Deuteronomy 32:4) that moors reality, the fount of light and life (Psalms 36:9). The biblical Creator is not some ruddy Vulcan pounding at his unruly materials. Theists find grace and wisdom in the make up of things. So naturalism is their ally: Science sees the wisdom; religion, the grace. But grace and wisdom interpenetrate. The cosmos is intelligible because it is coherent. Its constituents have value in themselves and in their contributions to the whole. The intrinsic value of each being is vouched for by its project; its instrumental value, by the projects of others. But if creation is a miracle, life's miracle is compounded by evolution.

Does finding God at work within nature, not against it, render divinity otiose? Clearly some might fear, if natural causes explain natural effects, God becomes a fifth wheel; and if they don't, aren't we thrown into the lap of superstition? Why, asks Jaegwon Kim, does an event need two sufficient causes?[12] Perhaps God is not the sort of cause that scientists seek, but a source of value – beauty, goodness, purpose, or being itself, the broadest of values, as we've said. Ultimate causality does not displace proximate causality, and mechanics doesn't answer value questions. The forces that explain, say, jet propulsion don't reveal why a jet plane is made, or used. But purposes and structures intertwine: We won't get far in shaping airplanes by knowing nothing of their uses – just as Maimonides said about needles. Still, jets, like needles, are tools. Do living beings have purposes?

Teleology

Darwin is often praised for purging teleology from science, but he did no such thing. As his son wrote:

> One of the greatest services rendered by my father to the study of Natural History is the revival of Teleology. The evolutionist studies the purpose or meaning of organs with the zeal of the older Teleologist, but with far wider and more coherent purpose.[13]

Many purists, spurred by positivism and the youthful rivalry of genetics with evolution, called Darwinism unscientific for having too much truck with purpose, chasing unverifiable hypotheses instead of collecting field data and experimenting in the lab. Adaptation, they declared, was an unscientific notion. Erik Nordenskiöld's once respected history of biology scored Darwinians for asking why a cat has claws, foolishly seeking purposes, not mechanisms: "Darwin and his contemporaries are constantly putting such wrong questions to nature."[14] Hadn't Bacon cautioned that "the most general principles of nature ought to be held merely positive, as they are discovered," not sought in purposes? Aims belong to human plans. Injected into studies of "the nature of the universe," final causes have only "strangely defiled philosophy."[15]

Bacon made a fair case for curbing purpose mongering. The teleology he spurned was typically anthropocentric, as Spinoza's complaints make clear. But Nordenskiöld drowns all natural purposes in the same tub with naive quests for a motive behind every event – as if nature had nothing better to do than plot for or against human fortunes: We shouldn't look for purposes, even in a kitten's claws. Darwin should not have speculated about sexual selection to explain why some male birds are colorful or indiscriminate about mates while the females are drab but selective: "Internal secretions" and the linkage of courtship behavior to secondary sexual characteristics are all the explanation needed.[16]

Dodging teleology, Nordenskiöld trips over tautologies that Renaissance critics thought they'd buried, "causal" factors named for their function – as though "secondary sexual characteristics" were an explanation and not just the name for a bundle of effects. Darwin, by contrast, did explain courtship behavior and sexual dimorphism – but only by imputing interests to birds and finding purposes in their behavior. Nordenskiöld stands by his guns: Natural selection "is really of no practical importance; the phenomenon cannot be observed and it is therefore not possible to fit it into a subject of research that is based on exact observations."[17]

Emanuel Rádl, similarly, chastised Darwin for seeking adaptive value in secondary sexual characteristics rather than pursue their physical causes in glandular secretions.[18] Charles Singer accused Darwin of hiding a teleology behind the idea of random variation. Science should deal with "things seen and proved," not with "might" and "may be."[19] Even Thomas Hunt Morgan, a founder of modern genetics but a partisan in its early rivalry with Darwinism, chafed at Darwinian teleology and complained that natural selection sounds too intentional.[20] Niko Tinbergen, as a student, was "told off firmly" by a professor for having the temerity to suggest that selection pressures might have influenced birds' flocking more densely when attacked by a raptor.[21] Anatomy, not behavior, was science. Purposes are invisible, the stuff of metaphysics.

I well remember A. J. Bernatowicz's lingering impact on science teaching even in the 1980s, and the anxious circumlocutions he prescribed, lest instructors say that eyes are for seeing or ears for hearing. "Each of us is for good and against evil," he wrote in *Science*.[22] So one dasn't speak of the purposes roots serve in a plant or mention the reproductive functions of gametes, or the nutritional value of food. "Beware the infinitive form of the verb," he warned, and shun even innocent-sounding phrases like "Cells of the archesporial tissue divide and redivide at various angles to form a massive sporogenous tissue." Astronomy lecturers must never say that rings of gas and dust "condense to form a planet." The word *to* might suggest intent, letting unwary students "slip into uncritical acceptance of overt as well as subtle teleology"!

'*And,*' Bernatowicz counseled, can replace '*to*' avoiding "infections of animism or anthropomorphism." Hydrogen and oxygen combine *and* form water, not *to* form water. Seeds are not "modified to function as agents in the distribution of species." "Sporogeneous" passes, since it names only a possible outcome. But one mustn't say that each strand of the double helix, once disentangled from the other, is "free to attach to itself nucleotides or their precursors" – lest that suggest an event somehow different from the compounding of hydrogen with oxygen that forms water. "The danger" is "not that we teach 'unscientific' terminology but that we are actually thinking teleologically and communicating these modes of thought to students."

But *can* we explain the shape of a bladderwort or pitcher-plant or the snapping shut of a Venus flytrap, without *implying* that its "leaves are modified for the capture of insects"? Can we do physiology without assuming that roots are *useful* for taking up materials, and kidneys for filtering the blood? Galen, in a celebrated demonstration, traced to the brain the nerves controlling six throat muscles. He inveighs against Aristotle's siting consciousness in the heart. Only "those who know nothing of what is to be seen in dissection" would assign voluntary actions to the heart. Galen's dissections "established for all time that the brain is the organ of thought and represented one of the most important additions to anatomy and physiology, being probably as great as the discovery of the circulation of the blood."[23] So is it wrong to call the brain an organ used in voluntary control? Is that as bad as saying it "refrigerates the radical heat"? Can doctors diagnose or treat disease without knowing the proper function of hearts and lungs? Bernatowicz prescribed "accumulate," not "store," when tracking nutrients. But does the approved diction block teleology or only mask it? Can we tiptoe around the fact that portulaca leaves store water? It doesn't "accumulate" there by accident.

Bernatowicz aims to make biology safe for mechanists. Teleology, he insists, is never parsimonious, "probably never heuristic," distracting at best, answering pseudo-questions with "meaningless" pseudo-hypotheses laden with "hints at the supernatural." In an unguarded moment, he confesses, he once said in a lecture "that an excited electron has to give up the absorbed energy when it returns to a lower energy level." Well, we're all of us only human. But "A bright student should have pointed out that the electron doesn't *have* to give up the energy, it just *does*."[24] Of course electrons don't give up energy because they feel they must. But it's certainly not the case that they just *do*. There is a necessity here, although necessities, like purposes, are not perceived directly. Ban necessities and dispositional properties and explanation is crippled beyond recovery. That puts science out of business, with grievous collateral damage to our ordinary practice in issuing cautions and making predictions. The procrustean project of conforming language, thought, and science to the prejudices of a crabbed metaphysics has had its day. Its yield in impoverished discourse is well known now and deservedly discredited.

As Aristotle saw, we can't fully describe an organ without reference to its work (*ergon*). Organisms are integrated systems of organs, tools serving the interests of the whole and the survival of its kind. Leave out the interests and physiology collapses. We'd as soon be describing a corpse. Darwin doesn't extinguish Aristotle's idea. Biological functioning is what natural selection is meant to explain. No account of species change, Darwin writes, would be adequate without explaining "how the innumerable species inhabiting this world have been modified, so as to acquire that perfection of structure and co-adaptation which most justly excites our admiration."[25]

Organic functions are readily lumped together under the heading of survival. But the word is inadequate. A lineage splayed out over time is not a static type but a population, linked to ancestors by descent, and to progeny as well. Organisms have needs, continuous with those once met in specific ways but now, perhaps, in new ways. Futurity, rarely *consciously* pursued, is a goal in every organism. True, purposes are not visible. They aren't mechanisms, although mechanisms serve them. They are ends or aims, goods sought by individuals and their progeny, a fluid natural line, persistent by its stability but also, we now know, by its plasticity.

Purposes don't register on positivistic radar, but it's hard work to overlook them. I think of Keats here, writing to his brother and sister: "I go among the Fields and catch a glimpse of a Stoat or a fieldmouse peeping out of the withered grass – the creature hath a purpose and its eyes are bright with it."[26] The vole's purpose is not the stoat's. Each has its own ends. But there's a sense of 'good,' that even competing goals share, reflecting life's diversity. Conflict is also complementarity, as ecologists understand – the inter-dependence of parasite and host, predator and prey. We humans find higher complementarities, reflectively. We form communities and project interests beyond our most immediate needs.

Function, a teleological concept, remains critical. It's what biologists study: the nexus of form and use. Darwinism sees this link dynamically, quanti-fying its yield in reproductive success. Explicitly or tacitly biologists posit inter-ests, ends that organisms pursue, elaborate, and, increasingly, direct and make their own. To purge such assumptions robs evolution of its dynamic. To retain them destroys one advertised outcome of Darwin's work. Many reductionists keep the postulates but try to keep them quiet, hooded in their cages.

It may offend theists that biology presumes no overarching plan, especially when evolution is made out to be the explanation of all explanations. Still, reducing all events to mechanism is not just different from Darwin's project, it's inconsistent with it. There is no evolution unless there's value in survival. The teleology is immanent, but insistent. In an environment made ever more challenging by competition, evolution is progressive – although hardly uni-linear. Darwin, chary of talk about progress, lest it foster thoughts of some inexorable life force, questions any distinction between higher and lower life forms. "It is absurd," he wrote in his notebooks, "to talk of one animal being higher than another."[27] But Dobzhansky freely describes what the record reveals: "viewing evolution of the living world as a whole, from the hypo-thetical primeval self-reproducing substance to higher plants, animals and man, one cannot avoid the recognition that progress, or advancement, or rise, or ennoblement, has occurred."[28] Purposes diverge; many an interest is left behind, displaced by new ends alien to the ancestral stock. Purposes evolve, but they don't become irrelevant.

Immanent and emergent values are nothing new in philosophy. The Stoics saw them in moral growth, as avoidance and pursuit give way to con-scientiousness and principle. The neoplatonists localized value, denying that all things exist for mankind's sake: Each being has a sake and stake of its own. But evolution charts the emergence of new values in the rise of higher organisms. Mechanists speak of greater complexity, as though complexity were a master key and not another effect disguised as a cause, a mask for embarrassing value terms like autonomy, sensibility, and community. Reductionists don't take it lying down when they hear talk of Darwinian teleology. All this talk of purposes, they say, boils down to narratives about past history and differential reproduction.[29] Value and purpose are expected to evaporate. "Characteristic c is an adaptation for doing task t in a popu-lation," Elliott Sober writes, "if and only if members of the population now have c because, ancestrally, there was selection for having c and c conferred a fitness advantage because it performed task t."[30]

"Fitness advantage" might sound like a value term. But fitness is just differential reproduction. Pay no attention to "advantage"! Still, if fitness is really just a way of waving at past facts, if we have equivalence here, of fitness with numbers, we don't yet have an explanation. Tautologies don't explain. When Darwin subtitled his book, *The Preservation of Favoured Races in the Struggle for Life*, he didn't mean, as Kass puts it, "The Preservation of Preserved Races."[31] Surviving types endured *because* they coped. That's a value judgment, compounded when explained further by the adequate or superior working of some organ system. The teleology remains.

To have explanatory power, evolutionary narratives need ideas of efficacy and success, an *un*-reduced idea of fitness: *c* was *useful* to those ancestors. When we call a trait an adaptation, as Robert Brandon explains, it always makes sense to understand that it is *for* something – it had a function.[32] The value idea has not disappeared. Unless this trait was useful in some way, calling it adaptive explains nothing. Its bearers might have out-reproduced others by chance. Perhaps the governing allele was linked to another that *was* beneficial. We need to know *how* it gave good results. Here mechanism is critical: how did *c* sustain the interests of the taxon?

Suppose we vow never to say that webbed feet facilitate swimming, just that past aquatic birds were more prolific when their feet were webbed. Ditto with oil glands, *not* (God forbid!) to waterproof the feathers. Is the new just-so story any less teleological than Darwin's? Or are purposes now just left to the imagination? Omit them and the narrative is no longer explanatory.

Does teleology dissolve?

Ernest Nagel experimented with purging teleology, to make a more perfect science. Sentences like 'Woodpeckers peck so as to find insect larvae for food' were fine – so long as their telic content could be analyzed away. This, Nagel was confident, could be done. Teleology, he explained, puts the cart before the horse. It treats an outcome as a cause, reversing the flow of time. Where talk of purposes is proper, in describing goal seeking by humans and "possibly some higher animals," the reversal is only apparent. For "it is not the *goal* that brings about the action," but an intent, typically attended by a belief or representation.[33] But in biology intent is rarely in question: We can't assume that a tadpole dreams of its future as a frog.

Wary of externally assigned purposes in nature, some biologists favor the term 'teleonomy' in place of teleology. Ernst Mayr defines as teleonomic processes that proceed toward a certain end even when disrupted. They're guided, Mayr stipulates, by an internal code or program, perhaps even adjusting to new circumstances. They're not mere effects of general causal laws: The waterfall just flows, but the swallow swoops and soars and builds its nest. Mayr is unfazed that by his account a clock is just as teleonomic as the swallow. But Nagel is dissatisfied: Meiosis, like the waterfall, is governed by natural law; and uranium decay is just as internally directed as, say, metamorphosis in a butterfly.

Nagel finds a cleaner account in work by Gerd Sommerhoff, bolstering Mayr's criteria by explaining that teleonomic regulation is *in principle* independent of what it regulates: A steam engine's governor, say, has weights that spread as they spin, throttling back a speeding engine. But no general law of nature connects engine speed to governor speed.[34] Similarly, water uptake by the kidneys and release by the muscles keep our blood's water content around 90 percent. Uptake and release are linked to water concentrations in the bloodstream – but only by that regulatory function. Otherwise, the two are independent. Sommerhoff's model lets one explain how an end like regulation is achieved, without mention of that end: Teleonomy, Nagel concludes, has been reduced to mechanism. So "the concept of being goal-directed can be explicated without employing in the analysis any specifically biological notions, and in particular without using any expressions that have a teleological connotation."[35] Q. E. D.

There's just one thing, as Columbo used to say: The idea of a set point. If the body overheats, critical proteins might cook and death ensue; if an engine runs too hot, it can explode. So Sommerhoff is still teleological: Set points and safety zones are defined by interests that an engine maker (or saboteur) assigns – or, in organisms, by *their* interests – or volitions.

By Nagel's account, "all material processes of nature must be explained by 'merely mechanical laws'." So is there nothing more to say about heliotropism, once we know that hormones make sunflowers track the sun? Is the evolutionary narrative complete once it says that ancestral plants that faced the sun outbred congeners that didn't – ours not to ask the reason why? It's not magic. If we don't relate solar tracking to energy economy, we haven't explained a thing. Teleological explanation *is* the evolutionary account. If webbed feet aren't *good* for swimming and waterproofing doesn't *help* our feathered friends, nothing is gained by harking back to rival lineages that lacked such traits.

Some philosophers sheepishly suggest that talk of purposes might help us toward a better grasp of mechanisms. Granted. But finding a mechanism doesn't obviate grasping its use. As Kass says, the Lilliputians might have figured out exactly what made Gulliver's watch tick (or boom, to them) without forming the foggiest idea of what it was for. (Swift leaves them with the notion, based on Gulliver's behavior, that his timepiece was his god.)

Form follows function in living beings, as in tools. So goods are part of the given. We *do* at times discover mechanisms by following their functions. But, like Galen, we also learn about functions by tracing their mechanisms. Physiologists study the structures that do the body's work, and physicians hunt for processes that went wrong. Medicine is scientific and physiology fruitful only by linking the search for mechanisms with the search for functions. In today's life sciences that's a two-way street, increasingly well lit, where understanding moves ever more freely. One could hardly wish to see the lanes impeded in either direction. But banning talk of purposes blocks the flow completely. Meiosis, unlike a waterfall, can fail or succeed. Much as some might like to see biology reduced to chemistry or physics, life needs a language of its own.

Nagel quotes Carl Hempel, once known as America's last unrepentant positivist, for trying to eliminate teleology by saying that a beating heart is generally needed to keep a body in "proper working order." Nagel prefers to say "flourishing." But neither phrasing eliminates the implicit reference to values. As J. B. S. Haldane famously remarked, "teleology is like a mistress to a biologist: he cannot live without her but he's unwilling to be seen with her in public."[36] We needn't anthropomorphize natural selection, let alone assign it foresight, to see that medicine and physiology describe good hearts and bad. Some circulatory systems work better or worse than others. That's where natural selection takes hold. It doesn't consult the affected population or visualize their interests, present or future, or sweep back the flow of time to make outcomes into causes. But interests are served: Some individuals survive and thrive, others perish; new types emerge. Evolution tells us how. But it doesn't erase purposes. It presupposes them.

Teleology and history

Theism is the eight hundred pound gorilla in the room when the talk turns to teleology. Pure minded naturalists want no hints of divine design secreted in biology. But theists too should balk at that kind of special pleading. Ascribing adaptations to artisanship hides behind a metaphor and obviates the real work of natural theology, which is not to presume or plump for design but to seek an ultimate cause of what we see. What we do see are emergent interests. Being has worth, and beings press their interests, often toward further interests: What was good in the barest sense becomes better in higher senses. Individuality makes way for personhood and personality. We need not make humanity the be-all and end-all of creation to recognize in personhood, conscience, and consciousness peaks in evolutionary processes still underway.

Clearly, evolution is no mere product of chance. It's driven by what Darwin called the struggle for survival. That has two sides. Externally it means natural selection, not a causally empty concept at all but a portmanteau term standing for the sum of environmental challenges. What energizes the struggle from within is the claim to life that every living being makes. The struggle, in its inner dimension, then, is pursuit of a good. Hence, Darwin's kinship with Aristotle – and with Genesis. Like Aristotle, Darwin finds nature comprehensible. Like Genesis, he does not find it pointless or devoid of value. For Darwin, as for Aristotle, what makes sense of life forms is capability. For Darwin, as for Genesis, there is a good in every living being: local means serving local ends.

Nature, Aristotle says, does nothing in vain. Genesis too takes a global view: God sees the world and calls it good. Darwin does not negate the goods that Genesis envisions. He situates them: "Man selects only for his own good," he writes – "Nature, only for that of the being which she tends."[37] What Darwin adds to the Genesis narrative is a plotline, the trajectory by which species win their local good. What he adds to Aristotle's faith in nature's purposes is a sustained dynamic: Survival extends beyond the life of the individual but also beyond the invariance of species. The teleology remains robust.

The good of a species is still an interest in survival. But Darwinian survival is not immutability. Species enlarge their interests. They endure not just by constancy but often by finding the openings to transgenerational change that a dynamic environment demands. Dinosaurs do survive – only not as reptiles but as birds. Animals and plants change forms and strategies. They overtop the channels that Aristotle thought it destruction to abandon. Species arise or die, or change when it's destruction for a population to remain what it has been.

"Teeth," Aristotle writes, "have one invariable office, reduction of food. But besides this general function they have other special ones ... in some animals as weapons. ... In man the number and character even of these sharp teeth have been determined mainly by the requirements of speech."[38] Uses here are general and specialized, not early or late: Human incisors are shaped for articulacy, an essential, thus eternal, human trait. Function does determine form. But with Darwin form and function interact in the natural arena. Adaptation is no longer just the suitability of organs to their tasks. It's a shift in the make up of a population. Where Aristotle saw adaptation fixed in the traits of each species, for Darwin it's a process. Science is no longer just the study of what must be as it is. History takes its place alongside nature's laws.

Aristotle often speaks of organs "pressed into service" (*katachretai*) for some new use: The elephant's trunk becomes a sensitive tool, not just a breathing tube.[39] It "compensates" for the stout legs that bear a massive frame but can't grasp a piece of fruit, harvest sheaves of grass, spray cooling water over back and head, or trumpet a greeting. But trunks remain a timeless variant on a timeless theme. Aristotle does expect to get "the clearest view of things," by considering "their first growth and origin."[40] But real essences, for him, don't change. Empedoclean natural selection, he insists, would muddle causal regularity, sink nature in the play of chance, and turn her steady purposiveness to helter-skelter.[41] Against Anaxagoras, he argues, it's not because we humans stand erect and have hands that we're intelligent. We have hands because we're intelligent!

For hands are instruments, and nature's invariable plan in distributing organs is to give each to such animal as can use it, as any prudent man would do. For it's a better plan to take someone who's already a flute player and give him a flute, than to take one who owns a flute and teach him flute playing.[42]

Aristotle here slights his own insight, that teleology and naturalism need not compete. He does not yet see what Darwinians must constantly remember: that intelligence and dexterity, organs and the skills to use them, must emerge pari passu. That's the real meaning of Darwinian gradualism, the central point that just-so stories overlook.

Realistically, we probably owe the opposable thumb to our arboreal ancestry, the likely origin also for the advanced sight brain in which our reasoning and language skills took hold. But human hands, erect stature, and higher brain functions could take their present form only by myriad steps, each dependent on the rest – not the vicious circle that ID signposts but a spiral staircase of interlocking, often opportunistic, adaptations. Our higher functions are not degraded by their humble origins. Nor (pace Aristotle) is handwork necessarily all that humble. But teleology is not eliminated when Darwin gives it a history.

Is evolution progressive? Darwin must say yes and no: There's no "innate and inevitable tendency towards perfection in all organic beings." But nature does demand adaptation.[43] There's no single goal toward which all strivings bend. Advantage will vary, since environments shape need. Yet complexity does emerge; integration will advance in the dialectic of life's struggle. If any goal drives the process, it's not envisioned in organisms that lack consciousness. And no goal, of course, is both specific and universal. Since creatures exist for their own sakes, the values that we humans favor, or the ones that favor us, won't capture every dimension of organic advance, or every salient of grace.

F. D. Por offers an overview of evolution, starting about a billion years ago: Gray-green algae subsist with the bacteria that feed on them, perhaps some nematodes, and a rare mollusc. Fast forward to a mangrove forest just a hundred thousand years ago: There are flowering trees, swarms of bees, small birds like the honey guide, actually able, with help from an intestinal bacterium, to digest beeswax, and prone, like the cuckoo, to poach on other birds' brooding instincts. A honey badger, led by the bird, breaks open a beehive. They feast on honey and bee larvae, until Australopithecus, summoned by the bird's commotion, frightens off the badger but is welcomed by the bird, since the intruder's stick can open the hive still wider. The whole sequence, from pond scum to proto-human, was made possible by animals and their first predecessors.[44]

Eukaryotes, organisms whose cells have a well-defined nucleus and organelles limited by membranes, can't live in isolation. Their prokaryote bacteria-like ancestors had the earth to themselves for nearly two billion years, until the first Protozoans appeared. Cyanobacteria ("blue-green algae"), flourished, along with other photosynthesizers, in ancient lagoons, their bodies recycled by bacteria. But "huge amounts of unrecycled organic material" became the coal deposits of the Precambrian. For "redistribution of resources was left entirely to the whim of the natural elements: currents, waves, and winds" – and the steady force of gravity, sinking organic matter under tons of sediment. The constant shortage of minerals needed by living synthesizers, and the relative dearth of organic matter to feed the decomposers, left every population at risk of crashing. There was "no premium on rapid metabolism." This "clumsy, uncoordinated, and wasteful ecosystem could have gone on forever" – or "succumbed to heat death," had synthesizers and decomposers not somehow kept up their wobbly tandem bicycle ride. But the appearance of animals picked up the pace, "constantly mending and improving" the ecosystem, "importing" goods in short supply. The biosphere became "less and less dependent on external energy," ever more reliant on energy supplied by animal metabolism.[45]

Animal life creates intensive feedback loops between oxygen users and oxygen yielders, earth's free oxygen being "almost exclusively a biogenic product of photosynthesizing bacteria and later of the plant-like eukaryotes" – now seconded by plants. Animals, in turn, generate the CO_2 plants need. Oxygen, toxic to the primordial anaerobes, was released slowly, allowing ample time for oxygen-tolerant forms to emerge. But aerobic respiration proved fifteen times more efficient than its alternative: It "extracts all the chemical energy from the food in a rapid sequence, and within one cell," leaving only CO_2 and water. The oxygen plants generate produced the ozone layer, our natural sunscreen; coral reefs and other living populations have thus far trapped most of the earth's carbon in carbonates (seashells, coral skeletons) or fossil fuels.[46] So the greenhouse effect has not made Earth an oven like Venus, where all the CO_2 is atmospheric, and the surface temperature, 480° C.

Eukaryotes could appear only when oxygen-dependent biochemical pathways opened the way to steroid and lipid synthesis and the formation of membranes, collagen, "the universal glue of all multicellular animal tissues," and the myosin, actin, and dynein active in the movement of animal cells. That made predation possible, and "endosymbiosis," one organism engulfing another, to use not just its matter but its substance. Mitochondria, the powerhouses of animal cells, and the chloroplasts where photosynthesis takes place in plants, are the classic cases.[47]

Rapid movement meant that responses to environmental challenges need not await a new generation. And animal grazing pushed the evolution of plants, yielding the indigestible cell wall, the spines and ridges, chemical poisons and irritants plants deploy. The most primitive plants receded in variety and range: "the large mats of blue-greens disappeared gradually from the open sea," surviving "only in very extreme and exceptional environments such as hypersaline lagoons or hot springs," safe from grazers.[48]

Animals, Por writes, are catalysts, "traders" ecologically, speeding other organisms' evolution. Animals did not annihilate the rest. Indeed, they "offered a rich choice of sheltered environments" to parasitic and symbiotic forms that fanned out in their wake or miniaturized within their bodies. Given the many functions each free-living eukaryote must perform, the genetic information it carries grows immensely, as do the mechanisms that access and activate that information. One protozoan even has an eye organelle, complete with crystalline lens and light-sensitive pigment. In the end, though, "cooperative specialization," a multicellular strategy, "won the day over multi-talented individualism," allowing greater size, swifter movement, more efficient energy economy and heat transfer than single cells can manage. Plants, needing protection more than animals, outgrew the animals, as witness the redwoods, and the ocean's giant kelp forests. Animals relied on movement; plants fortified. Animal cells can migrate before differentiating fully; but plant cells' fates are fixed, like their positions. So animal reproduction was more focused in the germline, shielding offspring from somatic mutants. Since mutant cells in plants stay put, plants remain more capable of asexual reproduction, individual cells still totipotent. Thus many plants will propagate from a cutting.[49]

Size matters. In predators, a doubling of length permits an eight-fold increase in the biomass of prey. But larger predators need a larger range. So there are fewer of them, and they're competitive and territorial. Prey too ramp up in size – more formidable, but more tempting. Some herd together or rely on speed or camouflage, or the special defenses of skunks, porcupines, and the many toxic toads. Predation and greater body mass allow, even demand, increased brain size. So even fish are lifelong learners, adding neurons that make them ever abler hunters and school swimmers: "a shoal of herring may contain 150 million fish" and extend over a mile.[50]

Animals moved onto land, following plant pioneers. Insects and other arthropods developed hard skeletons, protecting their body moisture. Often, like the dragonfly or mosquito, the larvae remained aquatic. But other insects, and the spiders, developed eggs permeable to gases but safe from water loss, as vertebrates' eggs would be. Plants grew taller; spores and seeds, spinier. But insects left amphibians behind. For some 100 million years they were the only airborne animals.[51]

Fish, traversing lagoons and estuaries, needed osmoregulation to handle varying salinities, and ample energy to gain phosphorous for proper vertebrate bones, not the calcium carbonate of seashells. The bony girdles that support two pairs of fins would prove invaluable when fish first left the water.[52] But the aqueous birthplace of vertebrates is evident in tadpole metamorphosis. Reptile eggs can hatch on land, and scales of keratin preserve the body moisture. Better lungs and circulatory apparatus complete the shift from amphibian roots: Reptiles become the keystone of the first terrestrial ecosystem: plants, insects, insect-eaters, predators.[53]

Summing up his story, Por writes:

> The flow of animal evolution is ultimately not chance-dominated ...
> mutations are streamlined by the accumulated ineffaceable limitations of
> previously acquired morpho-physiological body plans. ... Perhaps the
> evolutionary success of the morpho-physiological type called phylum
> Chordata resides in the fact that it was able to find the answers to a
> maximal number of environmental requirements without losing the lib-
> erty to find the response to a host of new situations; or, in other words, it
> maintained the best capacity among the phyla for an open-ended evo-
> lution ... it would take a global catastrophe unequaled even by the great
> Permian extinction to wipe out the vertebrates: not only are they present
> in a wide variety of environments, but they have an inherited ability to
> cope with new challenges.[54]

One almost wants to read "we," not "they." But Por's story is not anthropocentric, and the human talent for coping is part of what our environment
continues to test.

The means to survival and the meanings of flourishing take different
turnings in different species. Broad terms like complexity afford no uniform
metric of advance. Increasing size can be a trap when food grows scarce.
Longevity may cramp transgenerational change and exacerbate inter-gen-
erational competition. Some types simplify over time, becoming sessile, or
dependent, as parasites are in their cosseted environments, reduced, perhaps,
to little more than a mouth and gut. Darwinian progress is always situa-
tional. Higher-order systems do emerge – a food chain, an ecosystem. But
Darwin was right to insist that no species lives just for another, like Al
Capp's schmoos. That would undercut the very idea of identity. Each species
is its own project. Yet we do see evolutionary advance: Every living species
has a lineage that has endured eons of testing. The most archaic "living
fossil" has its modus vivendi. It is as adapted as any other creature that
holds its own in the struggle for survival. So "primitive" forms persist. But
even elegant or powerful forms perish when they fail to meet the challenges
of their environment.

Intrinsic and instrumental goods

Genesis and Darwin meet in the idea of the good. Genesis thematizes creation in terms of goodness – the goodness God saw in light and life, the
teeming animals and luxuriant plants, the humans, fashioned from the earth
and animated with God's own spirit. Darwin does not scan quite so vast a
range. But he weaves the finer threads of life into a vivid tapestry, imaging
the course and causes of evolution – "on almost every page" using terms like
'useful,' 'profitable,' 'advantageous,' 'important,' 'beneficial,' 'harmful,' 'fit,'

'adapted,' 'purpose,' 'tendency,' 'welfare,' 'success,' 'improvement,' 'perfection.'[55] The appraisals are critical to Darwin's enterprise: These goods are what evolution will explain. Each one portends a telos – staying alive, for openers, and procreation, the biblical *be fruitful and multiply*. But procreation, we now know, is not just continuation. Pace Jacques Monod, it is not "invariant reproduction." Even the term 'reproduction' is a misnomer. For constancy is perilous. What survives is not sameness.

Like any good writer, Darwin writes what he knows. That means living things. The good he thematizes is *their* good. We humans are proud of our ideas of the good, although our values can be narrow, skewed, or murky – as Maimonides confesses in glossing the story of Eden. Survival is a fair name for the general goal, and it's natural to call the individual the beneficiary. But the benefits of an adaptive trait extend far beyond its first bearers and give larger meanings to their struggles, accruing to a lineage that may differ strikingly from its forebears.

From the first stirrings that lift and sift living from non-living matter, to the emergence of consciousness, it's not just organisms that evolve but purposes. Thought and caring arise, communities, based ultimately not on instinct but on dignity and the regard that moral subjects can confer – or, tragically, withhold. The goals of planaria are not those of porcupines. The human good is not captured in the aims of a chimp. All organisms are kin. Some biochemical pathways persist through long stretches of life's pedigree. So we can study life in general and find common themes even where interests diverge. But deep differences in capacities for control culminate in the latitude of choice that humans share with no other species on our planet. We choose our purposes and create realms of activity in the sciences and arts, play and sport, where, within measure, we shape our own goals and forge the character that pilots our vessel.

Reductionists try to boil down life processes to the few they deem most basic: The artist, scientist, statesman or ecologist, virtuoso violinist and fullback, are all just after reproductive success. Psychological Darwinism becomes a kind of conspiracy theory, as Jerry Fodor puts it, all behavior traced to sub rosa interests. Denying agency to selves, reductionists typically make heredity and environment jointly omni-competent. They're in denial about self-initiated action. So they give agency to genes or memes – new demons invoked to bar the old, that is, human purposes and intentions, substantive minds or souls. Conscious goals are mere window dressing, cloaking a mindless quest for gene replication. But in human actions at least, intentions are of the essence: The accused, Fodor writes, "wasn't making confetti, he was shredding the evidence."[56]

Purposes are still in play when genes are anthropomorphized. But the new trope seems benign to mechanists, since we know genes don't literally hatch plans. Besides, there's a certain frisson in making genes, not persons, the loci and foci of intent. Describe adaptations broadly enough and specific challenges and solutions are swept up in the abstraction: Animals, described as if they were plants; plants, as if they were machines; humans, as if we were not just kin but no different ultimately from amoebas – the course of evolution, at once cele-brated and dismissed, as if life has gotten nowhere. The genes are just fielding ever trickier strategies to achieve their undistinguished, undistinguishable goal.

Genes, we're told, "want" to survive. But the most successful, we note, rarely survive unchanged. They "persist" in progeny often quite unlike their forebears. They "use" the phenotype to proliferate *not themselves* but new DNA sequences. Why, then, focus on the genes? Why does the teleological buck stop here, when purposes are otherwise embargoed? If teleology is arbitrary or otiose, why give genes alone objective purposes? Why not say the nautilus lives to build its shell, or that the birds nesting for centuries on Nauru flew there not to breed but to deposit the tons of guano that made the atoll so rich, if rapidly depleted, a phosphate quarry?

Genes are favored purposers because they're small and physical. They sustain the Democritean dream of deriving quality from quantity, explaining all things by atomization. But if purposes are to retain explanatory force, small parts will yield only fractional explanations. For no organ functions by itself. If it's acceptable to cite purposes at all, explanations should look beyond com-ponents, to organisms, and their lineages. Evolution must consider outcomes, not just origins – not to reverse the flow of time but simply because genes, like any other organ or organelle, are understood by the benefits they confer. Before Sutton saw the role of chromosomes, no one really knew just what they were.

Holism, not reductionism, is the lesson here, as Mayr saw: We need to study an organism and its life cycle and environment, its history and futurity, not just its parts. The need to see the larger picture is one reason why science is empirical: Just as we can't readily reconstruct a recipe by taking apart a cake, we can't tell much about a cake's purpose by fingering its ingredients in their canisters. We haven't grasped the whole story of wing buds, regardless of their primal function, until we know that wings is what they became. But beyond the growth of efficacy, if we're studying evolution, we confront the rise of intrinsic value, aims not reducible to utility, objects *not* in service to reproductive ends.

Kittens are learning their moves when they tussle together or play with a ball of yarn. They're reinforcing social bonds when they groom each other, or their keepers. But cats also enjoy their play. They love interaction and crave attention. They enjoy their food and don't eat just to survive. Kass paints the picture of emergent intrinsic interests:

> The mockingbird delights in its own imitative sounds … a coyote howls at the moon, the otter turns identical underwater somersault after som-ersault for hours on end … the dog sniffs the ground for traces of his pals, the young deer engages in ceremonial duels, the lizard sunbathes on a rock, the penguin struts and parades, the peacock shows off his plumage.[57]

Some of these behaviors have clear utilities. That doesn't erase their intrinsic value. Peacocks display and stags duel, as a mating ritual. Many birdcalls declare territory or entice prospective mates. But otters frolic and dolphins follow ships for the sheer joy of it. Lizards seem to like basking in the sun, much as we do. They don't know that reptile homeostasis needs sunshine. It just feels good to them – and to the cat that stretches out each morning in a sunbeam.

We all pursue intrinsic values, strikingly in choosing a mate or plotting a career. The bison bulls in Yellowstone, when too old to defend their status in the herd, wander off to live alone or join small bachelor groups. They lose their teeth and starve, or fall prey, as they weaken, to wolves or even bears, the demolition teams that follow up on wolf kills. But humans need far fewer offspring than our ancestors did to sustain a population. In industrial socie-ties, more than half our years are post-reproductive. Most of our actions pursue what appeals to us – all the more so once offspring are launched. The shift is distinctive. But we make choices throughout life about how to define ourselves and contribute to others, how we shall be known or remembered. The salience of the ethical in human lives is unique. But the prominence of values pursued for their own sake is not unprecedented.

Charles Hartshorne reports spending far more of his life studying birdsong than in his philosophical profession. Surveying four to five thousand singing species worldwide, he argues that birds sing partly because they enjoy it. His case is Darwinian in spirit: Our own penchant for music is either "entirely unique to human life, or there are precedents or analogies in older forms of animal life."[58] But that would leave our musical interests and skills unaccountable in evolutionary terms.

Hartshorne faults intellectual austerity for prompting behaviorism in ethology. The reductionism rampant in the 1950s, when he began publishing about birds, valued observation but shunned talk of purposes, thoughts or feelings – even when the bias left ethologists impoverished of language to distinguish, say, courtship from aggression. Hartshorne does not veer to an opposite, anthropomorphic extreme. But he does find it appropriate, given what he sees and hears, to predicate aesthetic feelings of birds. We need to know when a baby is wet or hungry, cooing happily, or recognizing a famil-iar face. We can tell something about a cat's feelings when it purrs, and when it arches and spits. An animal "acts sexually," Hartshorne writes, "at least partly because it enjoys doing so."[59]

Animals do experience pleasure and pain. So it's hard to say they don't pursue at least some ends for their own sake. They don't court and couple simply because they (or their genes!) aim to reproduce. Omitting the internal dimension may lend a scientific patina to descriptions, but it doesn't make them more accurate, or more explanatory. Long before Thomas Nagel wrote his essay "What is it Like to be a Bat?" (1974), Teilhard championed the neglected "within" of things, the "radial," rather than "tangential" dimension.[60]

Naturalists naturally focus on physical relations – impacts and effects. But consciousness and caring arise in the within of persons. Like other emotions, these must have had precedents before they took flight in humans.

Many birds signal distress or alarm, urgent if not especially tuneful vocalizations. But birdcalls, Hartshorne argues, verge into rhythmically punctuated, complex sequences of clear tone and melodic structure. Some birdsongs are learned, often by imitation. Others seem to be instinctual, perhaps refined by learning. Birdsongs are used in courtship and declaring territory, in sustaining pair bonds or keeping contact with a flock. Some songs, unique in style or detail, identify individuals to one another. Some birds answer songs only of their own kind or their own mate, others mimic a wide variety of songs.[61] The brilliant duets of some bird pairs, the extensive repertoires of others, the lightning execution of melodic (or non-melodic) patterns, and the concomitant elaboration of syrinx muscles and the auditory and neural capacities to produce, perceive, and recall subtle song sequences (and filter out extraneous songs as mere noise), all argue for the evolutionary value of birdsong, but also for the mediation of taste and skill. Utilities would go unserved without the rise of intrinsic interests.

In some birds, colorful markings matter; in others, courtship rituals – dancing, bower building, presentation of nesting materials or shiny, brightly colored gifts. In songbirds, musical quality seems critical in attracting and holding a mate. "Counter-singing," answering a neighbor or prospective rival, demands that successful breeders become musical adepts and afficionados. Birds may sing yearlong, or through the day or night, varying song patterns to stave off ennui in themselves or their avian audience.[62] Originality is not salient. Symbolism, pivotal in human arts, is irrelevant. But virtuosity is often a value, along with variety, clarity, and volume. Birds seem to prize such features for themselves, just as they care about the right plumage.

Intrinsic value takes on new meanings at every stage of evolution. But in a broad sense it reaches to the roots of the evolutionary tree. We see it in the emergence of explicit beauty, beauty that announces itself as such, beyond the silent beauty of the natural order. Correspondingly, we see autonomous choice in the love of beauty – in the hen that chooses a brilliantly plumed or tuneful mate. All unaware of evolutionary interests, she knows what she likes. Her tastes can shift the course of evolution.

An elderly socialist friend of my grandmother's used to ask an old question: "I know why flowers are brightly colored," she said. As a child she'd gathered wild mushrooms in Russia before the Revolution. In old age she read *Scientific American* religiously. "They need to attract the birds and insects to carry their pollen. But why are flowers beautiful?" The functionalist answer: What we call beauty just marks a landing site; symmetry and contrast point to the sexual spot. We humans too are sexually adapted. But flowers, as Darwin saw, not least in his study of orchids, complement the habits and anatomy of the moving partners in their sessile sexual dance.

They tease and educate bird or insect sensibilities with scents or mimicry, advertising a free feed, or falsely promising seduction. Blatant, bright, sometimes in wavelengths invisible to us but neon to their porters, blossoms are profuse and insistent. Genes are calling out for continuance and the variation that paradoxically promises continuance. Insects and birds, fed or fooled, pursue the promised reward. Each on-site display flashes its ensign and wafts its perfumes. The customers like what they sense, or they wouldn't come. So beauty arises, evanescent, extravagant, as if echoing Lear's whisper: "Reason not the need." Hues and scents plash. Ornament, wheedling avian tastes and teasing the insects, far outruns pale necessity.

Darwinists speak of runaway sexual selection. The peacock's tail, lion's mane, bower bird's mating house, brilliant markings, courtship songs and dances, outstrip sheer need – and yet become obligatory. Sexual selection pushes phenotypes well beyond utility. Purist adaptationists, following Zahavi's "handicap" conjecture, explain the seeming extravagance: What is not adaptive directly is obliquely so, a marker of vigor, good nutrition, some subtle determinant of reproductive promise. I doubt that's true in every case. But even here the choosers' tastes are the proximate agency, promoting values beyond utility: These birds trade safety for display. And even utility is not unidimensional, as the branchings of the taxonomic tree reveal.

Hormones prime stags to fight, just as they cause horns to sprout. Instinct tells the fighters when to yield. The ritual is rooted in natural and sexual selection. But, as Kass says, "faculties which are at first preserved for the sake of living" now have a life of their own. Stags are not machines. They fight because it feels right to them and yield when they feel they must. In humans, interests exfoliate without clear limit. Propensities that once made living possible are preserved for the sake of living well.[63] As Fodor says, "Not all of one's motives could be instrumentalized" – "there must be some things that one cares for just for their own sakes." He mentions friendship, for one, or the arts. Steven Pinker cashiers friendship: It's just mutual exploitation. Like Epicurus, who pressed that case, he probably knows better. "Fictional narratives," Pinker writes, "supply us with a mental catalogue of the fatal conundrums we might face someday and the outcomes of strategies we could deploy in them. What are the options if I were to suspect that my uncle killed my father, took his position and married my mother?" "Good question," Fodor responds: "Or what if it turns out that, having just used the ring I got by kidnapping a dwarf to pay off the giants who built me my new castle, I should discover that it is the very ring that I need in order to continue to be immortal and rule the world? It's important to think out the options betimes, because a thing like that could happen to anyone and you can never have too much insurance." Isn't it more sensible, to recognize "there are lots of things that we care about simply for themselves"?[64]

Long before concerted, subjective interests found any proper sphere, living populations faced crossroads between individual and reproductive success, between longevity and swift generational turnover, between size and agility, genetic flexibility and genetic stability, qualitative versus quantitative investment in offspring. But subjective factors come into prominence in tradeoffs between courtship and camouflage. Evolution continually opens new doorways to the framing of intrinsic interests. Most striking in the human case are the interests we make our own – beauty or learning, science or piety, music, mathematics, painting or the dance, procreation, wealth or politics, philosophy, charity or service, athletic prowess, fame or honor, pleasure of one kind or another, spelunking, mountain climbing, skydiving, equitation, or conservation. Human beings, distinctively, choose aims expected to give meaning to their lives. Rarely do we passively accept the putative minima of our nature. Self-expression has biological parameters, of course. It also faces social boundaries and psychological barriers, some fringed with high voltage fencing. We may yield or grapple, but our ends are never the mere dictates of our genes. We are always, in some measure, who we make ourselves, reaching for a good defined in part by our own efforts.

Looking back across the evolutionary vista from our own modest plateau, surveying the ground life has covered, we can judge the emergence of intrinsic values as an achievement of evolution. Just as Genesis reports the goods God saw, we see in nature an openness to emergent goods of many kinds, as natural selection sculpts living species, interpreting and letting them interpret *their* good dynamically and interactively. Teilhard sees consciousness as evolution's goal. Its rise guides us, like Ariadne's thread, through the taxonomic labyrinth. Some pathways are dead ends: Insects teem and swarm. But heavy exoskeletons dwarf them, stunting the nervous system, so higher functions emerge only through social strategies that sacrifice individuality to instinct, regimenting behavior and confining fertility to a tiny caste. Even the queen is never free.

For Kass, like Teilhard, soul is evolution's yardstick. Asking if there is any "natural term to evolution, at least in its tendency of ascent," he replies:

> The answer would appear to be man ... both in possessing the *highest*, and also in possessing the most *complete range* of faculties of soul. Even looking to the future, what could be higher than man?[65]

Well, we humans do hold a summit here on earth, in powers, and responsibilities. That can't make us the be-all and end-all of creation. Persons, I've often argued, stand on a plateau. If humanity grounds personhood, humanity is unsurpassed. Even if personhood has emerged in more advanced species elsewhere in the universe, they are our moral peers, not lesser or greater morally, since we share subjecthood. But here on earth life flourishes in many ways, not all answering our needs. Darwin, like the neoplatonists, sees all natural kinds as existing for their own sakes. It's because the good is sought in so many ways that we can read the vast history of evolution as a series of experiments, groping for the light, finding all sorts of self-definition. That's what I hear when Genesis speaks of God's creation of animals and plants *after their kind* (1:11, 21): All being is beautiful, although not all creatures are equal. Life flourished long before we came to taste the fruits, or plant their seeds. Human uniqueness does not fade with the recognition that every being holds a goodness and beauty of its own.

Value in nature

Genesis names light, not matter, the first object of creation – good, not yet for its uses or the joy it will give, but intrinsically: Good in itself, but pregnant with possibilities. The same is true of elementary particles, teeming with energy. Space, as Einstein showed, is more than a backdrop. It shapes nature and is shaped by it. Light is the metric of our physics, but matter and the world's geometry make room for life and motion. Teilhard saw cohesion as love's natural harbinger. Spinoza sees the conatus not just in inertia or solidity but in patterns and rhythms of motion and rest that reveal the drive of each complex to persist, to express its nature and even enhance its perfection. He calls that striving providence.[66] For as the Hebrew liturgy puts it, God rejoices in His creatures' joy – His love expressed in theirs.[67]

Value does not start from nothing, or remain just where it started. Each being makes claims recognizable *as* claims by their dynamism. Humanity is a way station on life's journey – from the electron to *Hamlet*, as George Wald used to say – and perhaps beyond, in a course not fully charted for us but one that we, increasingly, must chart. The journey was never a passive play of particles: The creative work of evolution wins ground and continues in pursuit of further goals. The quest, as worthwhile as we creatures make it.

God's purposes, if God is timeless, are as aptly conceived to beckon from the future as to set creatures afloat from the past. Choices remain ours, and evolution is neither predestiny nor abandonment. When Infinite Goodness calls, its message to finite beings is scaled to their capacities. These vary, but they're not fixed. The message to all conscious subjects is freedom and an invitation to emulate not God's ipseity but his creativity and grace. A larger, less pointed message is nature's silent, polyphonic song calling creatures of all sorts toward horizons that are open but remain their own, filled with real risk, and real opportunity.

It's because open-ended advance is the thrust of living nature that Teilhard can see the Alpha of creation in the Omega of evolution. The Hebrew liturgy illuminates a kindred thought: *Sof ma'aseh be-mahshavah tehilla* – What was last in the making was first in intent.[68] Outcomes are prefigured, not preordained. Otherwise, creaturely actions are not actions, and our efforts are not our own. Nature is no craft project or game but a world, given light and life from a Creator with agency to spare, imparting creativity to creatures without diminution of the Source.

Aristotle spoke for creativity when he made the actual prior to the potential – no egg without a chicken. We know now, with Darwin's help, that the old chicken–egg puzzle rests on false premises. The first chickens didn't hatch from eggs laid by other chickens. They evolved from ancestors not quite chickens – ultimately, not birds at all. But is Aristotle right in calling the actual prior causally to the potential? Should that thought too be turned upside down, or inside out? It was not Darwin but Plotinus who saw the repair that was needed. The actual is rich, but its wealth is not stasis but living, creative power. Potential, then, is not sheer passive receptivity. It is fecundity. Matter, we now know, is never utterly inert. God, whom Aristotle called most fully actual, must be most fully active – and therefore, most fully puissant. So *dynamis* entails creativity; potency no longer need imply limitation.

Robust in Aristotle's insight is his confutation of the notion that more can come from less. That thought, for Aristotle, rules out creation. Parmenides believed as much. So did Democritus, and the Epicureans, all the way down to many a materialist today. But theists read the idea rather differently: To us it means that strict materialists must either posit an eternal world or bootstrap a world from bare facticity, ignoring (or hoping others will ignore) the values secreted in the primitives they posit – the vibrant dance and resilience of matter, the struggles of life forms, the rise of purposes. Mechanists ignore the play of grace in constituting interests as interests. But, without that, something is derived from nothing – value from dull neutrality.

In our efforts to make sense of things, part of what cries out for explanation is the rise of value, starting with the bare value of existence and moving on to the emergent purposes of organisms. Values, I've stressed, are not explained mechanically. That's why Genesis celebrates light and the life that light makes possible: These are gifts, not neutral facts – but also, not self-sufficient, not divine. None of this need have been; none of it need be as it is. A monotheist who studies evolution will celebrate not just the fact of life but its dynamic, opening ever new gifts: This intricate Fabergé egg opens outward, to a world. The sky opens up. The future too is open – as the text of Genesis suggests, to be made.

There's a tendentious rhetoric in scientistic accounts that pin evolution to uncaring chance, but also a kernel of truth, or such accounts would not exercise their broad appeal. The play of genes that promises evolution also yields Down's Syndrome and Tay-Sachs disease. But put the shoe on the other foot: The same processes that cause cancer fire up evolution.[69] Serendipity does not explain why beings should have interests at all, let alone means of enhancing them. Our would be mechanists quietly presume persistence as a universal appetite. But if there is such an appetite, it's not passive or static. Evolution, as we've seen, does not mean simply that what survives survives. What survives makes claims and gives survival ever-new means and meanings.

To trumpet the hostility or indifference of nature is to miss the fact that much within the natural system is a resource, niche, or opportunity – exploited from one standpoint, a precious good from another. Anti-evolutionists worry out loud that Darwinism paints natural laws as cruel. Any God who would permit them must be mindless or neglectful. Darwin himself was troubled by such thoughts:

> With respect to the theological view of the question: This is always painful to me. I am bewildered. I had no intention to write atheistically, but I own that I cannot see as plainly as others do, and as I should wish to do, evidence of design and beneficence on all sides of us. There seems to me too much misery in the world. I cannot persuade myself that a beneficent and omnipotent God would have designedly created the Ich-neumonidae with the express intention of their feeding within the living bodies of caterpillars or that a cat should play with mice. ... On the other hand, I cannot anyhow be contented to view this wonderful universe, and especially the nature of man, and to conclude that everything is the result of brute force. I am inclined to look at everything as resulting from designed laws, with the details, whether good or bad, left to the working out of what we may call chance.[70]

The problem of evil here, with no serpent but a tiny wasp as its emblem, prompts Darwin to cast nature's details into the lap of chance – or "what we may call chance" – for Darwin is too devoted to science to surrender the natural order to any ultimate disorder. "The birth both of the species and of the individual," he writes, "are equally parts of that grand sequence of events, which our minds refuse to accept as the result of blind chance."[71]

What, then, of the problem of evil? Start with moral evil. Critics of evolution blame the theory for the abuses of its pretended heirs, who use the ancient Sophists' rationale, calling right what nature seems to sanction. Evolution, if true, they argue, gives nature's mandate to "brute force" – victimizing the weak, exploiting the strong – a free pass to vicious rivalries, promiscuous engrossment of goods, mates, habitats, prestige, or power – as if conscience too did not arise in evolution. The abuses are hardly confined to soi-disant Darwinians. The pious too can be self-serving, their piety a fig leaf ill concealing wanton aggression. Bloodletting and the rape of nature, a penchant for self-righteous dogma, sectarian fanaticism, self-deception, and triumphalism are charged against them, even as they charge Darwinians with inhumanity. The crimes are real. But in neither case are they sound inferences from the beliefs invoked to justify them – or rejected for supposedly implying them. Theists desecrate their ideals and atheists blaspheme against their humanism when they cloak ferocity and invidious exploitation in the aura of what they hold most sacred. Violence has a false grip on value, whether sacred or secular ideals are its mask. The ancient charges and countercharges don't reach the core of either of the targeted ways of life and thought.

With moral questions, intention is of the essence. So moral judgment awaits the rise of personhood. But how one thematizes nature is itself a moral question, alongside the cognate issue of how one thinks of God. Cruel, greedy, salacious, punitive gods reflect ill on their makers. Pictures of a nature ruled by cruelty, licentiousness, and violence, similarly, betray a jaundiced eye. The perverse images devised to justify a crabbed outlook or hide an oppressive lifestyle belong properly neither to science nor religion but to the mythologies and ideologies that human passions paint over scientific findings and spiritual insights. Racism, eugenics, sexism, and social Darwinism, are impostors flying false colors. They're not products of science but projections of human weaknesses tricked out in the emblems of discovery, just as fanaticism and chauvinism cloak themselves in false religious garb when they pretend to holiness.

The great theme of nature is not the law of the claw, any more than misanthropy is the great theme of spiritual life. The world is not a prison to be escaped, or a monster to be caged. Nature's great theme is grace, manifest in the gift of being and its dynamism – the possibility of life and growth, advantage and advance. Evolution is part of that: Granted, one creature's good may harm another. Such cycles are the sea anchor of life – and the engine of evolution. Without the grazing of animals on plants there would be no vegetation on earth, as Por explains – only pond slime. There is wildness in nature, but creation is a treasure house of openings to joy and pleasure, giving and growth.

We can't ignore predation, parasitism, and extinction. No one should whitewash natural violence, deficiency, and destruction. But evil has no meaning without a prior good. What destruction violates is prior ontically to the evil that attacks it. The very idea of evil is parasitic on the idea of the good, just as evils are parasitic on the goodness they exploit. It would make no sense to combat illness or mourn death unless there were something precious and prior to be lost. Theists see this and fault those who ignore it by reducing evolution to naked mechanism – and then, inconsistently, citing natural and human evils against theism, at once presuming and ignoring the values that such evils corrosively attack. But the same is true of those who find evolution troublesome because of death and suffering and extinction. Vulnerability is the price of creation. God did not create more gods. Either evolution is an achievement or it is not. If it is not, the problem of evil recedes. But in fact it is, and the achievement steals a march on the affront.

It is because exploitation presupposes generosity that the great theme of nature is not rapacity but generosity and love. The Jewish pietist known as the Hafetz Hayyim, the lover of life, thus finds a moral in natural history: It is in virtue of our power to bestow grace and favor on others that we humans are said to be created in God's image. We can emulate God's creativity and the grace we see in nature's governance.[72] That grace, biblically, was the focus of the Mosaic epiphany; its locus, Maimonides explains, was nature.

For when God permitted Moses to see "his back," the vision (since God has no body) was of nature's panoply, flowing, as it were, in the wake of God's creative act and the ongoing grace of his governance. Nature's meaning, then, is voiced in the names we find for God's attributes: mercy, goodness, truth, justice – the same attributes we are called to emulate.[73] Putting that thought in Darwinian terms: If creation is an act of love, evolution is that love's dynamic. For God's gifts did not cease with the imparting of existence. Each existent, after all, has a nature. Creatures use what they receive, rise to address the challenges they face, as individuals and as living kinds.

What about the play of chance? It might help to say a word about that slippery term. Strictly speaking, chance events are uncaused. In that sense, science has little room for them, and Darwin is right to bracket the term. Even the behavior of electrons, which we describe these days as undetermined, statistical, cloudlike rather than mechanically determinate, is not disordered. And it's hardly unintelligible, despite the tendency of subatomic particles to elude familiar, Newtonian slots and berths. Informally, we ascribe random events to chance, events with causes so tightly balanced that we find prediction difficult or impossible: A coin toss is called random not because the outcome is indeterminate but because we can't readily predict which side a quarter will land on.

Countering Lamarckian notions that heritable variations arise in response to need, biologists like to stress that genetic variation is typically random with respect to an organism's interests. Mutations are unhelpful generally, often deleterious. So polemicists on both sides of today's creation–evolution struggle tend to stress the impact of chance in evolution. Three things should be said about that: First: Genetic changes are not entirely random with respect to the interests of a living population. Second: Randomness is not simply the opposite of order but often its prerequisite. It's random motion in the air that gives a balloon its even surface; glass differs from sand by the random arrangement of its molecules. That's what makes it smooth. Third: Living systems can and do incorporate randomness into their strategic repertoire. They make randomness a resource.

Putting chance to work

Gene control, sexual reproduction, and the rise of thought mark critical phases in the emergence of autonomy, defining identities that stand up to the play of forces indifferent or hostile to their being. Consider gene control. In the classic Jacob–Monod model, genes were bits of DNA that program production of life's protein machinery. "One gene, one polypeptide" was the mantra. But, like any figure of speech, the programming image carried risks: Metaphors age, lose their edge and power, even die. When imagery is taken literally, thinking no longer governs the language it uses and can stumble over it.

Mayr, simultaneously with Jacob and Monod, introduced the program imagery in 1961. The "Central Dogma" of genetics came to rest on the "ungainly metaphor" of "a computer reading software" – an image with "only superficial similarities" to what it represents.[74] Biological development became a "single sited" genetic determinism.[75] Dawkins even urged that the alternative to a dyslexia gene would be a gene for reading.[76] But there's no such gene. Genes are systemic. Many interact in governing a single trait, and one gene may affect many traits.[77] Enzymes, we now know, can actively manipulate DNA; and DNA changes can be induced environmentally.[78] The genome is not isolated from the feedback loops so prominent in life processes. Developmental pathways are more like electronic circuitry than they are like production lines. Outcomes aren't just dictated by DNA, itself knocked into place in a genetic pinball game. What evolution yields are increasingly sophisticated systems of inboard control.

Genes are interdependent. Their work is contextual: They are units of inheritance, but also of mutation and recombination. They're developmental master switches, RNA templates, silencers or enhancers of the work of other genes.[79] Often we identify alleles by their phenotypic effects. So we may focus on a point mutation implicated, say, in phenylketonuria. But genetic, cellular, and somatic factors work in concert.[80] The discovery of just how systemic gene expression is, has shaken genetic reductionism, with significant implications for evolution.[81]

Cyberneticists, early on, questioned the analogy of DNA to computer instructions: Information does pass to new generations, but it's also interpreted and applied.[82] Still, the computer imagery appealed powerfully. Excited by the genetic regulators they discovered in E. coli and entranced by the cybernetics of Norbert Wiener and Erwin Schrödinger, Jacob and Monod eagerly generalized the pattern: DNA was in command. A critic years later would call their operon model "absolutely true" but "also absolutely vacuous." The reason: "The paradigm does not tell us how to make a mouse but only how to make a switch."[83] The histones, hormones, and RNA that regulate differentiation were familiar in the 1960s. We now know a further host of enzymatic and metabolic pathways, transcription complexes, signals, and transduction sequences[84] – not to mention the transcription of RNA to DNA by retroviruses and the action of retrogenes in HIV and perhaps in the origins of life. Jacob knew that the famous model that earned him and Monod a Nobel prize told only part of the story. Even as he popularized it, he hedged, calling chromosomes a program that "makes sense only for the structures it has itself determined."[85] But science writers still often write as if DNA were flying solo. Yet no software runs without its hardware.

Had it been known in earlier days, DNA might have been called the Logos and bruited as proof of purpose and design. That's not the tack I want to take. Order is too readily dismissed, and intent too readily projected to sustain convincing arguments. Nature is no pocket watch, and organisms are not computers. We needn't dash to catch the programmer behind the screen. Like faces in the fire, design is too often in the eye of the beholder, and we humans all too readily fill the heavens with answers to our prayers, or malice toward our purposes. Of course Paley saw a designer and Dennett an algorithm in the play of DNA. Monod sees sheer chance. But rhetoric rarely captures the true nature of things.

Far less contentiously, the structures and networks we now recognize in the working of genes, and the holism they demand in our explanations, reveal the futility of efforts to erase value from biology. Like organs, organisms have purposes; like species, those purposes evolve. Emergent with the rest are enhanced capacities to control evolution itself. Living beings are not just heaps of atoms. Chance plays its part in their constitution; but, as organisms evolve and pursue futurity by ever subtler means, they put chance to work. As interests evolve, individuality acquires new meanings. Transcendence itself is transformed. Sex is at the heart of the transformation.

The sexual revolution

Sex is inefficient, compared to asexual procreation. Two partners need to find each other. Individuals unpaired are an evolutionary lost investment to their parents' reproductive energies. So why does sexual reproduction exist? Why is it so widespread in animals and plants? Darwin had no answer. He confessed: "We do not even in the least know the final cause of sexuality; why new beings should be produced by the union of the two sexual elements instead of by a process of parthenogenesis. ... The whole subject is as yet hidden in darkness."[86] This, in an 1861 paper about primroses and cowslips and how some varieties block selfing. It was commonly thought that barriers to fertilization served only against inter-species crosses. So why would flowers reject self-fertilization but accept pollen from another plant? Why do so many species procreate sexually, when a single hermaphrodite might have done the job?

Genetics raises the question pointedly. A gamete, as J. Maynard Smith explains, bears only half the parental endowment. So a sexually reproducing mother must produce twice as many ova as her asexual rival to transmit all her genes.[87] Genes transmitted asexually flow largely unchanged, but sexual reproduction splits up valuable combinations. So sexuality looks like a luxury. Yet it's found in all phyla and is "by far the most important mode of reproduction in such large and diverse taxa as molluscs, arthropods, echinoderms, and vertebrates."[88] Its precursors run back over a billion years. Why does it persist? Shouldn't natural selection have purged it long ago? The evidence is that every complex asexual organism now known had sexual ancestors. What connects sexuality to complexity?

Weissmann proposed in 1889 that sexual reproduction enhances genetic variability, promoting adaptability in the face of environmental change.

Graham Bell calls this idea, elaborated by Fisher, Muller, and others, "The Vicar of Bray," after the divine lampooned in a witty eighteenth century ballad for shifting his posture with the changing political tides. Rapid evolutionary adaptation works best in large populations, where beneficial genes readily meet potential complements. Sexual reproduction does tend to break up useful pairs. But strong selection pressures in a sizable group can fix helpful alleles "in the blink of an eye." Asexual populations "dodder along for aeons" without much change, but random segregation creates new, potentially valuable combinations in each new gamete.[89] Barring twins, the mixing and matching of human genes reduces the probability that a couple will produce genetically identical offspring to less than one in a trillion.[90] The likelihood of genetic uniformity across a population is far, far less. Crossing over enhances the effect. "The fate of a mutant gene which arises in an asexual clone is bound up with the fate of the clone itself." The same mutant in a sexual species finds new, potentially advantageous, settings in every generation.[91]

The impact of sex on adaptability was confirmed in 2005: In sexual and asexual yeast colonies, growth was about equivalent in low stress conditions, but in severe conditions the sexual type flourished.[92] Still, there is a weakness in the Vicar of Bray hypothesis: It takes multiple generations to fix a genetic change in a population. That won't impede yeast colonies, where generational turnover is swift. But it might be fatally slow for vertebrates. Leigh Van Valen of the University of Chicago framed a variant hypothesis that he named for the Red Queen in *Through the Looking Glass*, who cautioned Alice that in her world "it takes all the running you can do, to keep in the same place." The core idea: stasis is a grave disadvantage where pathogens and predators are constantly evolving new tactics of attack.

W. D. Hamilton tested the Red Queen in computer simulations. Asexuality far outpaced sexual reproduction, until parasites were added to the model: "antiparasite adaptations" were "in constant obsolescence." But sex "stores genes that are currently bad but have promise for reuse. It continually tries them in combination." Against emergent challenges, the Red Queen's reserves swiftly proved their worth. Sexuality, then, should predominate in species facing dynamic challenges. Curtis Lively and Robert Vrijenhoek confirmed that prediction in Mexican topminnows that hybridize with a related species: Asexual offspring suffer far more than their sexual cousins from the parasitic worms that cause "black spot disease."

Bell favored the Tangled Bank hypothesis suggested by Michael Ghiselin in 1974, and named for Darwin's image of "an entangled bank clothed with plants of many kinds, with birds singing in the bushes, with various insects flitting about, and with worms crawling through the damp earth."[93] To the casual eye all is disorder, but complex relations of interdependence are everywhere: In a diverse, dynamic environment, natural selection, over time, favors diversity. The model is economic, as ecological models should be: A clever button maker, Bell explains, will diversify as competition saturates the market. A well-ensconced asexual population expands to the "carrying capacity" of its niche. But sexual populations in a complex environment will diversify, despite the costs: Their progeny can exploit niches untouched by more uniform, asexual clones.[94]

The hypotheses are complementary: Diversity aids defense, as any switch hitter knows. Life conditions vary. So populations do evolve varied tactics. In a stable niche, asexual species thrive. But a dynamic and diverse environment, filled with challenges and opportunities, favors flexibility. Sexual reproduction promotes adaptive radiation and the diversity of the Tangled Bank. Species under pressure from pathogens, parasites, and predators cannot await each rare beneficial mutation. They need sexual reproduction to pick up the pace of genetic change, as the Red Queen would urge. It's not surprising, then, that higher organisms reproduce sexually. Their complexity arose through sexual reproduction. It's not just a source of new numbers. It's an evolutionary tactic, enhancing the responsiveness of populations to emergent challenges and arming them with traits not yet fully exposed in competition and thus not yet countered by an adversary. Sexual reproduction allows taxa to exploit and modulate the play of chance, shuffling the deck without shredding the cards, regrouping genes and remodeling the chromosomes in new, potentially profitable combinations. Past gains are conserved but not invariant. Mutants get new chances, purged, typically, only when doubled up, but held in reserve in heterozygotes. Populations remain stable, their genomes coherent but not brittle with uniformity. And breeding strategies remain flexible, favoring adaptability or stability in diverse circumstances.

Alongside the colorfully named hypotheses, least apt is the image of a simple lottery. Monod lightly lists the effects of sex as "Various kinds of 'scrambling' of the genetic text by inversion, duplication, displacement, or fusion of more or less extended segments." And then: "We call these events accidental, we say that they are random occurrences."[95] But sexual reproduction is as much an adaptation as lungs or wings – and far more general. Chance *is* active in genetics: Mutant alleles don't just pop up to meet new challenges. DNA polymerase does edit and correct copying errors, putting a brake on mutation and limiting genetic variance. But sexual reproduction enhances variance – conservatively. Just as college roommates may mix and match their clothes to vary their wardrobes, Richard Colling writes, "individuals acquire *variant forms* of established genes rather than always relying upon random variations to create *new genes.*" Sex modulates "the wildness of the universe."[96]

Consciousness

Sexual reproduction, as we've noted, inscribes clear distinctions between parents and offspring. So it defines death more sharply than, say, budding does. By the same token, it enhances individuality. The offspring of a sexual pair are typically contemporary with their parents. That can give parents new interests in their progeny and in values beyond the imperatives of pro-creation, new opportunities for selfishness, and selflessness. Advancing com-plexity demands ever greater parental investment. But discrete identities make way for interests in community that are not merely protective, interests in mates that are not merely procreative, interests in offspring that lift par-enthood beyond the sheer demands of survival. As evolution traverses the terrain between paramecia and primates, emergent individuality creates the theater for thought. Swifter to adapt than chromosomes and far more flexible than instinct, thought gives individuality new meanings. It nurtures person-hood and personality, language, culture, art, religion, and morals, and is nourished by them in turn.

The capacity for thought evolves phyletically. But it grows in individuals too. Thought escapes genetics only in the sense that flight escapes gravity: A bird is still subject to gravitation. Indeed, flight needs gravity, just as wings need air. But birds are not pinned to the ground by G-forces. Biology, as the Malbim, saw, is not *beyond* physics; life does not violate physical laws. But organisms are not adequately described in the very general, very abstract, terms that physics or chemistry affords. Fish don't breach the Second Law of Thermodynamics when they swim upstream. Like all living beings, they *use* the energy flow which that law describes. But that's not something pebbles on the beach can do.

All organisms on earth take energy, flowing in abundance, ultimately from the sun, and make it a resource, staking claims in the environment. The flow of energy allows life to hold entropy, locally, at bay. The living eddies in the stream persist. They become selves. Claims are pressed to ever higher planes. Life gives birth to use. Identities emerge, making ever more effectual claims to autonomy. Control is internalized, and with it, an ever clearer sense of value. This too is a gift. As Conrad Hyers writes, "An ideal father ... is hardly one who attempts to decide and determine everything ... the ideal father is one who gives increasing amounts of freedom and responsibility" – even with the risks that might involve.[97]

All beings are active, but life processes are recursive from the start, using ever subtler tactics to win a firmer grip on futurity and fate. Just as life does not halt entropy, consciousness does not escape electrochemistry but uses it, winning autonomy in ways definable only in mental terms. Thought makes the brain its organ, not its cause, wiring and rewiring neural circuits, flexible channels beyond the grooves and gullies of the given. Thought exercises its heritage of command in choices with no set outcome, charting its own course, giving visible expression to mental creativity. All this is lost on those who confuse creativity with chance and miss the affinity of ampliative rea-soning to divine creativity that helps make the human mind an image of God. In their accounts of invention and discovery reductionists generally presume that intelligent beings pursue their own interests. But they soft pedal the presumption. The Democritean myth ascribing invention to accident, like its counterpart that lays evolution at the door of chance, is a piece of indirection, distracting attention from the values presumed in the story.

A mind, Dennett will say, is a brain infested by memes, gremlins modeled on the very selves they were meant to displace. But selves are not clay, nor are they passive to the pleas said to constitute them. It is *we* who act and think our thoughts, who dream, wonder, love, hate, or fear, compose, desire, intend. It is we who grasp meanings, not meanings that grasp us. Memes, like genes, have no aspirations: They are ours; we don't belong to them. We're not absolute masters of our destiny, or even our ideas. But neither are we driftwood. We share in agency and freedom, as in creativity. Our learning is active, not a passive inscription. We build our language as we learn it. Only so can we frame new sentences, and new thoughts.

Our three cases, then: gene control, sexuality, and thinking, argue for holism in biology. They show us evolution enhancing the autonomy of living beings. Nature does not smother our liberty, as if there were no self-determination, no feedback from the whole to its parts, from the person to the organism.[98] Living beings work as systems. In some measure they take charge of their own fate and remake their environment. Feedback of the kind seen in homeostasis makes way for thought and choice. Far from a mere whirl of particles, life reaches for order, stability, growth, and awareness. Theists see the handiwork of God here. Darwin was far too keen an observer to overlook the higher order systems that arise when evolution calls the genes to order. Here's what he said about the tangled bank:

> It is interesting to contemplate an entangled bank, clothed with many plants of many kinds, with birds singing on the bushes, with various insects flitting about, and with worms crawling through the damp earth, and to reflect that these elaborately constructed forms, so different from each other, and dependent upon each other in so complex a manner, have all been produced by laws acting around us ... from the war of nature, from famine and death, the most exalted object which we are capable of conceiving, namely, the production of the higher animals, directly follows. There is grandeur in this view of life, with its several powers, having been originally breathed by the Creator into a few forms or into one; and that, whilst this planet has gone cycling on according to the fixed law of gravity, from so simple a beginning endless forms most beautiful and most wonderful have been, and are being evolved.[99]

The Creator here is hardly anthropomorphic. Darwin, in fact, was sorry in the end, that he had even used that word.[100] He clearly didn't mean some anthropomorphic craftsman god. The breath of life that Darwin spoke of here, like God's breath of life in Genesis, stands for all the powers of growth, generation, variation, and adaptation. Darwin, of course, resists notions of a single purpose impressed upon nature. But it remained his "inmost conviction" that "the Universe is not the result of chance." Our animal origins caution us to remember that all our convictions are fallible, he wrote. But he welcomed the thought that theism and evolution are compatible.[101] His scientific focus, fittingly, was on nature seen in its own terms, life arising in the struggle for survival. And there is no rise, after all, without a slope. Natural variation and natural selection, in tension with each other, drive evolution: Natural selection, a paradigm case of causal law; natural variation, cast in the role of chance. Both are necessary, not as rivals but as complements. The two may seem to exile God. But they may also be God's tools, the hammer and anvil on which living species are forged.

Chance and necessity

Seeing random mutations as "the *only* source of modifications in the genetic text," Monod infers that "chance *alone* is at the source of every innovation, of all creation in the biosphere." His conclusion: "Pure chance, absolutely free but blind at the root of the stupendous edifice of evolution," is "the *sole* conceivable hypothesis," never to be revised.[102] Dawkins speaks up for necessity: "I want to persuade the reader not just that the Darwinian worldview *happens* to be true, but that it is the only known theory that *could*, in principle, solve the mystery of our existence."[103] The rhetorical opposites, chance and necessity, both press in the same direction. Either account makes God otiose. And yet, necessity and chance have long been seen as God's right and left hands – chance deals the cards, natural law sets the rules of play.

Maimonides saw futility in all attempts to capture and contain the Infinitely transcendent. Our descriptors inevitably reflect our values. That's why one can judge a theology by the values it projects and gauge its subtlety by its awareness of an inevitable debt to poetry. What we understand in nature, the principles and laws, Maimonides wrote, we attribute to God's wisdom. But since biblical times, what we fail to bring under a general rule we readily call chance and ascribe to God's will. Form was immanent wisdom; matter grounds "what we call chance," scripturally ascribed to God's will. Ultimately, in God's perfect unity, will and wisdom are one.

Arthur Peacocke writes a sequel to Maimonides' story. For him, as for Plato in the *Timaeus*, matter is the locus of necessity – and thus, of order, as the substrate of natural law. But chance preserves its role. Evolution, Peacocke writes,

> is the process *par excellence* of the manifestation of emergence. This is the in-built creative potentiality of all-that-is, which we have now to see *as* God at work, continuously creating in and through the stuff of the world he had endowed with those very potentialities. ... Instead of being daunted by the role of chance in genetic mutations, as the manifestation

of irrationality in the universe, it would be as consistent with the observations to assert that the full gamut of the potentialities of living matter could only be explored through the agency of the rapid and frequent randomization that is possible at the molecular level of the DNA. Indeed, the role of "chance" is what one would expect if the universe were so constituted that all the potential forms of organization of matter (both living and non-living) might be explored.[104]

Chance is nature's doorway to creativity, breaking the monotony of iteration. Chance is at play in the choreography of the stars and the dance of the electron, and, tellingly, in the genes, where nature's exuberance is judged continually, each strategy tested by its outcomes in the world.

The Midrash speaks of God's aspects of mercy and justice. But in nature, as in God, the two lock hands: There's economy in nature's prodigality. In higher organisms, where offspring are costly, selection is heaviest among the gametes. Natural selection steers evolution. But conscious subjects project a standard by which even nature will be judged. Human purposes will seem to eclipse all rival goods. But values other than our own don't vanish when we squint.

God, Peacocke argues, built into nature the propensities that favor life and "increased complexity, awareness, consciousness and sensitivity"[105] – Ariadne's thread, leading out into the open air, finding its goal in thought and freedom. Liberty and consciousness are not the sole aims of every striving. But if autonomy is of value, thought, besides its intrinsic worth, will be a means to it – and to worlds of further goods to be pursued, and ills to be avoided. Peacocke figures God's work on the model of a composer who marshals spontaneity and rule, but begins:

> with an arrangement of notes in an apparently simple subject, elaborates and expands it into a fugue by a variety of devices ... always the consequent interplay of sound flowing in an orderly way from the chosen initiating ploy.[106]

Variety here means creativity but also divine delight, in which creatures share.[107] Peacocke tells of Bach's improvising on a theme set by Frederick the Great and following next day with a six-part fugue on matter of his own, miraculous not for violating nature but for working so creatively with matter Bach gave himself.

Nature too works up its matter:

> The way in which what we call 'chance' operates within this 'given' framework to produce new structures, entities and processes can then be seen as eliciting the potentialities that the physical cosmos possessed *ab initio*. ... God acts to create in the world *through* what we call 'chance' operating within the created order.[108]

Peacocke complements the biblical images of God's work and rest with Hindu thoughts of divine play, *lila*.[109] Peter Forrest uses the same Sanskrit word, naming an activity grounded not in need but in overflowing joy in "things which are good as ends."[110] Again God delights in his creation. Comparing divine creativity to the use of chance by artists like Jackson Pollack, Hyers cites Zen painters' playful spirit and Zen potters' use of "controlled accident":

> highly prized was not precise and intricate detail, filled in completely and in full accord with a prearranged plan or established rules. Instead the Zen artists used sketchy, suggestive brushstrokes which, to some extent, had a life of their own. ... The focus was the present moment and immediate, spontaneous interaction with the materials.
>
> The same aesthetic was applied to the development of raku. ... The very process of firing and the materials and techniques used have resulted in vases and tea bowls which are intentionally rough, irregular, and cracked. Even the glazes oxidize and run in unpredictable ways. Judged by the standards of fine china, such a result may appear crudely misshapen ... yet it is seen as having a beauty and fascination all its own.[111]

What these artists were discovering, and discovering to their audience, was no trivial dimension of nature, but the same that Kant called freedom. As Peacocke writes, the "unfolding of the hidden potentialities of the world is not a predetermined path." The future lies open, "but not inchoate and without purpose."[112] Whether in joy or beauty or freedom, the idea holds steady: Finite value bespeaks a higher Source.

God's play is serious work, like the play of a composer at the keyboard, or the play Einstein saw in scientific thinking. God's work is also play, being joyful – and art, because it is creative. Natural beauty is no longer the unending choric dance that Aristotle saw in the life cycle, the seasons, the spheres, all celebrating their unreachable Goal. It becomes an upward, outward groping toward Goodness, still always out of reach, but realized, by facets, in every self-defining movement of a creature. Peacocke hears just the right note in Aubrey Moore:

> Darwinism appeared, and, under the disguise of a foe did the work of a friend. It has conferred upon philosophy and religion an inestimable benefit, by showing us that we must choose between two alternatives. Either God is everywhere present in nature, or He is nowhere.[113]

Natural ebullience

When theists contemplate creation, in the explosive first moment of time, the coalescence of galaxies, the rise of life, thought, and love, we don't think that of this just happened. We look for causes. But the questions we ask aren't answered by tracing things back to their first motions or stripping bodies down to their least particles, or parts too elementary even to be called particles. We see value and want to know why it arises, persists, and grows. Why is light beautiful? Why does life arise? Why do organisms struggle and survive? Why does evolution take a direction, not favoring *us* perhaps, but toward the good each living kind pursues?

Monotheists ascribe each finite good to the infinite Goodness where immanence and transcendence meet: God is not one of the bodies down there on the field, jarred by equal and opposite recoil in every movement, checked or borne along by other bodies or their own inertia. The explanations we're looking for point to a cause that transcends the natures it explains, an ultimate source, shining through the veil that guards our finitude from sizzling to nullity in the light of overpowering value. The Infinite does not stand aloof and apart. It acts not *upon* things but *through* them, *in* them – not transitively, as Spinoza put it, manhandling things with Vulcan's maul and tongs. As Peacocke writes: "the natural, causal, creative nexus of events *is* itself God's creative action. It is this that the attribution of immanence to God in his world must now be taken to convey."[114] Yet God is transcendent, not dragged into the action like a deus ex machina in a bad play, as Aristotle put it, silent unless invoked at some existential or epistemic crisis.

In Isaiah's language transcendence is called holiness; its expression, glory. So the poet-prophet will say: *Holy, holy, holy!* – the Transcendent, removed by infinite powers above all that is touched or tried – is also immanent, manifest in his work: *The fill of all the earth is His glory* (6:3). God acts not by heating and annealing matter but by imparting an idea – a word, as Philo put it, an idea embodied, and so apprehensible, active and at work in nature's energies. For all natures are God's resources.

Reduction disappoints when it tries to bar all but mechanistic explanations and ignores emergent purposes. Equally disappointing is the rival reduction that talks of spirits but imagines them corporeally, picturing their work only in mechanistic images. Some theists, as if at a loss, punt toward indeterminacy, asking God to massage quantum deviations, in the interest of free will, or providence.[115] That's a cosmic loss of cosmological nerve, another way of exiling God to the gaps, copying the Epicureans' banishment of *their* anthropomorphic deities to the intermundia and laying off on the clinamen all thoughts of creativity. Our own view is more confident of God and more trusting of nature. To a monotheist all things express God's grace, but none exhausts his powers. All rise to his command, but not one consummates his purpose. All intelligibility is God's wisdom, but human wisdom is mere babbling beside nature's profundity. We can only study, celebrate, and contemplate the natures God created and creates.

Value is *here*, in nature, from the start. Being is given, not withheld, but small, seedlike at first, alongside what will follow. Even the first ray of light is precious, active, beautiful. It doesn't just hang in space. What the world gets at the start is its first week's allowance. Nature's goodness won't lie in the cookie jar to get stale. Light is out there in the world, piercing the void, spending itself, showing itself, frolicking, with only God to see. It's in deference to that liveliness that the Torah made light, not matter, the paradigm of God's first creative work, harbinger of the life that will crown the work of creation and, by its evolutionary play, give nature higher meanings and purposes than its origins foretold.

Purpose, as I say, is emergent in evolution. There's variation and selection. But even as selection carves the lineaments of life on a rock face that was never quite inert, purpose too evolves. Value grows. In a post-Copernican world we find inertia, not inertness: The sheerest mass of matter is, not alive to be sure, but dynamic. There's motion in every particle, insistent enough to demand our utmost efforts to bring it even close to a stop. And there's solidity, persistent enough to look heroic in massive mountains or the great torrents that will inspire a Bible or a Bierstadt, or the Chinese landscape painters – but more than rock solid at its smallest. Vast energies course through the cosmos, dangerous, sublime, breeding galaxies, some that will never nurse a seed of life. But, as the psalmist says, *above the torrent's roar, the mighty breakers of the sea, the Lord is far exalted* (93:4) – they're all his work, his expression, a soundless voice and wordless message – *whose ray runs all through the earth* (19:5; 19:4 in the ASV).

Masses combine, fuse in the stars, each element with its distinctive signature. Are their chemical couplings and uncouplings active or passive? The question beggars meaning. Chemical affinities are both active and passive. But compounds reveal properties as yet unseen – emergent properties, risen from the potentials with which the stars have stocked the cosmos. Life arises from this chemistry. We don't yet know how, but it's foolish to make a virtue of the mystery and lock God in the dark, taking ignorance for piety. For now, perhaps, it's enough to know the parts from which all living things on earth are made. We name them, as Adam named the animals. Like the child playing with mother's pocket watch, we can take some of these things apart, even if we don't always know how to put them back together. There's marvel enough in their making.

Afterword

A few final words about science and religion. Using the acronym NOMA, Stephen Jay Gould proposed a kind of truce in the creation–evolution wars, NOMA meaning non-overlapping magisteria. The use of an acronym makes it clear that what's intended is a program rather than, say, a fully developed synthesis. Given the valence evolutionary thinking has borne from its origins, peace overtures like Gould's are unlikely to inspire the most ardent belligerents to lay down their arms. Clarity and understanding are more modest, more winnable goals, helpful, perhaps, to those most deeply committed at once to science and religion.

Gould sees no overlap between the scientific and religious domains. Scientists focus on the empirical constitution of the universe; religion, on the search for ethical values and spiritual meaning. "The attainment of wisdom in a full life requires extensive attention to both domains."[1] Gould's irenic stance harks back to Descartes' proposing a line of demarcation even more telling than the line Pope Alexander VI drew in 1493, assigning Brazil to Portugal and western South America to Spain. To science Descartes assigned physical nature. Consciousness, the mind or soul, would be described in its own terms, in the language of conviction and doubt, sensing, willing, imagining. The soul in a more familiar sense was left to the divines. Wasn't it the task of theology to show us the way to heaven?[2]

In the 1996 message that prompted Gould's proposal, Pope John Paul II suggested a similar division of responsibilities. Pius XII in 1950 had found evolution not inimical to "the doctrine of the faith about man and his vocation." John Paul went further: Evolution was well attested (albeit open to revision and disconfirmation). But the theory, he insisted, applies to the body, not the soul.

The problem Descartes bequeathed to his successors is that sensing and willing do seem somehow to connect consciousness to a world independent of it. What, then, are their relations? Shouldn't we heed James Iverach's cautions against sundering the unity of human nature? Descartes himself was keenly alive to such concerns. Similarly with Gould's peace proposals: How do we deal with areas where science and religion do seem to overlap, or make competing claims, or where advocates contest the terrain for rights of exploration – or explanation?

Gould's magisteria, he admits, "bump right up against each other, inter-digitating in wondrously complex ways along their joint border. Many of our deepest questions call upon aspects of both for different parts of a full answer – and the sorting of legitimate domains can become quite complex and difficult" – witness questions about our responsibilities toward other species, or about the meaning of human life. It's easy to say science deals with facts, religion with values. But Gould wisely avoids reducing religion to its moral role. He includes wisdom and spiritual meaning in the province of the religious quest. In broaching questions about our responsibilities toward other species, he's acknowledging that there are facts about values – and values about facts. Otherwise, nature is stripped of interest, and the values that draw our eye are emptied of any content of their own. We have no *contractual* obligations to the environment, or to life itself, or future generations. Reflecting on that fact might help us see being itself as a value, a proper subject for spiritual (and aesthetic) contemplation. We've seen some "interdigitation" here in this book, in the large question of purposes – not unrelated to questions about the meaning of life in general, and human life specifically.

Purposes, I've argued, are manifest in nature. Darwin could explain organic purposes by recasting adaptation in dynamic terms, as a process, not just a fact about unchanging essences. Theists find meaning in purposes. They see the same nature as scientists but focus on different facets of the jewel. They rebel at any fusing of objectivity with a dead neutrality, or stolid denial of purposes. The philosophically inclined may even spot a category error in trying to reduce purposes to a narrative. Clearly the purpose of the heart, or brain, or kidneys is very different from the story of its origins. It doesn't take keen analysis to see that.

Religion isn't just reflection or meditation. Its norms are more than mere demands. They point to values in the world and rest on an understanding of the world that learns and adapts, as science does, growing more or less accurate, but also more or less open to the world's richness and complexity and beauty. Spiritual insights do address human nature and relations. But they also address the larger, natural world. Religions may seek a wider world still. But they don't get far until they're well familiar with the world we inhabit.

Religious norms and insights are corrigible. Like scientific hypotheses they need to be checked, against each other and all the rest of what we know. Even when we look beyond the world we need to be careful about our inferences: If the truths we seek (in scripture, say, or in spiritual experience) are in any sense more than merely human, we need to winnow and sift proposed epiphanies carefully, for that very reason, to ensure that what we cull is more than just a projection of our personal or parochial passions or desires. That, I think, is part of what we're meant to learn from the story of the loss of Eden.

A biologist who tried to describe human life without mentioning thought or culture would be doing bad ethology. Similarly, a biologist can't responsibly ignore the values found in nature – just as a philosopher can't responsibly ignore the realities of joy and suffering, guilt and generosity, beauty and rapacity, natural and human goods and evils. I well remember famous Oxford philosophy dons seriously maintaining that one needn't know anything about the brain to do philosophy of mind. But that was in the day, now happily ended, when philosophy was widely deemed a metadiscourse, a discourse about discourse. Ethical philosophy today is freely normative, religious philosophy tackles religious questions, no longer hiding behind the clinical, analytical mask, bracketing religious experience, to be pinned and studied and not candidly engaged as an integral part of life, to be made sense of and dealt with along with all the rest.

When theists speak about the world, as they must, they too take risks. Their claims are open to the challenge of counter-evidence. If theists found evidence that supported their faith, Dawkins argues, they wouldn't reject it because of NOMA; so why can't that work in reverse?[3] Dawkins lards his rhetoric with abuse and ridicule. He caricatures prayer and pillories scripture. Even today, then, the animus of Huxley and Andrew Dickson White persists. But Dawkins is right that religions need to address the world as we know it and take scientific findings seriously. I think he's wrong in seeing no evidence of God. Wrong again, in a different way, in trying to debar even the asking of *why* questions and the pursuit of ultimacy – as if science could settle by fiat the issue that so vexes him. Wrong in yet a third way when he charges with inauthentic faith those who seek to reconcile religious beliefs with scientific understandings.[4]

But Dawkins is right (if inconsistent) when he says: "a universe in which we're alone except for other slowly evolved intelligences is a very different universe from one with an original guiding agent whose intelligent design is responsible for its very existence"[5] – inconsistent, since that second alternative clearly does not address a pseudo-question, as Dawkins pretends, when he says he has "as yet to see any good reason" to judge theology a subject. "Some questions," he writes, "simply do not deserve an answer." He seems to number many a *why* question among them: "What on Earth *is* a why question?" he asks. "Not every English sentence beginning with the word 'why' is a legitimate question."[6] Quite true. But surely there must be some that need an answer, or Dawkins would not so urgently propose his own replies to every why question, and then steam and fume and write another book insisting that his is the only proper type of answer and branding any other type ignorant, disingenuous, superstitious.

Dawkins readily finds eager strawmen. But Gould knows that many a serious monotheist reads the Bible as "illuminating literature, based partly on metaphor and allegory (essential components of all good writing) and demanding interpretation for proper understanding."[7] Only a fringe minority, he writes, fail to read scripture that way. Well, sophistication probably varies. But it's rude to impugn the sincerity of anyone who struggles with the questions (real questions!) that religions raise, and intolerant to ridicule any faith that seems less sophisticated than one's own. Humanism doesn't show to best advantage that way – any more than piety looks best in dogmatic garb, denouncing all beliefs less credulous than one's own.

Gould respects religion: "throughout Western history," he writes, "organized religion has fostered both the most unspeakable horrors and the most heart-rending examples of human goodness in the face of personal danger."[8] It's clear why. Religions articulate socially and notionally some of our highest values, and we humans are capable of holy and unholy acts in the name of what we hold most dear. The same is true, of course, of organized atheism, as anti-Darwinists are fond of pointing out. Religion and its secular surrogates function in much the same way, then. So faiths and anti-faiths should be judged accordingly, individually, not globally. As it says in the Good Book, Part Two: "By their fruits shall you know them."

Gould stands fast in his "cold bath," insisting "nature can be truly 'cruel' and 'indifferent'" – even as he adds that such terms are "utterly inappropriate," since they invoke standards that have no bearing on nature at large, which "didn't know we were coming"and "doesn't give a damn about us." He finds the cold bath "liberating, not depressing." It leaves us free "to conduct moral discourse"on our own, "spared from the delusion that we might read moral truth passively from nature's factuality."[9] There's the moral nub of Gould's agnosticism. A deep humanism anchors him as firmly as piety might serve others. Gould knows his stance alarms some, and he respects *theirs*, perhaps in part for its kinship to his own. (For sacred texts and the spiritual epiphanies that bear moral fruit are hardly read off passively from nature's book or any other!) A good Darwinian would recognize the history behind such structural affinities.

History itself holds as many ironies as nature. One is the secularization and sublimation of spiritual values in moral and social outlets. The rhetoric of the Enlightenment demands that its children mask the spiritual roots of their moral certitude. When a scientist posits inviolability and intelligibility in nature's laws, naturalism pays tacit tribute to theism: The scientist is treading on, even trading on, sacred ground, righteously and rightfully unwilling to cede an inch of forthright commitment in his spirited defense of objective, inviolable truth. When a naturalist vows that nature is not chaos, that chance itself, the random play of particles and their constituents, is itself ordered, and a source of order, even a tool of the self-ordering systems that give rise to life and allow its further rise, to consciousness, autonomy, and community, the naturalist is not sowing moral categories where they don't belong but watching their emergence – not justifying facticity in the name of some self-constructed idol, an icon of the appetites and passions. What's glimpsed fleetingly, through nature's veil, is something real, absolute and ideal. Of course there's plenty of misprision of such notions. The truest, highest values are the most vulnerable. Nature, like scripture, demands careful, active, thoughtful and responsible reading and readily falls prey to misinterpretation. Morally, spiritually, intellectually, such is the human condition: Evolution has brought us to this point, which Genesis pictured long ago: We are what we decide. That's the freedom creation gives.

Notes

1 Backgrounds

1 Agathias, *History of the Reign of Justinian* 2.30–31; deVogel, *Greek Philosophy* 3.590–91.
2 Aristotle, *De Sophisticis Elenchis* 5. 167b 14–15; cf. 166b 37; *Physics* 8.1; *Topics* 2.2, 109b23; 4.6, 128b7–9; 6.2, 139b20; *De Generatione et Corruptione* 1.3, 317b 3, *De Anima* 3.7, 431a3–4.
3 Parmenides frg. 8 in Simplicius, ad *Phys.*; 145, in Kirk and Raven, 249–50, § 296, *ll.* 6–9.
4 Aristotle, *Metaphysics* I 5, esp. 986b 15; cf. 1.2–3, esp. 983b 6.
5 Aristotle, *Physics* I 3, 8; *De Caelo* III 1, 298b 11–24; *De Sophisticis Elenchis* 33, 182 b; *Topics* I 11, 104b18.
6 Thus Averroes, *Tahafut al-Tahafut*, ed. Bouyges, 5; tr. Van Den Bergh, 1.
7 See Proclus' Eighteen arguments for eternity; tr. Taylor, 38; ed. Badawi, 55; ap. Shahrastani, ed. Cureton, 338.
8 Philoponus, *De Aeternitate Mundi*; cf. Plato, *Statesman* 270D; see Sambursky, *The Physical World of Late Antiquity,* 170–75; Walzer, *Greek into Arabic,* 190–96.
9 See Simplicius ad *Phys.* and *De Caelo.*
10 Maimonides, *Guide to the Perplexed* I 74–76, II 6–18, 25.
11 Aquinas, *Summa Theologica* I, 46–47.
12 Kant, *Critique of Pure Reason*, A 426/B454-A433/B461.
13 Ghazali, *Tahafut al-Falasifa*, Discussions 1–4, 10, and conclusion.
14 Maimonides, *Guide* II 19.
15 Aristotle, *Topics* I 11, 104b 12–18, echoed at Maimonides, *Guide* I 31.
16 Maimonides, *Guide* II 15, 17, 18, III 32.
17 Galileo, *Dialogue*, tr. Drake, 7.
18 Galileo, *Dialogue*, 47–56, 72, 97–99.
19 Galileo, *Dialogue*, 19–32, 37–100.
20 Ikhwan al-Safa, *Animals vs Man.*
21 Descartes, *Principles of Philosophy,* esp. § 3.16, 17, 24, 26, 32, 47, 111, 112, 114, 115; 4.1, 189, 199, tr. Haldane and Ross, 272–74, 277, 280, 289–93; Kenny, *Descartes*, 12.
22 *Origin*, 15.344–45; cf. Ernst Mayr, *The Growth of Biological Thought*, 71.
23 Turner, *Commitment to Care* 126; cf. 25–26, 66–67, 377 n. 1.
24 Dawkins, *The Blind Watchmaker*, 6.
25 Marsh, *Variation and Fixity in Nature*, 28, 35; cf. Boardman, Koontz, and Morris, *Science and Creation*, 68.

26 Marsh, *Variation and Fixity in Nature*, 37–38.
27 Howe, "Homology, Analogy, and Creative Components in Plants"; Shute, "Remarkable Adaptations"; Clark, "The Plants Will Teach You," all in Lammerts, ed., *Scientific Studies*, 243–68, 303–7; Lammerts, "Mutations Reveal the Glory of God's Handiwork," in *Why Not Creation?* 299–311.
28 *Descent*, 21.148–49; cf. 21.95–96; Moore, *The Post-Darwinian Controversies*, 221–22, 231–32. Even as Darwin read proofs of the *Origin*, Lyell was reporting that Hugh Falconer and Joseph Prestwich had found Stone Age tools in association with extinct fossil mammals. By 1863 he was ready to argue for the "antiquity of man," as he put it. Browne, *Darwin*, 2.80, 130, 218–19.
29 Morris, *Scientific Creationism*, 171.
30 Boardman, Koontz, and Morris, *Science and Creation*, 41.
31 Kofahl, *Handy Dandy Evolution Refuter*, 81–84.
32 Davidheiser, *Evolution and Christian Faith*, 337; cf. Howe, "Evolution and the Problem of Man."
33 Cf. Gillespie, *Charles Darwin and the Problem of Creation*, 120, 139, 152.
34 *Descent*, 21.107.
35 *Descent*, 21.103.
36 *Jackson's Oxford Journal,* July 7, 1860, p. 2; *The Athenaeum*, 30 (June, 7, 14, July 1860), in Lucas, "Wilberforce and Huxley," 319–20, 325. For the varied accounts of the debate, see Richards, *Darwin and the Emergence of Evolutionary Theories*, 549–51. Richard Owen quietly assisted Wilberforce with the science for his review condemning the *Origin* as atheistic – much as Huxley aided Kingsley's support of the opposite conclusion. Browne, *Darwin*, 2.114, 120–25, 137.
37 *Descent*, 22.644; cf. 21.107.
38 Wilberforce, review of the *Origin,* 270, 279.
39 John Roach Straton, *Evolution versus Creation*, in Numbers, ed., *Creation–Evolution Debates*, 2.120; cf. Gish, *Evolution: The Fossils Say No!*; Boardman, Koontz, and Morris, *Science and Creation*, 47–94; Lammerts, ed., *Why Not Creation?*; Wilder-Smith, *Man's Origin, Man's Destiny*, 160–269; Rushdoony, *The Mythology of Science*, 32.
40 Wilberforce, per *The Atheneum*, 14 July 1860, p. 65, col 1; cf. his review of the *Origin*; see Lucas, 315–20.
41 Morris, *Scientific Creationism*, 172–75.
42 Moore, *The Post-Darwinian Controversies*, 198.
43 Hodge, *What is Darwinism?* 132, 169–80; Moore, *The Post-Darwinian Controversies*, 212; Overman, *Evolution and the Christian Doctrine of Creation*, 98; Russett, *Darwin in America*, 27.
44 Overman, *Evolution and the Christian Doctrine of Creation,* 109.
45 Le Conte, *Evolution*, 301.
46 Le Conte, *Evolution*, 351–53.
47 Savage, "perhaps the first clergyman in America to accept evolution from the pulpit," was, again, more Spencerian than Darwinian. For him matter was one manifestation of an "infinite, eternal spirit and life," Moore, *The Post-Darwinian Controversies*, 229.
48 Madden, *Chauncey Wright*, 82–88.
49 Wright, "Natural Theology as a Positive Science," (1865); letter to Lesley, January 19, 1865, in Thayer, ed., *Letters*, 67–71; to Charles Eliot Norton, October 1, 1865, quoted in Madden, *Chauncey Wright*, 149.
50 To Abbot, October 28, 1867, Wright confesses: "concerning the existence of a God and the immortality of the soul. The verdict of 'not proven' is the kind of judgement I have formed. ... Practical grounds are really the basis of belief in the

doctrines of theology. The higher moral sentiments have attached themselves so strongly to these traditions that doubts of them seem to the believers like contempt for all that is noble or worthy. ... " Wright repudiates "dogmatic atheism"; it expresses the "bad motives" of "the meanest and narrowest of men." But he brands Kant's moral postulate of immortality a paralogism grounded in undervaluing this present life; *Philosophical Writings*, 43–44.

51 Osborn, *Evolution and Religion in Education*, 45–67.
52 Clark, *Genesis and Science*, 115–24; Morris, *Biblical Cosmology*, 16; Rushdoony, *Mythology*, 41; "The Premises of Evolutionary thought," in Lammerts, ed., *Scientific Studies*, 1–8.
53 Davidheiser, *Evolution and Christian Faith*, 111–14.
54 Morris, *Biblical Cosmology and Modern Science*, 57.
55 Machen, *Christianity and Liberalism*.
56 Browne, *Darwin*, 2.100–106, 115, 136.
57 Russell, *Inventing the Flat Earth*.
58 Boardman, Koontz, and Morris, 43–44; cf. Davidheiser, "Social Darwinism," in Lammerts, ed., *Scientific Studies*, 338–43; Morris, *Scientific Creationism*, 179–80; Wilder-Smith, 187–97; Rushdoony, *Mythology*, 53.
59 Davidheiser, *Evolution and Christian Faith*, 350.
60 *Descent*, 21.162; cf. 21–22, 26, 187–88.
61 Marsden, *Understanding Fundamentalism and Evangelicalism*, 9–10.
62 Straton, *Evolution versus Creation*, ed. Numbers, 99.
63 Morris, *Biblical Catastrophism and Geology*, 12–13.
64 Richards, *Darwin and the Emergence of Evolutionary Theories of Mind and Behavior*, 543.
65 Robert Richards, 4–5, quoting Ernst Mayr, Richard Lewontin, Susan Cannon, et al. in *Science in Culture*, 276.
66 Richards, *Darwin and the Emergence of Evolutionary Theories*, 545.
67 James Moore, *The Post-Darwinian Controversies*, 213.
68 McCosh, *The Religious Aspect of Evolution*, 7, 110; Moore, *The Post-Darwinian Controversies*, 245–49.
69 Iverach, *Christianity and Evolution*, 86, 95, 128–29, 172–76; Moore, *The Post-Darwinian Controversies*, 253–58.
70 Aubrey Moore, *Science and The Faith*, 166–67; James Moore, *The Post-Darwinian Controversies*, 263.
71 Aubrey Moore, *Science and The Faith*, 87–88.
72 Aubrey Moore, *Science and The Faith*, 208–11; James Moore, 266–68.
73 Aubrey Moore, *Science and The Faith*, 180.
74 Aubrey Moore, *Science and The Faith*, 184.
75 Moore, *The Post-Darwinian Controversies*, 327.
76 Moore, *The Post-Darwinian Controversies*, 303.
77 Moore, *The Post-Darwinian Controversies*, 339; for the ideological Darwinism of the liberals, 343–44.
78 Numbers, *The Creationists*, 19–27.
79 Numbers, *The Creationists*, 33–50.
80 The charge was made even in Darwin's time. He laughed off a Manchester newspaper's satirical charge that his theory would justify Napoleon's wars and the chiseling of every dishonest tradesman. Browne, *Darwin*, 2.109.
81 *Capital*, 1.341, 372. Marx wrote Engels June 18, 1862, "Although developed in the crude English fashion, this is the book which in the field of natural history, provides the basis for our views." To the socialist leader Ferdinand Lasalle, he wrote: "Darwin's work is most important and suits my purpose in that it provides

a basis in natural science for the historical class struggle." *Collected Works*, 46.246, 543; cf. 234; Giuliano Pancaldi, "The Technology of Nature: Marx's Thoughts on Darwin." Browne (*Darwin*, 2.403) finds "scant evidence" that Marx sought to dedicate a book to Darwin. He did send *Capital* in 1873, inscribed as a "sincere admirer." Darwin acknowledged the gift and the importance of political economy, different as the subject was from his own. The book remained in his library "uncut and unopened."

82 Numbers, *The Creationists*, 56.

83 Numbers, *The Creationists*, 55.

84 Numbers, *The Creationists*, 57.

85 Numbers, *The Creationists*, 55–59, 67–68.

86 Larson, *Summer for the Gods*; Numbers, *Darwinism comes to America*.

87 Numbers, *The Creationists*, 58.

88 Numbers, *The Creationists*, 194–204.

89 Numbers, *The Creationists*, 368–72.

90 Price, *The Fundamentals of Geology*, 13–15. Bryan had hoped to call Price as an expert witness in Dayton. But Price was teaching in England at the time and disliked the Tennessee statute on constitutional grounds. He had counseled Bryan to avoid scientific claims. But Bryan cited Price's young earth arguments, although personally disclaiming their conclusions. Price never forgave the betrayal of his flood geology. Numbers, *The Creationists*, 116.

91 See Morris, *The Remarkable Birth of Planet Earth*; Whitcomb, *The Early Earth*; Howe, ed., *Speak to the Earth*; Daly, *Earth's Most Challenging Mysteries*. Biostratigraphy is structurally inconsistent with a single worldwide deluge, and Morris and Whitcomb's notion that higher animals are found in higher strata because they could flee the flood to higher ground is embarrassingly ad hoc; Prothero, *Evolution*, 57–72.

92 Segraves, *The Great Dinosaur Mistake*; Wheeler, *Two-Taled Dinosaur*, 35; Coffin, "A Paleoecological Misinterpretation," 165–68; Meister, "Discovery of Trilobite Fossils in Shod Footprint"; Cook, "W. J. Meister's Discovery of Human Footprint with Trilobites in a Cambrian Formation of Western Utah" – both in Lammerts, ed., *Why Not Creation?* 185–93.

93 Segraves, *The Creation Report*, 17; Moore and Slusher, *Biology*; Numbers, *The Creationists*, 270–72.

94 Morris, *Scientific Creationism*, 8–16; and in Lammerts, *Why Not Creation?* "Science versus Scientism in Historical Geology," esp. 119–23; John W. Klotz, "The Philosophy of Science in Relation to Concepts of Creation vs. The Evolutionary Theory," 11, 14, 20; A. F. Williams, "The Genesis Account of Creation," 36; Daly, *Earth's Most Challenging Mysteries*, 387; Rushdoony, *Mythology*, 13; Wheeler, *The Two-Taled Dinosaur*, 47; Numbers, *The Creationists*, 274–75.

95 As Donald Prothero explains, geological faunal sequence was observed well before the ascendance of evolution. The stratigraphy is now attested at thousands of drilling sites: Older strata lack higher types, although many early types persist, some down to the present. Evolution explains the sequence, but the first geologists did not use evolutionary assumptions; Prothero, *Evolution*, 54–72.

96 Price, *The Phantom of Organic Evolution*, 5–6.

97 Morris, *Scientific Creationism*, 210–11; cf. Whitcomb and Morris, *The Genesis Flood*. Lee Tiffin responds in *Creationism's Upside-Down Pyramid*, 176–80.

98 Schneerson, "The Weakness of the Theories of Creation" (1962).

99 See O. Bakar, *Critique of Evolutionary Theory*; Numbers, *The Creationists*, 421–27.

100 Morris, *Scientific Creationism*, 59–60.

101 Morris, *Scientific Creationism*, 61.

102 Morris, *Scientific Creationism*, 62, citing questions raised by the evolutionary biologist Frank Salisbury, "Doubts about the Modern Synthetic Theory of Evolution," 336.

103 Dembski, *The Design Inference*, 1–9.

104 E. Melendez-Hevia, et al., "The Puzzle of the Krebs Citric Acid Cycle," and M. A. Huynen, et al., "Variation and Evolution of the Citric-Acid Cycle."

105 *Descent*, 21.11–12.

106 Morris, *Scientific Creationism*, 37–58.

107 Morris, *Scientific Creationism*, 43–45.

108 Morris, "Science Versus Scientism in Historical Geology"; "The Power of Energy"; Barnes, "A Scientific Alternative to Evolution," all in Lammerts, ed., *Scientific Studies*, 107–18, 66–68, 331–37.

109 Morris, *Scientific Creationism*, 211.

110 Morris, *Scientific Creationism*, 211–12.

111 Gregory of Nyssa, "Catechetical Oration," §§ 21–24; Clement of Alexandria, *Paedagogus* 1.12.98; Irenaeus, *Against the Heresies* 3.23.5; Athanasius, *De Incarnatione Verbi* 20. For John of Damascus Christ is the Healer; incarnation was an act of healing – not redemption from original sin; *De Imagine* 3.9; Origen, *De Principiis* 1.8.3, 3.6; Lossky, *In the Image and Likeness of God*, 97–110, 125–39.

112 Wilson, *Sociobiology*, 562.

113 Wilson, *Sociobiology*, 120.

114 Monod, *Chance and Necessity*, 160–80.

115 Gallup Poll, May, 2008.

116 Chambers, "Why a Statement Affirming Evolution?," 23.

117 See Hofstadter, *Gödel, Escher, Bach*.

118 Sagan, *The Dragons of Eden*, 150; John Skoles and Dorian Sagan's sequel, *Up from Dragons*, pursues Sagan's theme, tempered, by focusing on human distinctiveness and cerebral plasticity.

119 Frye, *The Secular Scripture*, 6–20.

120 Voegelin, *Order and History*, 4.112–13.

121 Kass, *Beginning of Wisdom*, 54.

122 Thomson, "Turin Shroud," 2.

123 Saadiah, *Amanat wa-'l-Itiqadat*, I, Exordium, tr. Rosenblatt, 28–29.

124 Overton, in McLean vs. Arkansas, in Ruse, *But is it Science?* 307–31.

125 Morris, *Impact* 3 (September, 1982) 1.

126 See Goodman, *In Defense of Truth*, 374–76.

2 Leaving Eden

1 *Targum Onkelos*, the ancient Aramaic translation, renders *Elohim* here by the tetragrammaton, meaning God Himself, lest one imagine some other deity is meant.

2 As the exegete Rashbam, Rabbi Shmuel ben Meir explains (at Genesis 1:1), the Hebrew Bible often uses summary statements that anticipate the subsequent narrative. Sasson notes summary sentences here and in 2:3: All was God's work. If there were prior existents, that "in no way deters God from creating many things out of nothing. For example, light … is created *ex nihilo*, and then simply contrasted with darkness. … In fact, no item which God orders into being by using the jussive *y'hi* (let there be) within a *va-yo'mer* (He said) statement can be said to emerge from preexisting materials," "Time … to Begin," 187–90.

3 Bible critics know Rahab as a turbulent goddess. In the Psalms (89:10) and Isaiah (51:9) she is cut to pieces – a deity no more. Here she is simply absent. "It is now

practically impossible to locate a biblical commentary which does not devote many pages to *Enuma Elish*. ... I doubt, however, that Israel was much interested in the theologies of other nations, if only because its own theologians did not have ready access to Pritchard's hefty *Ancient Near Eastern Texts Relating to the Old Testament* from which to mount their polemics. Linguistically *tehom* [the deep] could be related to Tiamat [the pagan goddess] only indirectly, through a link which is missing from the evidence at hand. *Tehom* as an adversary for God makes fullest sense only in creations where the combat metaphor is dominant. While this particular metaphor appears frequently in Scripture, it is not featured in Genesis where there are metaphors of rearrangement and of craftsmanship. Therefore we should recognize that here, as elsewhere, *tehom* is a poetic term for bodies of water ... theogony or the birth and emergence of God from preexisting matter is a theme which the Hebrew writer could not profitably discuss. It is this reluctance which makes the Hebrews so different from their more mythopoeic neighbors who repeatedly retold how deities emerge either from unformed matter or from each other." Sasson, "Time ... to Begin," 188–91.

4 Ginzberg, *Legends of the Jews*, 57, following Ezekiel 37:14.
5 Plotinus, *Enneads*, V 3.17, VI 9.11.
6 Philo, *De Opificio Mundi* 33–34, ed. Colson, 24–27.
7 Sasson, "Time ... to Begin," 191.
8 Nahmanides, on 1:4, citing Ecclesiastes 2:13.
9 Cf. Rashbam, *On Genesis*, 34–35.
10 Kass, *Beginning of Wisdom*, 36.
11 Genesis Rabbah 13.10; cf. Resh Lakish at 13:11, citing Psalms 135:7.
12 Saadiah, *The Book of Theodicy*, at Job 37:11, tr. Goodman, 192, cf. 377.
13 Philo, *De Opificio* 38, ed. Colson, 1.29.
14 Cf. Sasson, "Time ... to Begin," 193; Augustine, *De Genesi ad Literam*, 175.
15 John Roach Straton, *Evolution vs Creation*, in R. Numbers, ed., *Creation–Evolution Debates*, 2.120.
16 The *tahash*, variously identified as a seal, dugong, dolphin, or badger, is homiletically problematic, its skin used in the biblical tabernacle (Exodus 25:5, 26:14, 35:7, 23) but its flesh unfit as food. Later it is romanced as a fabulous creature, but Ezekiel (16:10) mentions *tahash* soled sandals. Rashi (at Exodus 25:5, following B. Shabbat 28B) deems it extinct. Israel Gedaliah Lipschutz is well aware of extinction; see Shuchat, "Attitudes Towards Cosmogony and Evolution among Rabbinic Thinkers," 25.
17 Tosefta Bekorot, Second Alphabet of Ben Sirah 25a – 27a, 34a – 36a; Sanhedrin 108AB.
18 In Aristotle's *Politics* I 8, 1256b 15 plants do exist for animals' sake. But that hardly seems their sole purpose. Teleologically, Aristotle looks to outcomes and not always to intentions; cf. Nussbaum, *Aristotle's* De Motu Animalium, 74–99.
19 Sanhedrin 38a, citing Proverbs 9, where wisdom invites the simple to her feast; cf. Tosefta Sanhedrin 8.7–8.
20 Rosenbloom, "Mysticism and Science in Malbim's Theory of Creation," 81.
21 Philo, *De Opificio* 45–46, ed. Colson, 1.34–37; cf. Genesis Rabbah 6.1.
22 Kass, "Evolution and the Bible," *Commentary* 86.5 (November, 1988) 35.
23 Plato, *Apology* 26D; Anaxagoras was the proper target of the charge; see Hippolytus, *Ref.* 1.8.3–10 = DK 59A 42, Kirk and Raven § 502.
24 The Torah, similarly, numbers the months, bypassing their pagan names.
25 Cf. Nahmanides at Genesis 1:18.
26 Benamozegh, *Israel et l'Humanité* 154.
27 Cf. Philo, *De Opificio* 69; *Quis rerum Divinarum Heres*, 231; *Legum Allegoriae* 3.96.

28 Kass, *Beginning of Wisdom*, 37–38.

29 Pesikta de R. Kahana, Supplement 1.11, to Genesis 5:2.

30 Almosnino, Sermon on *Eleh Pequde* (1568) in Saperstein, *Jewish Preaching*, 228.

31 Cross reads *These are the generations* ... as introducing what follows; *Canaanite Myth and Hebrew Epic*, 301. But what follows is about Adam and Eve, not heaven and earth. So Hyers sees a closing summary: *these* are the generations – *this*, and no theogony, is the history of heaven and earth; *The Meaning of Creation*, 45, 197 n. 2.

32 Kass, *Beginning of Wisdom*, 31–33, 39–40.

33 Jacob Agus, in *Jewish Identity in an Age of Ideologies*, 232–81, indicts Babylonian myth, and Bergson's *elán vital* idea, for reducing the divine to functionality.

34 Heschel, *The Sabbath*, xxxx.

35 Philo, *Legum Allegoria* 1.2, 1.20; cf. *De Opificio* 13, 26, 28, 67.

36 *Mekhilta*, ed. Lauterbach, 2.255–56.

37 Kass, *Beginning of Wisdom*, 55.

38 Sanhedrin 38a, citing Psalms 139:16, Zechariah 4:10.

39 Klein, *Etymological Dictionary*; *American Heritage Dictionary*, s.v. *human* and the "zero-grade form" *dhghem-*, earth, the source of *cthonic, chameleon, chamomile, humus, humble, homage, hombre*, the Russian *zemlya* (land), and Persian *zamin*, earth or land.

40 *Descent*, 21.171.

41 Naphta'Halevi, *Toldot Adam* (The History of Adam), citing Genesis Rabbah 2.7.

42 Orlinsky, *Notes on the New Translation of the Torah*, 60.

43 Philo, *De Specialibus Legibus* 4.24, *De Legum Allegoria* 1.13, *De Opificio Mundi* 51, ed. Colson and Whitaker, 1.115, 171, 8.85. Cf. Ecclesiastes 12:7; Nahmanides at Genesis 2:7.

44 Samuel ben Nahman in Genesis Rabbah 8.1, Midrash on Psalms, 139:5, Tanhuma Tazria 1, B. Berakhot 61A, Eruvin 18A. Eusebius, *Praeparatio Evangelica* 585c, complains that Plato assigns Aristophanes a distorted version of Eve's formation from Adam's rib. But the comedian was "used to scoffing even at sacred things."

45 Philo, *De Vita Contemplativa* 7.63.

46 Cf. Ginzberg, *Legends of the Jews*, 5.88–89 n. 42.

47 B. Bava Batra 16A, Genesis Rabbah 13.15; cf. the *Nishmat* prayer.

48 Benamozegh, *Israel et l'Humanité*, 168.

49 Philo, *Legum Allegoria* 1.91.

50 Lawler, "Manliness," 156.

51 Hartman, Lecture delivered in Jerusalem, June 9, 2008.

52 Origen, *Contra Celsum* 4.38.

53 Philo, *Legum Allegoria*, 2.19.

54 Nemoy, "Two Controversial Points in the Karaite Law of Incest," 247.

55 Philo, *Legum Allegoria* 1.105–8.

56 J. Makkot 2.6; cf. Philo, *Legum Allegoria*, 1.88–89.

57 Kass, *Beginning of Wisdom*, 94–96.

58 Benamozegh sees more: the unity of all living things; *Israel et l'Humanité*, 148, 168.

59 Maimonides, *Guide*, Introduction, Munk 1.4; "Eight Chapters," 8; Genesis Rabbah 15.5.

60 "The Murdered Brother," Niles 10 (Child 13) in Niles, *Ballad Book*.

61 Goodman, *Islamic Humanism*, 162–65.

62 Goodman, *God of Abraham*, 101–2, 119–20, 125; Hammurabi's Code, tr. Driver and Miles, 1.17; 2.47, 79, 83, 500.

63 Similarly Levirate marriage and the laws of the suspected adulteress; see *On Justice*, 13; *God of Abraham*, 117–18, 137–38, 163.

64 Genesis Rabbah (28.8, citing Genesis 6:12) implicates the animals and even the earth in sin – the animals, for crossbreeding or growing fierce, the earth, for yielding sham grain – darnel or rye-grass. Biblically, the fault was clearly human.
65 Abbott, *Life and Literature of the Ancient Hebrews*, 80.
66 The Rabbis find seven laws in God's covenant with Noah, binding on humanity at large; Genesis Rabbah 34.14.

3 The case for evolution

1 *Origin*, 15.39.
2 Diderot, quoted in Rostand, *L'Atomisme en biologie*, 175.
3 Buffon, *Histoire Naturelle*, 10.
4 Ikhwan al-Safa, *The Case of the Animals vs Man*, Introduction.
5 *Origin*, 16.421.
6 Wallace conceived of evolution by natural selection independently while traveling in search of specimens. He anticipated humans' simian ancestry from the start, but in 1864 argued that human physical evolution had ceased; a spiritual power had taken over moral and spiritual development; Browne, *Darwin*, 2.23–36, 316–21.
7 *Origin*, 16.14–15.
8 *Origin*, 16.44–45, 90–91.
9 *Origin*, 16.15–24; Browne, *Darwin*, 2.205.
10 *Origin*, 16.22–23.
11 *Origin*, 15.25–29, 16.68–69.
12 *Origin*, 16.35.
13 *Origin*, 16.70.
14 *Origin*, 15.123, 140.
15 Poinar and Poinar, *What Bugged the Dinosaurs*.
16 *Origin*, 16.35–36.
17 *Origin*, 16.38–42.
18 *Origin*, 16.51.
19 *Origin*, 16.51–52.
20 Tennyson, *In Memoriam* (1850) 56, stanza 4, echoed in *Descent*, 22.521.
21 *Origin*, 16.52.
22 *Origin*, 16.53.
23 *Autobiography*, 29.144.
24 See Dennis, "Collective and Individual Rationality"; for the many connections of Malthus with Darwin's circle, reading, and thinking, Browne, 1.385–88.
25 *Origin*, 16.55–60.
26 *Origin*, 15.69.
27 *Origin*, 16.74–83.
28 *Origin*, 16.107–8.
29 Browne, *Darwin*, 1.186–90, 273–74, 287, 298–99, 317–18, 324; 2.73, 80, 86, 91, 96.
30 See Aristotle, *Physics* II 8, 198b 29; Lucretius, *De Rerum Natura* V 855–77. Where Epicureans lacked the cell biology that would supply the particles they posited, Darwin lacked knowledge of the genes and chromosomes.
31 Seeking the source of variation even in 1837, Darwin connected it in the end with sexual reproduction but remained ignorant of its basis; Browne, *Darwin*, 1.385, 516; 2.38–39.
32 *Origin*, 16.279–80.
33 *Origin*, 16.281, 285. Darwin miscalculated the time needed for the erosion of the Weald and withdrew the example from later editions of the *Origin*.

34 Lamarck was also among the first to speak of biology. Karl Burdach coined the term, applying it in the human case. Gottfried Treviranus gave it a general sense in 1802, in the title of a multi-volume work. Lamarck followed that same year.

35 Lamarck, *Philosophie zoologique*, 2.248.

36 Lamarck, *Philosophie zoologique*, 1.2.

37 Lamarck, *Philosophie zoologique*, 1.71.

38 Lamarck, *Philosophie zoologique*, 1.224.

39 Lamarck, *Philosophie zoologique*, 1.248–49; tr. Elliot, 119–20.

40 Lamarck, *Philosophie zoologique*, 1.235–38.

41 Darwin, "On the Evidences Favourable and Opposed to the View that Species are Naturally Favoured Races Descended from a Common Stock," in Francis Darwin, ed., *The Foundations of the Origin of Species*, 10.176–77; Notebook D: "Habits give structure," quoted in Browne, *Darwin*, 1.383.

42 *Origin*, 15.9.

43 *Origin*, 15.97–98.

44 *Origin*, 15.10; see Browne, *Darwin*, 2.201.

45 *Origin*, 16.397–98.

46 *Origin*, 16.11.

47 *Origin*, 16.388.

48 *Origin*, 16.378.

49 *Origin*, 16.47. William Herschel discovered moons of Saturn and Uranus in the late 18th century. In 1852 his son John Herschel, a versatile scientist whose work inspired the young Darwin, who first met him during the voyage of the *Beagle* while Herschel was in South Africa, confirmed those findings and named the two moons of Uranus that his father had identified.

50 *Origin*, 16.164.

51 *Origin*, 15.93–94, 16.110–11, 378–80.

52 *Origin*, 16.144.

53 *Origin*, 16.398.

54 Aristotle, *De Generatione Animalium* II 6, 743b 20–24.

55 *Origin*, 16.167–69.

56 *Origin*, 16.162; cf. *Descent*, 22.514, *Orchids*, 17.201.

57 Kant, *Critique of Judgment*, 346–47, 363–64, quoted in Richards, *The Meaning of Evolution*, 23.

58 *Origin*, 16.399.

59 *Origin*, 16.400.

60 Darwin, Notebook E, 83–84, ed. Barrett and Freeman, 418.

61 Darwin, to Hooker, *Correspondence*, 7.432, quoted in Browne, 2.105.

62 *Origin*, 16.xiii. Darwin courted the support of von Baer, whom Huxley had translated, Browne, *Darwin*, 2.86, 92.

63 Richards, *The Meaning of Evolution*, 12–14.

64 Tiedemann, *Zoologie*, 1.64–65, in Richards, *The Meaning of Evolution*, 45.

65 Owen's angry review of the *Origin* caused Darwin much pain; Richards, *The Meaning of Evolution*, 101–4, Browne, *Darwin*, 2.98–100, 110–12.

66 Darwin, Notebook D, 134e-135e, ed. Barrett and Freeman, 374–75.

67 Richards, *The Meaning of Evolution*, 105–6, 130–31.

68 *Origin*, 16.411.

69 *Origin*, 16.324; cf. the unpublished Essay of 1844; Gould, *Ontogeny*, 72; Richards, *The Meaning of Evolution*, 124–25, 170–71.

70 *Origin*, 16.411.

71 *Origin*, 16.388.

72 *Origin*, 16.413.

73 *Origin*, 16.415–16.
74 *Origin*, 16.380–81.
75 Richards, *The Meaning of Evolution*, 160–64; Storer and Usinger, 467.
76 *Descent*, 21.164.
77 Storer and Usinger, 211.
78 *Origin*, 15.117.
79 *Descent*, 21.17–19.
80 *Origin*, 16.315–16.
81 *Origin*, 16.295–300, 309, 312–13.
82 *Origin*, 16.306.
83 *Origin*, 16.327–28.
84 *Origin*, 16.303–9.
85 *Origin*, 15.227–28; cf. 10.111–12.
86 *Origin*, 16.303; cf. 16.276–77, 282–85.
87 Tudge and Young, *The Link*.
88 Prothero, *Evolution*, xix–xx.
89 *Origin*, 16.288. By current estimates, fewer than one percent of the species that have lived are represented among the fossils. Soft tissues rarely survive, and most bones and shells are crushed, dissolved, weathered away, or obliterated in metamorphic rock; Prothero, *Evolution*, 51–54.
90 *Origin*, 15.305; 16.43, 90–94, 141–42, 148.
91 *Origin*, 16.332.
92 *Origin*, 15.279.
93 *Origin*, 16.338, 362.
94 *Origin*, 16.358–59.
95 *Origin*, 16.345–46.
96 *Origin*, 16.366.
97 *Origin*, 15.283–84.
98 *Origin*, 15.284.
99 Darwin, *Journal of Researches* (2nd edition, 1845), quoted in Sulloway, "Geographic Isolation in Darwin's Thinking"; cf. his "Darwin and his Finches" and Lack, *Darwin's Finches*.
100 Browne, *Darwin*, 1.358–64; 2.31, 39, 61.
101 *Origin*, 16.151.
102 *Origin*, 16.155. No organism has both lungs and a swimbladder. Yet "modern biologists think that the recycling went the other way, the primitive lung being pressed into service as a swimbladder," Cronin, *The Ant and the Peacock*, 25.
103 *Origin*, 16.191–94.
104 *Origin*, 16.167–68.
105 *Origin*, 16.150, 365.
106 *Origin*, 16.164.
107 *Origin*, 16.201–2.
108 Kitcher writes: "It has taken more than a century of research on a wide variety of organisms to demonstrate that Darwin's hunch was basically right. Appearances to the contrary, organs and structures sensitive to light can be assembled piecemeal, with the intermediates enjoying some advantage over the competition." *Living with Darwin*, 80.
109 *Origin*, 16.212.
110 *Origin*, 16.153.
111 *Origin*, 16.176–77.
112 *Origin*, 16.221–24.
113 *Origin*, 16.225–29.

114 *Origin*, 16.226.
115 *Origin*, 16.229.
116 *Origin*, 16.230.
117 *Origin*, 16.230.
118 *Origin*, 16.236.
119 *Origin*, 16.240; Browne, *Darwin*, 2.203.
120 *Origin*, 16.247.
121 *Origin*, 16.248–49, 250.
122 *Origin*, 16.252–53.
123 *Origin*, 16.256.
124 *Origin*, 16.253.
125 Kelvin, "On the Age of the Sun's Heat."
126 When skeptics denied the sun was hot enough to fuse hydrogen atoms into helium, Eddington challenged them to show him a hotter place; *Observatory* 43.
127 Kelvin recanted to J. J. Thomson. For Kelvin's challenge, see Dalrymple, *Ancient Earth, Ancient Skies*, 26, 33; Hallam, *Great Geological Controversies*; 106–7, 111–13, 124; Lewis, *The Dating Game*, 19, 25–26, 35.
128 Unger, quoted in Fairbanks, *Relics of Eden*, 209.
129 See Browne, *Darwin*, 2.202.
130 *Origin*, 16.5–6, 16.415–16.
131 Joravsky, "Inheritance of Acquired Characteristics," 2.617–18.
132 *Descent*, 22.236–39, 478, 524–25.
133 Darwin, *Variations*, 20.303.
134 Jenkin, reviewing the *Origin* in *North British Review* (1867); Browne, *Darwin*, 2.282–83, 311, 314. Jenkin, a good friend of Robert Louis Stevenson's, who wrote a memoir of him, made the first graph of a supply and demand curve. In partnership with the later Lord Kelvin he pioneered in laying undersea cables.
135 Kekes, *In the Name of Eugenics*, 18; Fairbanks, *Relics of Eden*, 211; Bulmer, "Did Jenkin's Swamping Argument invalidate Darwin's Theory of Natural Selection?"
136 Sutton, "On the Morphology of the Chromosome Group ... ".
137 Rose, *Darwin's Spectre*, 45–47.
138 R. A. Fisher, *The Genetic Theory of Natural Selection*; D. S. Falconer, *Introduction to Quantitative Genetics*, 26–36, 286–307; L. L. Cavalli-Sforza and W. F. Bodmer, *The Genetics of Human Populations*, 71–88, 316–17.
139 Fairbanks, *Relics of Eden*, 125–30.
140 Kettlewell, "Selection Experiments on Industrial Melanism in the Lepidoptera"; "Further Selection Experiments on Industrial Melanism in the Lepidoptera."
141 Majerus, *Melanism*; Tutt, *British Moths*.
142 Rudge, "Did Kettlewell Commit Fraud?" responding to J. Hooper, *Of Moths and Men*.
143 Wright, *Evolution and the Genetics of Populations*, in Grant, "Fine Tuning the Peppered Moth Paradigm"; cf. Haldane, "The Theory of Selection for Melanism in Lepidoptera."
144 Kofahl, *Handy Dandy Evolution Refuter*, 54–55; cf. Davidheiser, *Evolution and Christian Faith*, 203–5.
145 Kitcher, *Living with Darwin*, 80.
146 Olson, *Evolution in Hawaii*, 15–19.
147 Fairbanks, *Relics of Eden*, 19–29, 88–99.
148 Fairbanks, Relics of Eder 53–59, 83–85.
149 Fairbanks, *Relics of Eden*, 69–70.
150 Fairbanks, *Relics of Eden*, 100.

4 Three lines of critique

1 Sedgwick, *The Spectator*, April, 1860, excerpted in Ruse, *But is it Science?* 100–104; Darwin, *Correspondence*, 7.396; Sedgwick even set a finals paper for his students calling on them to determine what was "inductive" and what was "hypothetical" in the *Origin*; Browne, *Darwin*, 2.93–94, 108.

2 Wittgenstein, *Culture and Value* 72e.

3 Maimonides, *Guide* III 13, 17.

4 Plantinga, "When Faith and Reason Clash," in Pennock, 131.

5 Plantinga, "Creation and Evolution," in Pennock, 779.

6 Plantinga, "When Faith and Reason Clash," in Pennock, 121–22; cf. 128. Ruse responds: "At the risk of sounding intolerant, any scientist – including any Darwinian – has to insist that there comes a point at which discussion is closed. No sensible person could or should possibly be convinced, after no matter how much careful and prayerful study of the Scriptures, that the Earth is the centre of the universe with the sun going around it in a circle. Such a belief is irresponsible and stupid, and if one's religion allows this, then the scientist (including the Darwinian) has to reject the religion. ... Darwinians today think their theory sufficiently well established that, if Christianity is a religion which would even allow the reasonable possibility of Darwinism's rejection on grounds of conflict with literal readings of Scripture ... then Christianity itself ought to be rejected." *Can a Darwinian be a Christian?* 59.

7 Huxley in Ruse, *But is it Science?* 106–7.

8 Browne, *Darwin*, 1.141, 337–38.

9 Ellegard, "The Darwinian Revolution"; Ghiselin, *The Triumph of the Darwinian Method*; Hull, *The Philosophy of the Biological Sciences*; Ruse, "Darwin's Debt to Philosophy." Whewell, however, was said to have banned the *Origin* from the Trinity College library at Cambridge. John Herschel, another formative figure in Darwin's methodological thinking, reputedly dismissed natural selection as "the law of higgledy piggledy." Mill, however, endorsed Darwinism in the 1862 edition of his *Logic*, labeling it not an induction in his sense but a hypothesis. Browne, 1.127–28, 372, 437; 2.107, 186.

10 In his 1831 Presidential Address to the Geological Society, Sedgwick had publicly recanted his early allegiance to "the Mosaic Flood"; Kitcher, *Living with Darwin*, 30–31.

11 Silvan S. Schweber, "The origin of the Origin revisited"; "Darwin and the Political Economists"; "The Correspondence of the Young Darwin"; Gould, *The Structure of Evolutionary Theory*, 59–60, 121–25, 193. Gould finds it a "delicious (and almost malicious) irony" that "the theory of natural selection is, in essence, Adam Smith's economics transferred to nature."

12 Evidence was the key to Darwin's strength, distancing him from more conjectural evolutionary views like those of his grandfather, or contemporaries like the more metaphysically inclined Herbert Spencer or the popular but highly speculative anonymous author of *Vestiges of the Natural History of Creation* (1844), later identified as the entrepreneurial publisher Robert Chambers. Darwin, uncharacteristically, entered the fray angrily and directly when his views were linked with speculations about spontaneous generation: His own theory linked "by an intelligible thread of reasoning a multitude of facts." Spontaneous generation could boast no "shadow of a fact." As matters stood, "one might as well think of origin of matter." Browne, *Darwin*, 2.213–14.

13 Morris, *Scientific Creationism*, 6–7; see Numbers, *The Creationists*, 274.

14 Popper, in Ruse, *But is it Science?* 144–46; cf. Popper's Spencer and Compton lectures, 1961, 1966. The charge seems as old as Samuel Haughton's comment

when the *Origin* appeared: "If it means what it says, it is a truism; if it means anything more, it is contrary to fact."

15 Popper, in Ruse, *But is it Science?* 147.

16 Popper, in Ruse, *But is it Science?* 148.

17 Darwin, *Orchids*, 17.173.

18 Mayr, *The Growth of Biological Thought*, 519, 523; cf. Williams, "Falsifiable Predictions of Evolutionary Theory"; Mills and Beatty, "The Propensity Interpretation of Fitness."

19 See Goodman, *In Defense of Truth*, 149–51.

20 Fleeming Jenkin, review of *Origin*.

21 *Origin*, 15.143–44.

22 *Origin*, 16.154.

23 *Origin*, 16.164, 174, 243, 431. Traced to a 1613 remark by Jacques Tissot, the saying was a favorite maxim of Leibniz's. Linnaeus gave it biological application. The underlying assumption, running back at least to Aristotle, acquires a variety of interpretations in physics, cosmology, metaphysics, and law. Even Huxley resisted Darwin's insistent gradualism and irked Darwin by calling evolution a working hypothesis, albeit a powerful one. Browne, *Darwin*, 2.58, 92–93.

24 *Origin*, 16.441.

25 Behe, *Darwin's Black Box*, 39.

26 Behe, *Darwin's Black Box*, 65.

27 Behe, *Darwin's Black Box*, 40, quoting Dawkins, *River out of Eden*, 83.

28 Behe, 72.

29 Sedgwick, in Ruse, 100.

30 Mivart, *On the Genesis of Species*, 21.

31 Cicero, *De Natura Deorum* II 85–86.

32 Cicero, *De Natura Deorum* II 87–88.

33 Aristotle, *Parts of Animals* II 9, 655b, *On Generation and Corruption* I 5, 321b 29–32, *Generation of Animals* II 5, 741a 10–11.

34 Aristotle, *Physics* II 4–8.

35 Gilson, *From Aristotle to Darwin*, 113.

36 *Origin*, 16.146–47,151.

37 Nilsson and Pelger, "A Pessimistic Estimate of the Time Required for an Eye to Evolve."

38 Nilsson and Pelger, "A Pessimistic Estimate of the Time Required for an Eye to Evolve."

39 Dawkins, *River out of Eden*; Berlinski, quoting a letter from Nilsson, "A Scientific Scandal," 34.

40 Behe, *Darwin's Black Box*, 71, 143.

41 Behe, *Darwin's Black Box*, 76.

42 Hume, *Dialogues Concerning Natural Religion*, 143.

43 Behe, *Darwin's Black Box*, 65.

44 Blackstone, 446; Roth, Mandrell, and Griffiss, 762–67.

45 Maupin-Furlow and Ferry, 28617–22.

46 Blackstone, 446, citing Driscoll, et al.; Gaczynska, et al.; Stuart and Jones.

47 Blackstone, 446, citing Buss, 82.

48 Thornton et al., *Science* April 7, 2006.

49 Shanks and Joplin, "Redundant Complexity."

50 Pigliucci, "Design Yes, Intelligent No."

51 Shanks and Joplin, 279, citing Cooke, Nowak, Boerlijst, and Maynard-Smith, 360–64.

52 Miller, "The Flagellum Unspun."

53 Miller, "The Flagellum Unspun," citing Hueck and McNabb.

54 Blackstone, 446, citing de Duve; Behe, 160.

55 Darwin, *Orchids*, 17.126.

56 Cronin, *The Ant and the Peacock*, 45.

57 Locke, *Essay*, IV xvii § 19.2, ed. Niddich, 686; ed. Fraser, 2.410–11; see Krabbe, "Appeal to Ignorance," 251–53.

58 Leibniz, *New Essays*, Bk. 4 Ch. 17, tr. Remnant and Bennett, 491–92.

59 Woods and Walton, *Fallacies*, 161; cf. 167.

60 Woods and Walton, 166.

61 Locke targeted Malebranche's claim that we will find no better account of experience than that we see all things in God. Fraser quotes the key passage from Locke's *Examination of Malebranche*, published posthumously (London, 1706).

62 Spinoza, *Ethics* I, Appendix, ed. Gebhardt, 2.80 *ll.* 30–37.

63 Spinoza, *Ethics*, ed. Gebhardt, 2.81 *ll.* 9–11.

64 Spinoza, to Oldenburg, 27 September 1661, Gebhardt, 4.12 *ll.* 7–9.

65 Spinoza, *Ethics*, ed. Gebhardt, 2.81 *ll.* 11–15.

66 Spinoza, *Ethics*, ed. Gebhardt, 78 *ll.* 28–38.

67 Maimonides, *Guide* III 12, glossing Genesis 1:15–18.

68 Spinoza, *Cogitata Metaphysica* II 7, in the Dutch, after Curley, 326, Gebhardt, 1.261, *ll.* 1–6, 13–14.

69 Spinoza, *Tractatus de Intellectus Emendatione*, §§ 29–32, 39; see Goodman, *In Defense of Truth*, 200.

70 Plantinga, "Evolution, Neutrality, and Antecedent Probability," 98.

71 Spinoza, *Cogitata Metaphysica* II 7, ed. Gebhardt, 1.260, *l.* 28 – 261, *l.* 1.

72 Job 38–39; cf. Isaiah 40:12; Proverbs 30:4.

73 Cicero, *De Natura Deorum* II 96.

74 Heschel, *God in Search of Man*, 44–46, 57.

75 Gilson, *From Aristotle to Darwin*, 57.

76 Aristotle, *De Partibus Animalium*, I 5, 645a 10–25; Gilson, *From Aristotle to Darwin*, 10.

77 *Origin*, 16.80, quoted at Gilson, *From Aristotle to Darwin*, 20–21.

78 Gilson, *From Aristotle to Darwin*, 24–25.

79 Aristotle, *De Partibus Animalium* I 1; Gilson, *From Aristotle to Darwin*, 26.

80 Aristotle, *De Caelo* II 11, 291b, 13.

81 Einstein, to Maurice Solovine, January 1, 1951, in *Letters to Solovine*, 119.

82 Einstein in Moszkowski, *Conversations with Einstein,* 46.

83 Einstein, *Ideas and Opinions*, 40.

84 Heschel, *God in Search of Man*, 33, 39–40.

85 Heschel, *God in Search of Man*, 48–49.

86 Heschel, *God in Search of Man*, 34.

87 Wittgenstein, *Culture and Value*, 5e (1930).

88 Heschel, *God in Search of Man*, 51.

89 Johnson, "Evolution as Dogma," in Pennock, 63.

90 Lewontin, "Billions and Billions of Demons," 31.

91 See Dembski, "What Every Theologian Should Know," 4.

92 Ruse, *Can a Darwinian be a Christian?* 128.

5 "That has its seeds within it"

1 McMullin, "Evolution and Special Creation."

2 See Rashi at Genesis 2:4.

3 Augustine, *De Genesi ad Literam*, tr. Taylor 1.150, 168, 180, 253–56, 259, 262–63, citing Ben Sirah 18:1 – *He who lives forever created all things together*, as

Augustine's Latin Bible has it; Taylor 2.244, n. 11. Cf. Aulie, "Evolution and Special Creation," 436.

4 *Origin* 15.346, 16.446.

5 Darwin, *Natural Selection*, ed. Stauffer, 224.

6 Malbim on Genesis 1:20, 25; cf. on Genesis 1:2–5, 11, citing Pinhas Elijah Hurwitz's comparison of apes and humans; see Rosenbloom, "Mysticism and Science in Malbim's Theory of Creation," 81.

7 McMullin, 328; Augustine echoes Genesis and Isaiah 45:18.

8 Plantinga, "Evolution, Neutrality, and Antecedent Probability"; cf. Van Till, "When Faith and Reason Cooperate." Plantinga writes: "Natural laws are not in any way independent of God, and are perhaps best thought of as regularities in the ways in which he treats the stuff he has made, or perhaps as counterfactuals of divine freedom. (Hence there is nothing in the least untoward in the thought that on some occasions God might do something in a way different from his usual way – e.g., raise someone from the dead or change water into wine." "Methodological Naturalism," 149.

9 Browne, *Darwin*, 2.95–96. Kingsley agreed to endorse evolution, and Darwin printed his words in every edition of the *Origin* after the first. The Harvard botanist Asa Gray also welcomed the work and pronounced it no threat to natural theology. Darwin hailed Gray as a "Lawyer, Poet, Naturalist, and Theologian" and underwrote the British reprinting of Gray's reviews arguing that theism and evolution were compatible. Browne, *Darwin*, 2.128, 155, 175.

10 Kant, *Lectures on Ethics*, tr. Infield, 252.

11 McMullin, "Evolution and Special Creation," 326.

12 Kim, *Supervenience and Mind*, 291.

13 Francis Darwin, introducing Darwin's *Autobiography*, 308.

14 Eric Nordenskiöld, *History of Biology*, 482.

15 Bacon, *Novum Organum* xlviii.

16 Nordenskiöld, *History of Biology*, 474.

17 Nordenskiöld, *History of Biology*, 594.

18 Rádl, *The History of Biological Theories*, 105–6.

19 Singer, *A Short History of Biology*, 305, 548.

20 Allen, *Thomas Hunt Morgan*, 314.

21 Tinbergen, "On the Aims and Methods of Ethology," 417.

22 Bernatowicz, "Teleology in Science Teaching."

23 Walsh, "Galen's Discovery and Promulgation of the Function of the Recurrent Laryngeal Nerve," 17; *De Usu Partium* VII 14, tr. May, 362–63; *De Placitis*, ed. C. G. Kühn, vol. 5.

24 Bernatowicz, loc. cit.

25 *Origin*, 2.

26 Keats, to George and Georgiana, February 14, 1819.

27 Darwin, Notebook: B, 214; cf. C, 166; M, 153; Browne, *Darwin*, 1.373.

28 Dobzhansky, "Chance and Creativity in Evolution," in Ayala and Dobzhansky, *Studies*, 310–11.

29 Millikan, *Language, Thought, and Other Biological Categories*.

30 Sober, *Philosophy of Biology*, 84.

31 Kass, *Toward a More Natural Science*, 265.

32 Brandon, *Adaptation and Environment*, 139, 165, 185–89.

33 Ernest Nagel, *Teleology Revisited*, 278–79.

34 Nagel, *Teleology Revisited*, 289.

35 Nagel, *Teleology Revisited*, 290, 313–16; cf. the discussion in Ruse, *Darwin and Design*, 255–89.

36 Haldane seems to have been quoting Freud's teacher, Ernst von Brücke.
37 *Origin*, 16.68.
38 Arisotle, *De Partibus Animalium* III 1, 661b 1–14.
39 Aristotle, *De Partibus Animalium* 659a 29–37, 662a 17–21.
40 Aristotle, *Politics*, I 2, 1252a 25–26.
41 Aristotle, *Physics* II 8.
42 Aristotle, *De Partibus Animalium* IV 10, 687a 10–14.
43 *Origin*, 16.103–6; cf. Richards, *The Meaning of Evolution*, 84–90.
44 Por, *Animal Achievement*, 6–9.
45 Por, *Animal Achievement*, 13–14, 129.
46 Por, *Animal Achievement*, 16–20, 58–59, 111.
47 Por, *Animal Achievement*, 20–22, 24–25.
48 Por, *Animal Achievement*, 25–26.
49 Por, *Animal Achievement*, 41–47.
50 Por, *Animal Achievement*, 139.
51 Por, *Animal Achievement*, 70–71.
52 Por, *Animal Achievement*, 72–75.
53 Por, *Animal Achievement*, 76–77.
54 Por, *Animal Achievement*, 266–67.
55 Kass, *Toward a More Natural Science*, 265.
56 Fodor, *In Critical Condition*, 211.
57 Kass, *Toward a More Natural Science*, 275.
58 Hartshorne, *Born to Sing*, xii–xiv, 157, 228.
59 Hartshorne, *Born to Sing*, 1–4.
60 Teilhard de Chardin, *The Phenomenon of Man*, 62–63.
61 Hartshorne, *Born to Sing*, 27, 61, 68, 70.
62 Hartshorne, *Born to Sing*, 46–47, 55, 59–60, 77, 101, 107–13, 119, 130, 134–35.
63 See Kass, *Toward a More Natural Science*, 274.
64 Fodor, *In Critical Condition*, 212.
65 Kass, *Toward a More Natural Science*, 272.
66 Spinoza, *Short Treatise* 1.5, Gebhardt, 1.40.
67 Birnbaum, ed., *Ha-Siddur ha-Shalem*: "*she-me-ahavatkha she-ahavta 'oto, u-mi-simatkha she-samakhta bo*"– "Out of thine own love didst Thou love him, and out of thine own joy didst Thou rejoice in him"; cf. Spinoza, *Ethics* 5, Props. 14–16, 32–37.
68 The line is from *Le-khah Dodi*, Solomon Alkabetz's sixteenth-century Sabbath epithalamion poetically celebrating the transcendent God's joyous union with his immanent manifestation, the Shekhinah.
69 Cf. Peacocke, "God's Action in the Real World," 466; Foster, *The Selfless Gene.*
70 Darwin to Gray, 1860, in F. Darwin and A. C. Seward, eds., *More Letters of Darwin*, 1.194.
71 *Descent*, 22.638.
72 Hafetz Hayyim, *Ahavat Hesed*, Part 2, chapter 2.
73 Maimonides, *Guide* I 54, glossing Exodus 33:17–23, 34:6–7.
74 Fogle in Beurton, 4, 11–12.
75 Evelyn Fox Keller, in Beurton, 162.
76 Gifford, in Beurton, 45.
77 Schwartz in Beurton, 28; cf. 36.
78 Beurton, x.
79 Fogle and Holmes in Beurton, 19–20, 137.
80 Beurton, xii, and Gifford in Beurton, 42.
81 Fogle, in Beurton, 14.

82 Fox Keller notes the cautions of Michael Apter and Lewis Wolpert and James Bonner in 1965; in Beurton, 163–66.
83 Sydney Brenner, quoted by Fox Keller, in Beurton, 172.
84 Fox Keller in Beurton, 169.
85 Jacob, *Logic of Life*, 275, 297.
86 Darwin, "On the Two Forms … in the Species of *Primula*," 94–96. Darwin saw adaptations against selfing in hermaphroditic species, but without knowledge of genetics was at a loss to explain their value. See Browne, *Darwin* 2.168, 170–80, 182, 211.
87 Bell, *The Masterpiece of Nature*, 62–64. Bell takes his title from Erasmus Darwin's fond, even Lucretian, appraisal of sexuality.
88 Bell, *The Masterpiece of Nature*, 26.
89 Bell, *The Masterpiece of Nature*, 59, 93.
90 Colling, *Random Designer*, 89; cf. Dobzhansky "Chance and Creativity in Evolution."
91 Bell, *The Masterpiece of Nature*, 45–46.
92 Goddard, Godfray, and Burt, *Nature* 434 (March 31, 2005) 636–40.
93 *Origin*, 15.347.
94 Bell, *The Masterpiece of Nature*, 128–29, cf. 351.
95 Monod, *Chance and Necessity*, 112.
96 Colling, *Random Designer*, 3, 89.
97 Hyers, *The Meaning of Creation*, 176.
98 Cf. Griffin, *Religion and Scientific Naturalism*, 250.
99 *Origin*, 15.347.
100 Browne, *Darwin*, 2.214.
101 Darwin, to William Graham, July 3, 1881, in *More Letters of Darwin*.
102 Monod, *Chance and Necessity*, 111–12.
103 Dawkins, *The Blind Watchmaker*, xiv.
104 Peacocke, "God's Action in the Real World," 467; cf. *Creation and the World of Science*, 94–95.
105 Peacocke, *Theology for a Scientific Age*, 119.
106 Peacocke, *Theology for a Scientific Age*, 174.
107 Peacocke, *Theology for a Scientific Age*, 113–14.
108 Peacocke, *Theology for a Scientific Age*, 118–19.
109 Peacocke, *Theology for a Scientific Age*, 119–20.
110 Forrest, *God without the Supernatural*, 55, 205–6.
111 Hyers, *The Meaning of Creation*, 173–74.
112 Peacocke, loc. cit.
113 Aubrey Moore, *Lux Mundi*, 73, quoted in Peacocke, "Welcoming the Disguised Friend," 471.
114 Peacocke, "God's Action in the Real World," 463.
115 Polkinghorne, *Science and Providence*; *Science and Christian Belief*. Cf. Ruse, *Can a Darwinian be a Christian?* 87.

Afterword Notes

1 Gould, "Nonoverlapping Magisteria," *Natural History* 106 (1997); cf. *Rocks of Ages*.
2 Descartes, *Discourse on Method* and *Meditations on First Philosophy*, tr. Cottingham, Stoothoff, and Mudoch, 1.114; 2.19.
3 Dawkins, *The God Delusion*, 55–61.
4 Dawkins, *The God Delusion*, 57.

5 Dawkins, *The God Delusion*, 61.
6 Dawkins, *The God Delusion*, 56–57.
7 Gould, "Nonoverlapping Magisteria."
8 Gould, "Nonoverlapping Magisteria."
9 Gould, "Nonoverlapping Magisteria."

Bibliography

Lyman Abbott, *Life and Literature of the Ancient Hebrews* (Boston: Houghton Mifflin, 1901).

Jacob B. Agus, *Jewish Identity in an Age of Ideologies* (New York: Ungar, 1978).

G. E. Allen, *Thomas Hunt Morgan: The Man and his Science* (Princeton: Princeton University Press, 1978).

Almosnino, "Sermon on *Eleh Pequde*" (1568), in Saperstein, ed., *Jewish Preaching*.

Erich Auerbach, *Mimesis: The Representation of Reality in Western Literature* (*1942–45*), tr. Willard Trask (Princeton: Princeton University Press, 1953).

Augustine, *De Genesi ad Literam*, tr. John H. Taylor as *The Literal Meaning of Genesis* (New York: Newman, 1982).

Richard P. Aulie, "Evolution and Special Creation: Historical Aspects of the Controversy," *Proceedings of the American Philosophical Society* 127 (1983) 418–62.

——. "The Post-Darwinian Controversies" (reviewing James Moore), *Journal of the American Scientific Affiliation* (1982) 24–29, 90–95, 163–68, 219–24.

Francisco José Ayala and Theodosius Dobzhansky, eds., *Studies in the Philosophy of Biology: Reduction and Related Problems* (Berkeley: University of California Press, 1974).

O. Bakar, *Critique of Evolutionary Theory: A Collection of Essays* (Kuala Lumpur: Islamic Academy of Science, 1987).

D. J. Bartholomew, *God of Chance* (London: SCM, 1984).

G. W. Beadle and E. L. Tatum, "Genetic Control of Developmental Reactions," *The American Naturalist* 75 (1941) 107–16.

Howard K. Beale, *Are American Teachers Free? An Analysis of Restraints upon the Freedom of Teaching in American Schools* (New York: Scribners, 1936).

Michael Behe, *Darwin's Black Box: The Biochemical Challenge to Evolution* (New York: Simon and Schuster, 1996).

Graham Bell, *The Masterpiece of Nature: The Evolution and Genetics of Sexuality* (Berkeley: University of California Press, 1982).

Elijah Benamozegh, *Israel et l'Humanité* (Paris: Ernest Leroux, 1914), tr. Maxwell Luria as *Israel and Humanity* (New York: Paulist Press, 1995).

David Berlinski, "A Scientific Scandal," *Commentary* 115 (April, 2003) 29–36.

A. J. Bernatowicz, "Teleology in Science Teaching," *Science* (December 5, 1958) 1402–5; repr. *Etc.: A Review of General Semantics* 17 (1959) 63–75.

Peter Beurton, Raphael Falk, Hans-Jorg Rheinberger, eds, *The Concept of the Gene in Development and Evolution: Historical and Epistomological Perspectives*, (Cambridge: Cambridge University Press, 2000).

Philip Birnbaum, ed., *Ha-Siddur ha-Shalem* (New York: Hebrew Publishing Company, 1949).

Neil W. Blackstone, "Argumentum ad Ignorantiam," *The Quarterly Review of Biology* 72 (1997) 445–47.

William Boardman, R. F. Koontz, and H. M. Morris, *Science and Creation* (San Diego: Creation-Science Research Center, 1973).

Peter J. Bowler, *The Eclipse of Darwinism: Anti-Darwinian evolution theories in the decades around 1900* (Baltimore: Johns Hopkins University Press, 1977).

Robert N. Brandon, *Adaptation and Environment* (Princeton: Princeton University Press, 1990).

J. T. Bridgham, Sean M. Carroll, and Joseph W. Thornton,, "Evolution of the Hormone-Receptor Complexity by Molecular Exploitation," *Science* vol. 312 no. 5770 (April 7, 1986) 97–101.

Janet Browne, *Charles Darwin: A Biography: Voyaging* (New York: Knopf, 1995); *The Power of Place – The* Origin *and After – The Years of Fame* (New York: Knopf, 2002).

Georges Buffon, *Histoire Naturelle générale et particulière*, in *Oeuvres philosophiques*, ed. Jean Piveteau (Paris: Presses Universitaires de France, 1954).

Michael Bulmer, "Did Jenkin's Swamping Argument Invalidate Darwin's Theory of Natural Selection?" *British Society for the History of Science* 37 (2004) 281–97.

L. W. Buss, *The Evolution of Individuality* (Princeton: Princeton University Press, 1987).

Umberto Cassuto, *A Commentary on the Book of Genesis*, tr. Israel Abrahams (Jerusalem: Magnes Press, 1961–64).

L. L. Cavalli-Sforza and W. F. Bodmer, *The Genetics of Human Populations* (San Francisco: Freeman, 1971).

Bette Chambers, "Why a Statement Affirming Evolution?" *The Humanist* (January/February 1977) 23–24.

Harold W. Clark, *Genesis and Science* (Nashville: Southern Publishing, 1967).

H. G. Coffin, "A Paleoecological Misinterpretation," in Lammerts, ed., *Scientific Studies* (1971) 165–68.

Richard Colling, *Random Designer* (Bourbonnais, Illinois: Browning Press, 2004).

Joseph Le Conte, *Evolution: Its Nature, its Evidences, and its Relation to Religious Thought* (New York: Appleton, 1897; repr., 1970).

Melvin A. Cook, "W. J. Meister's Discovery of Human Footprint with Trilobites in a Cambrian Formation of Western Utah," in Lammerts, ed., *Why Not Creation?* (1970) 185–93.

Jonathan Cooke, Martin Nowak, Maarten Boerlijst, and John Maynard-Smith, "Evolutionary Origins and Maintenance of Redundant Gene Expression during Metazoan Development," *Trends in Genetics* 13 (1997) 360–64.

Helena Cronin, *The Ant and the Peacock* (Cambridge: Cambridge University Press, 1991).

Frank Moore Cross, *Canaanite Myth and Hebrew Epic: Essays in the History of the Religion of Israel* (Cambridge: Harvard University Press, 1973).

G. Brent Dalrymple, *Ancient Earth, Ancient Skies: The Age of the Earth and its Cosmic Surroundings* (Stanford: Stanford University Press, 2004).

Reginald Daly, *Earth's Most Challenging Mysteries* (Nutley, N.J.: Craig Press, 1976).

Charles Darwin, *On the Origin of Species by Means of Natural Selection, or the Preservation of Favoured Races in the Struggle for Life*, 1859, vol. 15 of *The Works of Charles Darwin*, ed. Paul H. Barrett and R. B. Freeman (London: William Pickering, 1988); variorum text of the six editions, ed. Morse Peckham (Philadelphia: University of Pennsylvania Press, 1959).

——. *Autobiography*, ed. Francis Darwin (New York: Dover, 1958).

——. "On the Evidences Favourable and Opposed to the View that Species are Naturally Favoured Races Descended from a Common Stock" (1844) in Francis Darwin, ed., *The Foundations of the Origin of Species*, volume 10 of *The Works of Charles Darwin*, ed. Paul H. Barrett and R. B. Freeman (London: William Pickering, 1988).

——. *Various Contrivances by which Orchids are Fertilized* (1862), ed. Barrett and Freeman (London: Pickering, 1988) vol. 17.

——. "On the Two Forms, or Dimorphic Condition, in the Species of *Primula*, and on their Remarkable Sexual Relations," *Journal of the Proceedings of the Linnaean Society* (Botany) 6 (1861) 77–96, revised in *The Forms of Flowers* (1877) 14–30.

——. *More Letters of Darwin*, ed. A. C. Seward and Francis Darwin (New York: Appleton, 1903).

——. *Natural Selection: Being the Second Part of his Big Species Book, Written from 1856 to 1859*, ed. Robert C. Stauffer (Cambridge: Cambridge University Press, 1975).

Bolton Davidheiser, *Evolution and Christian Faith* (Grand Rapids: Baker Books, 1969).

Richard Dawkins, *The Blind Watchmaker: Why the Evidence of Evolution Reveals a Universe without Design* (New York: Norton, 1987).

——. *The Selfish Gene* (Oxford: Oxford University Press, 1976).

——. *River out of Eden* (New York: Basic Books, 1995).

——. *Climbing Mount Improbable* (London: Viking, 1996).

——. *The God Delusion* (Boston: Houghton Mifflin, 2006).

C. de Duve, *Vital Dust* (New York: Basic Books, 1995).

William Dembski, *The Design Inference: Eliminating Chance through Small Probabilities* (Cambridge: Cambridge University Press, 1999).

——. "What Every Theologian Should Know about Creation, Evolution, and Design," *Transactions* 3 (1995) 1–8.

Andy Dennis, "Collective and Individual Rationality: Robert Malthus's Heterodox Theodicy," City University of London, Economics Discussion Paper Series (2005) number 03/09.

René Descartes, *Principles of Philosophy* (1644), tr. Elizabeth Haldane and G. R. T. Ross (Cambridge: Cambridge University Press, 1967; first edition, 1911).

——. *Discourse on Method* (1637) and *Meditations on First Philosophy* (1641), tr. John Cottingham, Robert Stoothoff, and Dugald Mudoch (Cambridge: Cambridge University Press, 1992).

C. J. deVogel, *Greek Philosophy* (Leiden: Brill, 1964).

Theodosius Dobzhansky, "Chance and Creativity in Evolution," in Ayala and Dobzhansky (eds.), *Studies in the Philosophy of Biology* (Berkeley: University of California Press, 1974) 307–38.

J. Driscoll, M. G. Brown, D. Finley, and J. J. Monaco, "MHC-linked LMP gene products specifically alter peptidase activities of the proteasome," *Nature* 365 (1993) 262–64.

Sir Arthur Eddington, "Presidential Address to the British Association," *Observatory* 43 (1920) 353–55.

Manfred Eigen and Ruthild Winkler, *Laws of the Game* (New York: Knopf, 1981).

——. and P. Schuster, *The Hypercycle* (Berlin: Springer, 1979).

Albert Einstein, *Ideas and Opinions*, tr. Sonja Bargmann (New York: Crown, 1954).

——. *Letters to Solovine, 1906–1955*, tr. Wade Baskin (New York: Carol, 1993).

Alvar Ellegard, "The Darwinian Revolution and Nineteenth Century Philosophies of Science," *Journal of the History of Ideas* 18 (1957) 362–93.

Daniel J. Fairbanks, *Relics of Eden: The Powerful Evidence of Evolution in Human DNA* (Amherst, New York: Prometheus, 2007).

D. S. Falconer, *Introduction to Quantitative Genetics* (New York: Ronald Press, 1970).

Ronald A. Fisher, *The Genetic Theory of Natural Selection* (Oxford: Oxford University Press, 1930).

Peter Forrest, *God without the Supernatural* (Ithaca: Cornell University Press, 1996).

Charles Foster, *The Selfless Gene* (London: Hodder and Stoughton, 2009).

Northrop Frye, *The Secular Scripture* (Cambridge: Harvard University Press, 1976).

M. Gaczynska, K. L. Rick, and A. L. Goldberg, "Γ-Interferon and Expression of MHC Genes Regulate Peptide Hydrolysis by Proteasome," *Nature* 365 (1993) 264–67.

Galen, *De Usu Partium*, tr. Margaret Talmadge May as *On the Usefulness of the Parts of the Body* (Ithaca: Cornell University Press, 1968), 2 volumes.

Galileo Galilei, *Dialogue Concerning the Two Chief World Systems – Ptolemaic and Copernican*, tr. Stillman Drake (Berkeley: University of California Press, 1967).

Ghazali, *Tahafut al-Falasifa* (Incoherence of the Philosophers), ed. Maurice Boyuges, 2nd ed. (Beirut: Catholic Press, 1962); ed. and tr. Michael Marmura (Provo: Brigham Young University Press, 1997).

Michael T. Ghiselin, *The Triumph of the Darwinian Method* (Berkeley: University of California Press, 1969).

Neal Gillespie, *Charles Darwin and the Problem of Creation* (Chicago: University of Chicago Press, 1979).

Etienne Gilson, *From Aristotle to Darwin and Back Again* (Notre Dame: Notre Dame University Press, 1984).

Louis Ginzberg, *Legends of the Jews*, tr. Henrietta Szold and Paul Radin (Philadelphia: JPS, 1909), 7 volumes.

Duane Gish, *Evolution: The Fossils Say No!* (San Diego: Institute for Creation Research, 1973).

Matthew Goddard, H. Charles J. Godfray, and Austin Burt, "Sex Increases the Efficacy of Natural Selection in Experimental Yeast Populations," *Nature* 434 (March 31, 2005) 636–40.

L. E. Goodman, "Maimonidean Naturalism," in Robert Cohen and Hillel Levine, eds., *Maimonides and the Sciences* (Boston: Kluwer, 2000) 57–85.

——. "Respect for Nature," in Hava Tirosh Samuelson, ed., *Judaism and Ecology* (Cambridge: Harvard University Press, 2002) 227–59.

——. *Avicenna* (Ithaca: Cornell University Press, 2006).

——. *God of Abraham* (Oxford University Press, 1996).

——. *In Defense of Truth: A Pluralistic Approach* (Amherst, New York: Humanity Press, 2001).

Stephen Jay Gould, *The Structure of Evolutionary Theory* (Cambridge: Harvard University Press, 2002).

——. *Ontogeny and Phylogeny* (Cambridge: Harvard University Press, 1977).

——. "Nonoverlapping Magisteria," *Natural History* 106.2 (1997) 16–25.

——. *Rocks of Ages: Science and Religion in the Fullness of Life* (New York: Ballantyne, 1999).

Bruce S. Grant, "Fine Tuning the Peppered Moth Paradigm," *Evolution* 53 (1999) 980–84.

Asa Gray, "Natural Selection: Not Inconsistent with Natural Theology," *Atlantic Monthly* 6 (1860) 109–16, 229–39, 406–25.

David Ray Griffin, *Religion and Scientific Naturalism: Overcoming the Conflicts* (Albany: SUNY Press, 2000).

Hafetz Hayyim (Israel Meir Kagan), *Ahavat Hesed* (Warsaw, 1888; repr. New York: Pardes, 1946).

J. B. S. Haldane, "The Theory of Selection for Melanism in Lepidoptera," *Proceedings of the Royal Society* 145 (1956) 303–6.

Naphtali Halevi, "Toldot Adam" (History of Adam), *Ha-Shahar* 6 (1874) 3–60.

Anthony Hallam, *Great Geological Controversies* (New York: Oxford University Press, 1989).

Hammurabi's Code, tr. G. R. Driver and John C. Miles as *The Babylonian Laws* (Oxford: Oxford University Press, 1955).

Charles Hartshorne, *Born to Sing: An Interpretation and World Survey of Bird Song* (Bloomington: Indiana University Press, 1973).

A. J. Heschel, *God in Search of Man: A Philosophy of Judaism* (New York: Farrar, Straus, and Cudahy, 1955).

——. *The Sabbath* (New York: Farrar, Straus, and Young, 1951).

Charles Hodge, *What is Darwinism?* (New York: Scribner, Armstrong, 1874).

Douglas R. Hofstadter, *Gödel, Escher, Bach: An Eternal Golden Braid* (New York: Basic Books, 1979).

J. Hooper, *Of Moths and Men: An Evolutionary Tale* (New York: Norton, 2002).

George F. Howe, "Evolution and the Problem of Man" in Lammerts, ed., *Scientific Studies in Special Creation*.

——, ed., *Speak to the Earth: Creation Studies in Geoscience* (Nutley, N. J.: Presbyterian and Reformed Publishing Co., 1975).

C. J. Hueck, "Type III Protein Secretion Systems in Bacterial Pathogens of Animals and Plants," *Microbiolog. Mol. Biol. Rev.* 62 (1998) 379–433.

D. L. Hull, ed., *Darwin and his Critics* (Cambridge: Harvard University Press, 1973).

——. *The Philosophy of the Biological Sciences* (Englewood Cliffs: Prentice Hall, 1974).

David Hume, *Dialogues Concerning Natural Religion* (posthumous, 1779), Norman Kemp Smith, ed. (Indianapolis: Bobbs Merrill, repr. 1947).

M. A. Huynen, T. Dandekar, and P. Bork, "Variation and Evolution of the Citric-Acid Cycle: A Genomic Perspective," *Trends in Microbiology* 7 (1999) 281–91.

Conrad Hyers, *The Meaning of Creation: Genesis and Modern Science* (Atlanta: John Knox Press, 1984).

Ibn Khaldun, *Muqaddimah* (Prolegomena to the Study of History), tr. Franz Rosenthal (New York: Pantheon, 1958), 3 volumes.

Ibn Rushd, *Tahafut al-Tahafut*, ed. M. Bouyges (Beirut: Catholic Press, 1930); tr. Simon Van Den Bergh as *The Incoherence of the Incoherence* (London: Luzac, 1954), Volumes 2.

Ikhwan al-Safa, *The Case of the Animals versus Man*, ed. and tr. L. E. Goodman and Richard McGregor (London: Oxford University Press, 2010).

James Iverach, *Christianity and Evolution* (London: Hodder and Stoughton, 1894).

François Jacob, *Logic of Life* (New York: Vanguard, 1976).

H. C. Fleeming Jenkin (anonymous review), "The *Origin of Species*," *North British Review* 46 (1867) 277–318; reprinted in Hull, ed., *Darwin and his Critics*, 302–44.

J. V. Jensen, *Thomas Henry Huxley: Communicating for Science* (Newark: Delaware University Press, 1991).

Phillip Johnson, "Evolution as Dogma: The Establishment of Naturalism," *First Things* 6 (1990) 15–22, repr. in Pennock, 59–76.

David Joravsky, "Inheritance of Acquired Characteristics," in Philip Wiener, ed., *Dictionary of the History of Ideas* (New York: Scribners, 1973) 2.617–22.

Immanuel Kant, *Critique of Pure Reason* (1781/1787), tr. N. Kemp Smith (London: Macmillan, 1963).

——. *Kritik der Urteilskraft* (1790), ed. Wilhelm Weischedel (Wiesbaden: Insel, 1957); tr. as *Critique of Judgment*, J. H. Bernard (New York: Hafner, 1951).

——. *Lectures on Ethics* (1780–81), transcribed by T. F. Brauer; tr. Louis Infield (London: Methuen, 1930; New York: Harper and Row, 1963).

Leon Kass, *Toward a More Natural Science: Biology and Human Affairs* (New York: Free Press, 1985).

Leon Kass, *The Beginning of Wisdom: Reading Genesis* (New York: Free Press, 2003).

Daniel J. Kekes, *In the Name of Eugenics* (New York: Alfred Knopf, 1985).

Lord Kelvin (William Thomson), "On the Age of the Sun's Heat," *Macmillan's Magazine* 5 (1862) 288–93.

Anthony Kenny, *Descartes* (New York: Random House, 1968).

H. B. D. Kettlewell, "Selection Experiments on Industrial Melanism in the Lepidoptera," *Heredity* 9 (1955) 323–42.

——. "Further Selection Experiments on Industrial Melanism in the Lepidoptera," *Heredity* 10 (1956) 287–301.

Jaegwon Kim, *Supervenience and Mind: Selected Philosophical Essays* (Cambridge: Cambridge University Press, 1993).

G. S. Kirk, J. E. Raven, and M. Schofield, *The Presocratic Philosophers* (Cambridge: Cambridge University Press, 1983).

Philip Kitcher, *Living with Darwin: Evolution, Design, and the Future of Faith* (New York: Oxford University Press, 2007).

Ernest Klein, *A Comprehensive Etymological Dictionary of the Hebrew Language for Readers of English* (New York: Macmillan, 1987).

Robert E. Kofahl, *Handy Dandy Evolution Refuter* (San Diego: Creation Science Research Center, 1977).

Eric C. W. Krabbe, "Appeal to Ignorance," in Hans V. Hansen and Robert C. Pinto, eds., *Fallacies: Classical and Contemporary Readings* (University Park, Pennsylvania: University of Pennsylvania Press, 1995).

David Lack, *Darwin's Finches: An Essay on the General Biological Theory of Evolution* (Cambridge: Cambridge University Press, 1947).

Jean Baptiste Lamarck, *Philosophie zoologique*, ed. Charles Martins (Paris: Savy, 1873); tr. Hugh Elliot as *Zoological Philosophy* (London: Macmillan, 1914).

Walter E. Lammerts, ed., *Scientific Studies in Special Creation* (Grand Rapids: Baker Book House, 1971).

——. ed., *Why Not Creation?* (Nutley, New Jersey: Presbyterian and Reformed Publishing, 1970).

Edward J. Larson, *Summer for the Gods: The Scopes Trial and America's Continuing Debate over Science and Religion* (New York: Basic Books, 1997).

——. *The Creation–Evolution Debate* (Athens, Georgia: University of Georgia Press, 2007).

Peter Lawler, "Manliness, Religion, and Our Manly Scientists," *Society* 45 (2008) 155–58.

Joseph Le Conte, *Evolution: Its Nature, its Evidences, and its Relation to Religious Thought* (New York: Appleton, 1897; repr., New York: Kraus, 1970).

G. W. F. Leibniz, *New Essays on Human Understanding* (1704; first published, posthumously, 1765), tr. Peter Remnant and Jonathan Bennett (Cambridge: Cambridge University Press, 1996).

Jon Levenson, *God's Conflict with the Dragon and the Sea* (Cambridge: Cambridge University Press, 1985).

Cherry Lewis, *The Dating Game: One Man's Search for the Age of the Earth* (Cambridge: Cambridge University Press, 2000).

Richard Lewontin, "Billions and Billions of Demons," *New York Review of Books*, January 9, 1997, 28–32.

John Locke, *An Essay Concerning Human Understanding* (1689), Peter H. Niddich, ed. (Oxford: Oxford University Press, 1979).

Vladimir Lossky, *In the Image and Likeness of God*, John Erickson and Thomas Bird, eds. (Crestwood, New York: Saint Vladimir Seminary Press, 1974).

J. R. Lucas, "Wilberforce and Huxley: A Legendary Encounter," *The Historical Journal* 22 (1979) 313–30.

J. Gresham Machen, *Christianity and Liberalism* (New York: Macmillan, 1923).

Edward H. Madden, *Chauncey Wright and the Foundations of Pragmatism* (Seattle: University of Washington Press, 1963).

Maimonides, *Dalalat al-Ha'irin* (*Guide to the Perplexed*), ed. S. Munk (Paris, 1856; repr. Osnabrück: Zeller, 1964), 3 volumes.

M. E. N. Majerus, *Melanism: Evolution in Action* (Oxford: Oxford University Press, 1998).

George M. Marsden, *Understanding Fundamentalism and Evangelicism* (Grand Rapids: Eerdsmans, 1991).

Frank L. Marsh, *Variation and Fixity in Nature* (Mountain View: Pacific Press Association, 1976).

Karl Marx, *Capital*, from the third English edition, 1887 ed. Friedrich Engels, tr. Samuel Morre and Edward Aveling, with Engels additions from the fourth German edition. 1880. (Moscow: Progress, Publishers, 1965) 3 Volumes.

——. *Collected Works: Letters* (London: Lawrence and Wishart, 1985).

J. A. Maupin-Furlow and J. A. Ferry, "A Proteasome from the Methanogenic Archaeon *Meanosarcina thermophila*," *Journal of Biological Chemistry* 270 (1995) 28617–22.

Ernst Mayr, *The Growth of Biological Thought: Diversity, Evolution, and Inheritance* (Cambridge: Harvard University Press, 1982).

James McCosh, *The Religious Aspect of Evolution* (New York: Scribners, 1890).

Ernan McMullin, "Evolution and Special Creation," *Zygon* 28 (1993) 299–335.

R. M. McNabb, "The Bacterial Flagellum: Reversible Rotary Propellor and Type III Export Apparatus," *Journal of Bacteriology* 181 (1999) 7149–53.

W. J. Meister, "Discovery of Trilobite Fossils in Shod Footprint ..." in Lammerts, ed., *Why Not Creation?* (1970) 185–93.

Mekhilta de-R. Ishmael, ed. J. Z. Lauterbach (Philadelphia: JPS, 1976).

E. Melendez-Hevia, T. G. Wadell, and M. Cascante, "The Puzzle of the Krebs Citric Acid Cycle: Assembling the Pieces of Chemically Feasible Reactions and Opportunism in the Design of Metabolic Pathways during Evolution," *Journal of Molecular Evolution* 43 (1996) 293–303.

Midrash Rabbah (Commentary on the Pentateuch and the "Five Scrolls," – Ruth, Song of Songs, Ecclesiastes, Lamentations, and Esther), tr. H. Freedman and Maurice Simon (London: Soncino, 1961), 10 volumes.

Midrash Tanhuma, tr. John Townsend (Hoboken: Ktav, 1989–97), 3 volumes.

Kenneth Miller, *Finding Darwin's God: A Scientist's Search for Common Ground between God and Evolution* (New York: Cliff Street, 1999).

——. "The Flagellum Unspun: The Collapse of 'Irreducible Complexity'," (2004) http://www.millerandlevine.com/km/evol/design2/article.html.

Ruth Millikan, *Language, Thought, and Other Biological Categories*, (Cambridge: MIT Press, 1984)

S. K. Mills and J. H. Beatty, "The Propensity Interpretation of Fitness," *Philosophy of Science* 46 (1979) 263–86.

St. George Jackson Mivart, *On the Genesis of Species* (London: Macmillan, 1871).

Jacques Monod, *Chance and Necessity*, tr. Austryn Wainhouse (New York: Knopf, 1971).

Aubrey L. Moore, *Science and The Faith: Essays on Apologetic Subjects* (London: Kegan Paul, Trench and Trubner, 1889).

——. *Lux Mundi*, 12th edition (London: Murray, 1891).

James R. Moore, *The Post-Darwinian Controversies: A Study of the Protestant Struggle to Come to Terms with Darwin in Great Britain and America 1870–1900* (Cambridge: Cambridge University Press, 1979).

John N. Moore and H. S. Slusher, *Biology: A Search for Order in Complexity* (Grand Rapids: Zondervan, 1974).

Henry Morris, *Scientific Creationism* (El Cajon, CA: Master Books, 1985).

——. *Biblical Cosmology and Modern Science* (Nutley, N.J.: Craig Press, 1975).

——. *Biblical Catastrophism and Geology* (Philadelphia: Presbyterian and Reformed Publishing Co., 1975).

——. *The Remarkable Birth of Planet Earth* (Minneapolis: Bethany House, 1972).

——. *Impact* (Institute for Creation Research) 3 (1982).

Alexander Moszkowski, *Conversations with Einstein* (New York: Horizon 1970).

Ernest Nagel, *Teleology Revisited and Other Essays on the Philosophy and History of Science* (New York: Columbia University Press, 1979).

Nahmanides, *Commentary on the Pentateuch*, tr. Charles Chavel (New York: Shilo, 1971), 5 volumes.

Seyyed Hossein Nasr, *An Introduction to Islamic Cosmological Doctrines* (Cambridge: Harvard University Press, 1964).

Leon Nemoy, "Two Controversial Points in the Karaite Law of Incest," *HUCA* 49 (1978).

Reinhold Niebuhr, "The Truth in Myths," in J. S. Bixler, R. L. Calhoun, and H. R. Niebuhr, eds., *The Nature of Religious Experience: Essays in Honor of Clyde Macintosh* (New York: Harper, 1937).

John Jacob Niles, *Ballad Book* (Cambridge: Houghton Mifflin, 1961).

Dan-Erik Nilsson and Susanne Pelger, "A Pessimistic Estimate of the Time Required for an Eye to Evolve," *Proceedings of the Royal Society*, London Series B (1994) 253–58.

Erik Nordenskiöld, *The History of Biology: A Survey* (London: Kegan Paul, Trench and Trubner, 1929; first Swedish edition, 1920).

David Novak, *Natural Law in Judaism* (Cambridge: Cambridge University Press, 1998).

——. *Covenantal Rights: A Study in Jewish Political Theory* (Princeton: Princeton University Press, 2000).

—. *The Image of the Non-Jew in Judaism* (New York: Mellen, 1983).

Ronald Numbers, *The Creationists: From Scientific Creationism to Intelligent Design* (Cambridge: Harvard University Press, 2006).

——. *Darwinism comes to America* (Cambridge: Harvard University Press, 1998).

Martha Nussbaum, *Aristotle's* De Motu Animalium ... *Commentary* (Princeton University Press, 1985).

Steve Olson, *Evolution in Hawaii* (Washington: National Academies Press, 2004).

Origen, *Contra Celsum*, tr. Henry Chadwick (Cambridge: Cambridge University Press, 1965).

——. *De Principiis*, tr. G. W. Butterworth from the Koetschau text as *On First Principles* (New York: Harper and Row, 1966; first published, 1936).

Harry Orlinsky, *Notes on the New Translation of the Torah* (Philadelphia: JPS, 1970).

Henry Osborn, *Evolution and Religion in Education* (New York: Scribners, 1926).

Richard H. Overman, *Evolution and the Christian Doctrine of Creation: A Whiteheadian Interpretation* (Philadelphia: Westminster Press, 1967).

William Paley, *Natural Theology, or Evidences of the Existence and Attributes of the Deity collected from the Appearances of Nature* (1802) (Houston: St. Thomas, 1972).

Giuliano Pancaldi, "The Technology of Nature: Marx's Thoughts on Darwin," in I. B. Cohen, ed., *The Natural Sciences and the Social Sciences* (Dordrecht: Kluwer, 1994) 257–74.

Arthur Peacocke, *Theology for a Scientific Age* (Oxford: Blackwell, 1990).

——. "God's Action in the Real World,"*Zygon* 26 (1991) 455–76.

——. *Creation and the World of Science* (Oxford: Oxford University Press, 1979).

——. "Welcoming the Disguised Friend" (Idreos Lectures of 1997), repr. in Pennock, 5–23.

Robert T. Pennock, ed., *Intelligent Design, Creationism and its Critics: Philosophical, Theological, and Scientific Perspectives* (Cambridge: MIT Press, 2001).

Pesikta de R. Kahana, tr. W. G. Braude and I. J. Kapstein (Philadelphia: JPS, 2002).

Philo, *Opera*, tr. F. H. Colson and G. H. Whitaker (Cambridge: Harvard University Press, 1929, *etc.*), 12 volumes.

John Philoponus, *De Aeternitate Mundi contra Proclum*, ed. H. Rabe (Leipzig: Teubner, 1899).

Massimo Pigliucci, "Design Yes, Intelligent No: A Critique of Intelligent Design Theory and Neo-Creationism," http://www.infidels.org/library/modern/features/2000/pigliucci1.html.

Alvin Plantinga, "Evolution, Neutrality, and Antecedent Probability: A Reply to Van Till and McMullin," *Christian Scholar's Review* 21 (1991) 80–109.

Plotinus, *Enneads*, tr. Stephen MacKenna (New York: Pantheon, 1957).

George Poinar Jr. and Roberta Poinar, *What Bugged the Dinosaurs: Insects, Disease, and Death in the Cretaceous* (Princeton: Princeton University Press, 2009).

J. Polkinghorne, *Science and Providence* (Boston: Shambala, 1989).

——. *Science and Christian Belief* (London: SPCK, 1994).

F. D. Por, *Animal Achievement: A Unifying Theory of Zoology* (Rehovot: Balaban, 1994).

——. "A Ecological Theory of Animal Progress," *Perspectives in Biology and Medicine* (1980) 389–99.

Peter Portin, "The Concept of the Gene: Short History and Present Status," *The Quarterly Review of Biology* 68 (1993) 173–223.

George McCready Price, *The Fundamentals of Geology: And their Bearings on the Doctrine of a Literal Creation* (Mountain View: Pacific Press, 1913).

——. *The Phantom of Organic Evolution* (New York: Revell, 1924).

Ilya Prigogine, *From Being to Becoming* (San Francisco: Freeman, 1980).

——, with Isabelle Stengers, *Order out of Chaos* (London: Heinemann, 1984).

James Bennett Pritchard, *Ancient Near Eastern Texts Relating to the Old Testament* (Princeton: Princeton University Press, 1969).

Proclus, Eighteen arguments for the eternity of the world, tr. Thomas Taylor, in *The Fragments that Remain of the Lost Writings of Proclus* (London: Black, Young, and Young, 1825). The first argument, lost in Greek, survives in Philoponus ap. Simplicius *ad Phys.*, ed. A.-R. Badawi, in *Neo-Platonici apud Arabes, Islamica* 19 (1955) and Shahrastani, *Kitab al-Milal wa 'l-Nihal*, ed. Cureton (London: Society for the Publication of Oriental Texts, 1842).

Donald R. Prothero, *Evolution: What the Fossils Say and Why it Matters* (New York: Columbia University Press, 2007).

Emanuel Rádl, *The History of Biological Theories*, tr. E. J. Hatfield (Oxford: Oxford University Press, 1930).

Rashi, *Commentary on the Pentateuch*, ed. Harry Orlinsky, et al. (New York: SS and R Publishing, 1949).

Philip F. Rehbok, *The Philosophical Naturalists: Themes in Early Nineteenth-Century British Biology* (Madison: University of Wisconsin Press, 1983).

Robert J. Richards, *Darwin and the Emergence of Evolutionary Theories of Mind and Behavior* (Chicago: University of Chicago Press, 1987).

——. *The Meaning of Evolution: The Morphological Construction and Ideological Reconstruction of Darwin's Theory* (Chicago: University of Chicago Press, 1992).

——. *Science in Culture* (New York: Science History, 1978).

——. *The Romantic Conception of Life: Science and Philosophy in the Age of Goethe* (Chicago: University of Chicago Press, 2002).

Michael R. Rose, *Darwin's Spectre: Evolutionary Biology in the Modern World* (Princeton: Princeton University Press, 1998).

Noah Rosenbloom, "Mysticism and Science in Malbim's Theory of Creation" (Hebrew), *HUCA* 57 (1986) 39–86.

Jean Rostand, *L'Atomisme en biologie* (Paris: Gallimard, 1956).

R. I. Roth, R. E. Mandrell, and J. M. Griffiss, "Ability of Gonococcal and Meningoccocal Lipoligosaccharides to Clot *Limulus* Amebocyte Lysate," *Infection and Immunity* 60 (1992) 762–67.

David Wÿss Rudge, "Did Kettlewell Commit Fraud? Re-examining the Evidence," *Public Understanding of Science* 14 (2005) 249–68.

Michael Ruse, *Darwin and Design* (Cambridge: Harvard University Press, 2003).
——. *Can a Darwinian be a Christian? – The Relationship between Science and Religion* (Cambridge: Cambridge University Press, 2001).
——. "Darwin's Debt to Philosophy: An Examination of the Influence of the Philosophical Ideas of J. F. W. Herschel and W. Whewell on the Development of Charles Darwin's Theory of Evolution," *Studies in the History and Philosophy of Science* 6 (1975) 159–81.
——, ed., *But is it Science? The Philosophical Question in the Creation/Evolution Controversy* (Buffalo: Prometheus, 1988).
R.J. Rushdoony, *The Mythology of Science* (Nutley, N.J.: Craig Press, 1967).
Jeffrey Russell, *Inventing the Flat Earth: Columbus and Modern Historians* (New York: Praeger, 1991).
Cynthia E. Russett, *Darwin in America: The Intellectual Response 1865–1912* (San Francisco: Freeman, 1976).
Saadiah Gaon, *Kitab al-Mukhtar fi 'l-Amanat wa-'l-Itiqadat*, tr. S. Rosenblatt as *The Book of Beliefs and Opinions* (New Haven: Yale University Press, 1948).
——. *The Book of Theodicy*, tr. L. E. Goodman (New Haven: Yale University Press, 1988).
Carl Sagan, *The Dragons of Eden* (New York: Random House, 1977).
Frank Salisbury, "Doubts about the Modern Synthetic Theory of Evolution," *American Biology Teacher* 33 (September, 1971) 335–38.
Shmuel Sambursky, *The Physical World of Late Antiquity* (London: Routledge and Kegan Paul, 1962).
Marc Saperstein, ed., *Jewish Preaching 1200–1800: An Anthology* (New Haven: Yale University Press, 1989).
Jack Sasson, "Time … to Begin," in Michael Fishbane and Emanuel Tov, eds., *Shaarei Talmon* (Winona Lake, Indiana: Eisenbrauns, 1992) 183–94.
Minot J. Savage, *The Religion of Evolution* (Boston: Lockwood Books, 1876).
Menachem Mendel Schneerson, "The Weakness of the Theories of Creation," at www.daat.ac.il (1962).
Silvan S. Schweber, "The Origin of the *Origin* Revisited," *Journal of the History of Biology* 10 (1977) 229–316.
——. "Darwin and the Political Economists," *Journal of the History of Biology* 13 (1980) 195–289
——. "The Correspondence of the Young Darwin," *Journal of the History of Biology* 21 (1988) 501–19
Kelly Segraves, *The Great Dinosaur Mistake* (San Diego: Beta Books, 1977).
Nell Segraves, *The Creation Report* (San Diego: Creation-Science Research Center, 1977).
Niall Shanks and Karl Joplin, "Redundant Complexity: A Critical Analysis of Intelligent Design in Biochemistry," *Philosophy of Science* 66 (1999) 268–82.
Raphael Shuchat, "Attitudes Towards Cosmogony and Evolution among Rabbinic Thinkers in the Nineteenth and Early Twentieth Centuries: The Resurgence of the Doctrine of Sabbatical Years," *Torah u-Madda Journal* 13 (2005) 15–49.
Charles Singer, *A Short History of Biology* (Oxford: Oxford University Press, 1931).
John Skoles and Dorian Sagan, *Up from Dragons: The Evolution of Human Intelligence* (New York: McGraw-Hill, 2002).
Elliot Sober *Philosophy of Biology* (Boulder: Westview, 1993).
Baruch Spinoza, *Opera*, ed. Gebhardt (Heidelberg: Winter, 1925; repr. 1972).

John Roach Straton, *Evolution versus Creation*, Debate with Charles Francis Potter (New York: Doran, 1924); repr. in Ronald Numbers, ed., *Creation–Evolution Debates* (New York: Garland, 1995) 2.23–110.

D. I. Stuart and E. Y. Jones, "Cutting Complexity down to Size," *Nature* 386 (1997) 437–38.

Frank J. Sulloway, "Geographic Isolation in Darwin's Thinking: The Vicissitudes of a Crucial Idea," *Studies in the History of Biology* 3 (1979) 23–65.

——. "Darwin and his Finches: The Evolution of a Legend," *Journal of the History of Biology* 15 (1982) 1–53.

W. S. Sutton, "On the Morphology of the Chromosome Group …," *Biological Bulletin* 4 (1904) 24–39.

Pierre Teilhard de Chardin, *The Phenomenon of Man* (London: Collins, 1966; First French ed., 1955).

Dietrick Thomson, "Turin Shroud: Nature and Supernature," *Science News* (October 3, 1981).

Friedrich Tiedemann, *Zoologie: zu seinen Vorlesungen Entworfen* (Landshut: Weber, 1808).

Lee Tiffin, *Creationism's Upside-Down Pyramid: How Science Refutes Fundamentalism* (Amherst, New York: Prometheus, 1994).

Niko Tinbergen, "On the Aims and Methods of Ethology," *Zeitschrift für Tierpsychologie* 20 (1963) 410–33.

Colin Tudge and Josh Young. *The Link: uncovering our Earliest Ancestor* (New York: Little Brown, 2009).

Dean Turner, *Commitment to Care: An Integrated Philosophy of Science, Education, and Religion* (Old Greenwich: Devin-Adair, 1978).

J. W. Tutt, *British Moths* (London: Routledge, 1896).

Howard Van Till, "When Faith and Reason Cooperate," *Christian Scholar's Review* 21 (1991) 44–45.

Eric Voegelin, *Order and History* (Baton Rouge: Louisiana State University Press, 1974).

Joseph Walsh, "Galen's Discovery and Promulgation of the Function of the Recurrent Laryngeal Nerve," *Annals of Medical History* 8. (1926) 176–84.

Richard Walzer, *Greek into Arabic* (Oxford: Cassirer, 1962).

Gerald Wheeler, *Two-Taled Dinosaur* (Nashville: Southern Publishing Association, 1975).

John C. Whitcomb, *The Early Earth* (Grand Rapids: Baker Book House, 1972).

——and H. M. Morris, *The Genesis Flood* (Phillipsburg, New Jersey: Presbyterian and Reformed Publishing, 1961).

Samuel Wilberforce, reviewing the *Origin of Species*, *Quarterly Review* 108 (July, 1860) in Reginald B. Johnson, ed., *Famous Reviews* (London, 1914; repr., Freeport, New York: Books for Libraries, 1967).

A. E. Wilder-Smith, *Man's Origin, Man's Destiny* (Minneapolis: Bethany Fellowship, 1975).

Mary B. Williams, "Falsifiable Predictions of Evolutionary Theory," *Philosophy of Science* 40 (1973) 518–37.

E. O. Wilson, *Sociobiology: The New Synthesis* (Cambridge: Harvard University Press, 1975).

Ludwig Wittgenstein, *Culture and Value* (1948), G. H. von Wright and Heikki Nyman, eds.; tr. Peter Winch (Chicago: University of Chicago Press, 1980).

Caspar Friedrich Wolff, *Theorie von der Generation* (Berlin: Brinstiel, 1764).

J. Woods and D. Walton, *Fallacies* (Dordrecht: Foris, 1989).

Chauncey Wright, *The Philosophical Writings*, ed. E. H. Madden (New York: Liberal Arts Press, 1958).

——. "Natural Theology as a Positive Science," *North American Review* (January, 1865), repr. in C. E. Norton, ed., *Philosophical Discussions* (New York: Holt, 1877).

——. *Letters*, ed. James Bradley Thayer (1878; repr. New York: Burt Franklin, 1971).

Sewell Wright, *Evolution and the Genetics of Populations* (Chicago: University of Chicago Press, 1978).

J. A. Zahm, *Evolution and Dogma* (Chicago: McBride, 1896).

Index